WOMEN, CRIME
AND POVERTY

WOMEN, CRIME AND POVERTY

Pat Carlen

OPEN UNIVERSITY PRESS
Milton Keynes · Philadelphia

Open University Press
Open University Educational Enterprises Limited
12 Cofferidge Close
Stony Stratford
Milton Keynes MK11 1BY

and 242 Cherry Street
Philadelphia, PA 19106, USA

First Published 1988

British Library Cataloguing in Publication Data

Carlen, Pat
  Women, crime and poverty.
  1. Women criminals
  I. Title
  364.3'74

    ISBN 0–335–15870–6
    ISBN 0–335–15869–2 Pbk

Library of Congress Cataloging-in-Publication Data

Carlen, Pat.
  Women, crime, and poverty/Pat Carlen.
      p.   cm.
  Bibliography: p.
  Includes index.
  1. Female offenders – Great Britain – Case studies.
  2. Poor women – Great Britain – Case studies.   I. Title.
  HV6046.C29   1988
  364.3'74'0941 – dc19

    ISBN 0–335–15870–6
    ISBN 0–335–15869–2 (pbk.)

Typeset by Scarborough Typesetting Services
Printed in Great Britain by The Alden Press, Oxford

CONTENTS

LIST OF TABLES

ACKNOWLEDGEMENTS

Many individuals and organizations have assisted me in the production of this book. In particular, I thank:

The Economic and Social Research Council for a grant (No. EO6250010) of £14,200 to study women's criminal careers during 1985–6;

The University of Keele for allowing me leave of absence to pursue research on women and crime in the UK;

The Centre for Criminology, Keele University, for providing a stimulating environment in which to work;

The Prison Department and Ms U. McCollum, Governor of Bullwood Hall Prison and Youth Custody Centre for allowing me to interview the women in the Bullwood Group;

Jenny Hicks, Moira Honnan, Helen Kent and Josie O'Dwyer for putting me in touch with the women in the Contact Group;

Charlie Maynard of the National Association of Young People in Care (NAYPIC) for drawing the relevant publications to my attention and for arranging a discussion with NAYPIC members in Bradford;

The NAYPIC members who gave me information about their experiences in residential Care;

The National Association for the Care and Resettlement of Offenders (NACRO Information Service) for their usual generosity with their time, their information and their patience;

Josie O'Dwyer and Laurie Taylor who were forbearing (or at least polite) listeners while I repeatedly moaned about the difficulties of the research;

Peter, Daniel and Jill Carlen for cheerfully vacating rooms needed for interviewing and for performing innumerable clerical services and errands connected with the investigation;

Freda Mainwaring and June Poppleton who typed some of the tables;

x WOMEN, CRIME AND POVERTY

Florence Daniels who so efficiently transformed the tapes into transcripts;
and Doreen Thompson who typed the whole text with good humour and
much patience.

The book is dedicated to the thirty-nine women who in 1985 and 1986
entrusted me with some details of their criminal careers.

Pat Carlen, 1988

1

WOMEN, POVERTY AND SOCIAL CONTROL

Women are the poorest of all in our society. Making up over 40 per cent of the workforce, practically 100 per cent of the unpaid domestic workforce, they end up with only 25 per cent of the pay. Women are the largest group dependent on social security payments . . . two-thirds of supplementary pensions are collected by women; and some 13 million child benefit payments are made to women as a non-means tested right.

(Booth, 1985: 9)

JAILED FOR BEING POOR
One woman was threatened with jail a few days ago because she could not pay her library fines.

And another was actually jailed when she refused to give up smoking to clear unpaid fines for not having a television licence.

What on earth is the point of adding to our prison population – already one of Europe's largest – by jailing women whose only real crime is their poverty?

Our magistrates and judges should have the sense to keep prison for serious criminals and hand out those lesser penalties to such sad casualties of our divided nation as women too poor to pay fines.

(*Today* 28 March 1987)

PREAMBLE

Britain. End of the 1980s. Margaret Thatcher in her third term of office and current government policies on employment, taxation, tax allowances, social security and the social services resulting in women (especially the elderly and homeless new school-leavers) getting poorer all the time (see Bull and Wilding, 1983; Campbell, 1984; Pascall, 1986; Townsend *et al.*, 1987; Walker and Walker, 1987). Four main groups of women are in poverty: those 'who look after children or other dependants unpaid and receive insufficient income indirectly for these purposes; lone women with children, whether or not in paid employment; elderly women pensioners, especially those who live alone; and women with low earnings in households in which the earnings or income of others does not enable total household income to surmount the poverty line' (Townsend *et al.*, 1987: 63).

Those unwise enough to predict that Margaret Thatcher would 'do more for the advance of women than all the acts of parliament and all events of history' (Walden in Murray, 1978: 94) have been proved wrong. Government cuts in health and social services have pushed women back into the home to provide the care for the disabled and elderly nowadays denied them by the state.

Increases in the numbers of women working part-time (and therefore excluded from many of the benefits payable to full-time employees), together with the growing segregation of the female from the male labour force (thereby enabling employers to avoid regulation by the Equal Pay Act, 1974), have again widened the previously narrowing pay differentials between male and female employees (Pascall, 1986).

Over a million women head one-parent families and the majority of them live not only in poverty but also in fear – that due to official inefficiency the supplementary benefit cheque won't arrive; that the benefit will be withdrawn while their circumstances are reviewed; that they will be accused of any of a number of fraudulent practices relating to the claiming of supplementary benefit; that they are under constant surveillance, from both neighbours and officials watching to catch them out if they appear to be sharing household expenses with anyone else; that their children will be taken into residential Care if they themselves finally crack under the strain of bringing up kids in poverty (see Cook, 1987 for a summary account of the social control of women on supplementary benefit).

But this 'feminization of poverty' is not *just* a contingent consequence of economic recession aggravating women's powerlessness. It is also the logical result of a 'New Right' political economy that, in lauding the virtues of 'the market' and 'individual effort', also seeks to replace the 'cosseting' welfare state with the idealized, 'self-sufficient' nuclear family. As Lynne Segal succinctly puts it:

> Thatcherism's emphasis on family life, which is always about *women's* role in the family, fits neatly with Conservative policies of tight monetary controls and welfare cuts. But it is women's sacrifice, their toil and selflessness in the home which Conservative thought must encourage as spending cuts increase the demands of caring for the young, the elderly, the sick and disabled.
>
> (Segal, 1983: 9)

And, further to the Conservative Secretary of State's now notorious pronouncement that 'If the good Lord had intended us all having equal rights to go out to work and to behave equally, you know he really wouldn't have created man and woman.' (Patrick Jenkin, a former Secretary of State for Social Services, 1979, quoted in Coote and Campbell, 1982: 87), Bull and Wilding (1983: 10) comment:

> The televised invocation of divine disapproval for working mothers by Mr Patrick Jenkin, the Secretary of State for Social Services, is only the most famous of frequent demands for the return to domesticity of women at work. The 'caring professions' and the services they provide are seen as an unnecessary state appropriation of the proper functions of the home and family.

It is not surprising, therefore, that 'unemployment amongst women, especially young women, has increased more rapidly than that for men since the Conservatives were elected' (ibid.: 22), nor that Thatcher should present herself as being nothing more than the Great Housekeeper, an epitome of all the domestic virtues: 'It's not impossible to cut spending. Every housewife with a budget to balance knows that nothing is impossible, given the will, the character and the strength of purpose.' (Margaret Thatcher, Conservative Central Council Annual Conference, Solihull, 24 March 1979, quoted in Segal, 1983: 9 from an unpublished paper by Barry King entitled 'The image of the family in Thatcherism'.)

Yet, as the women in this study repeatedly asked, how would *she* know? Well, of course, she has not always been married to a millionaire and, ironically, she herself has said that it was a Labour government that was responsible for her initial decision to make a career in politics. 'The Labour Party were in Government and for the first time members of parliament were paid a living wage . . . from that moment on it became possible to think in terms of a political career.' (Margaret Thatcher, quoted in Murray, 1978: 42.) But, once the twins had arrived, Mrs Thatcher, was hardly the typical working mum. From the beginning she had help with the children and later they were packed off to boarding school. She admits that it was all made possible by her husband's enormous wealth. Showing a friend round the House of Commons during her early days as an MP, Mrs Thatcher remarked: 'I am very lucky because I have my own secretary. You know, I could only do it on Denis's money.' (Wapshott and Brock, 1983: 59; cf. Campbell, 1987.) In fact, Thatcher herself is a living witness to the very strong element of truth in one woman criminal's comment that: 'Really, if you're a woman from a working-class background, then the best way to get on is to marry some rich old geezer.'

WOMEN IN CRIME, COURTS, CUSTODY – AND POVERTY

Women, poor or otherwise, are on the whole a law-abiding lot. Although in both the USA and the UK there has recently been an increase in the female criminal conviction rates, in England and Wales in 1985 only 59.1 thousand females (as compared with 385.2 thousand males) were sentenced for indictable crimes, thus constituting but 13 per cent of the total (Central Statistical Office, 1987). Little is known about the social circumstances of those 59 thousand though, as is argued later in this chapter, it is most likely safe to assume that they were drawn from all income levels and social backgrounds. Slightly more is known about the average daily population of approximately 1,600 women locked up in the female penal institutions.

Women presently account for only 3 per cent of the prison population in England and Wales (Central Statistical Office, 1987), even though in 1985/6 the women's average daily prison population was 7 per cent higher than in 1984/5 (Home Office, 1986a). There is, nonetheless, grave cause for concern about women's imprisonment, and not least because the recent statistical analyses of female-incarceration rates reveal both that the proportionate use of imprisonment for women has more than doubled in the past ten years, and that women tend to be sent to prison for less serious offences than men (NACRO, 1987a and b).

Of all female receptions, approximately a quarter are remand prisoners of whom only 25–35 per cent can expect a custodial sentence. Of sentenced women prisoners, approximately 30 per cent of all receptions are for fine default, the majority of sentenced women prisoners being convicted of some relatively minor property offence. Less than 10 per cent of all female receptions have a conviction for violence (Home Office, 1985). More than four times the expected proportion of adult women in prison are from ethnic-minority groups (Home Office, 1986b). Healthwise, it is as likely today, as it was at the time of Professor Gibbens's 1967 study, that at least 15 per cent of the women will have a major physical ailment and 20 per cent a major health problem (Gibbens, 1971). A sizeable number will have been brought up in institutions since infancy; and the majority will have lived in poverty for the greater part of their adult lives (see Mandaraka-Sheppard, 1986; Genders and Player, 1987).

CLASS AND CRIMINALIZATION[1]

Despite the fact that the majority of people with long criminal records and most of those in prison come from the lower socio-economic groups, studies of white-collar crime (Sutherland, 1949), business crime (Carson, 1970, 1981; Braithwaite, 1983; Leigh, 1982; Levi, 1987) and crime across a variety of occupations (Ditton, 1977; Henry, 1978; Mars, 1982) lead to the conclusion that law-breaking is evenly distributed throughout all social classes. The same studies (together with those estimating the extent of unreported crime) indicate that a majority of all law-breakers from *all* social classes can expect to escape penal regulation altogether. Furthermore, of all those unfortunate enough to fall into the arms of the law, most can expect to escape the snowballing consequences of a stigmatizing criminal record. This is certainly not because the crimes of these law-breakers are less serious than those of their criminalized counterparts. It is because white-collar, business and occupational crimes are structurally difficult both to apprehend and successfully prosecute; and also because the crimes more usually committed by people from the lower socio-economic groups are those more visible crimes of theft and violence that are most feared by the public and most frequently portrayed by the mass media.

Throughout this book it will be argued that the different modes of social regulation of women have resulted in their patterns of law-breaking, criminalization and penal regulation being different again from those of men. Yet, even allowing for gender differences, when women *do* break the law, those from the lower socio-economic groups are more liable to criminalization than are their middle-class sisters (see Carlen, 1983a: 62–3). These relationships between crime and social class are neither new nor peculiar to the twentieth century.

Modern forms of policing had their inception in the nineteenth-century industrialists' need to discipline the workers of the new industrial towns by more peaceful, more ideologically effective and less socially divisive means than the sporadic use of the militia. Similarly, the primary aim of nineteenth-century imprisonment was to school the industrial workforce into regular working habits and the keeping of restrictive contracts (Rusche and Kirchheimer, 1939; Melossi and Pavarini, 1981). Since then, prisons have continued to confine and regulate disproportionate numbers of the poor, the unemployed, the unemployable, the socially disadvantaged and the socially inept (Foucault, 1977; Scull, 1979; Ignatieff, 1978; Mathiesen, 1980 and Williams, 1981). Whether or not these inequitable effects of policing and penal regulation were ever intended, it can be argued that, independently of any deliberate policy pursued by police, courts and prisons, today's working-class law-breaker is still more likely to be overcriminalized than is the middle-class offender. Precisely because the fundamental preconditions for this differential criminalization are economic and ideological, their earliest effects are often realized within social and political processes that overdetermine a working-class adolescent's criminalization, even prior to his or her first act of law-breaking.

By the mid-nineteenth century it was their poverty, rather than their lawbreaking that made working-class children prime candidates for incarceration.

By 1866 magistrates could commit to industrial schools children who were vagrant, who were said by their parents to be incorrigible or who were associating with criminals and prostitutes, so that they could be resocialized or reformed . . . By 1894 over 17,000 children from the 'perishing classes' were held in industrial schools compared with a mere 1400 delinquent children in the reformatories.

(Morris *et al.*, 1980: 5)

Yet although the forms of adolescent regulation have since been changed by a series of statutes striving to effect the moral rearmament of the family rather than the economic reconstruction of an inequitable social system, consecutive governments (Conservative and Labour) have continued to publish policy statements on crime that focus solely on the social and economic conditions of the lower socio-economic groups (Burton, 1980: 123–31). Instead of this emphasis resulting in any permanent gains for working-class people it has resulted in:

1 an extremely biased conceptualization of crime that all but ignores the institutionalized law-breaking of financial institutions and professional groups (Box, 1983);
2 a stereotype of 'the criminal' whose predominent feature is that (s)he is working class;
3 the early 'preventative' incarceration of large numbers of working-class children;
4 the 'saturation' policing of certain working-class areas (Scarman, 1982) and
5 the police harassment of certain suspect groups (McLeod, 1982; Cowell *et al.*, 1982; Smith and Gray,1983).

Taken together these factors have ensured that a greater proportion of poorer (rather than richer) law-breakers are brought before the courts. Once in court they are yet again disadvantaged by their poverty and powerlessness. Their inability to pay for adequate legal representation, plus their effective exclusion from judicial proceedings (Carlen, 1976), enhance their chances of conviction. Inability to pay a monetary penalty, together with factors such as homelessness or a previous history of institutionalization, increase the likelihood of a custodial penalty.

Working-class people are at further disadvantage in prison. Their too frequent and early institutionalization often produces a reaction to further imprisonment that instantly labels them 'difficult'. Consequently, they are more likely than white-collar criminals to be held in closed conditions. Upon release into the same social and ideological milieu that contributed to their criminalization in the first place, they are again subject to the complex but systematic processes which, in conjunction with each other, disproportionately increase their chances of being *overcriminalized*. If they are black, *overcriminalization* is even more likely to occur . . . and with a lower likelihood of actual lawbreaking being one of its preconditions.

RACISM AND CRIMINALIZATION

While children from ethnic-minority groups 'are disproportionately represented in the Care population', the numbers of children of mixed parentage in Care have been found to be *'alarmingly* disproportionate' (House of Commons,

1984, emphases added). Once in Care, young black people can expect to be exposed to the same risks of *overcriminalization* that threaten other state-raised youngsters – plus a few more (see Chapter 4). At the same time these general risks are aggravated by the police racism to which all young black people (in or out of Care) are subject (see Holdaway, 1983; Box, 1983; Smith and Gray, 1983; Benn and Worpole, 1986).

It is not possible within the confines of this book to document the immense amount of currently available evidence on police racism, but a quotation from Steven Box (1983: 218) may be suggestive of one of its effects:

> In the Metropolitan Police District in 1975, blacks represented only 4.2 per cent of the total population. Yet they constituted 37.1 per cent of those arrested for violent theft and 28.7 per cent of those arrested for robbery (Stevens and Willis, 1979: 32) – the relevance of these particular data being that nearly one-half of those convicted for these offences receive a prison sentence and the rate of incarceration for these same offences has increased during the last decade . . . a guesstimate that 40 per cent of young persons in prison are black 'errs on the side of caution'.

Young black people found guilty of a crime will also suffer from the effects of racism in areas of social life unrelated to crime, e.g. the effects of racism on unemployment, as well as from the biased stereotype of 'the criminal' that presents him as young, working class and black. Box again:

> Finally, there are reasons why ethnic minorities, particularly young males, would be treated more harshly by the judiciary. Not only is the unemployment rate amongst this group double or even treble that of its white counterpart (Stevens, 1979), but their demographic characteristics also signal potentially high levels of criminal behaviour. They are disproportionately aged between 15 and 25 years old. As a group, black British are then doubly vulnerable, first to higher levels of unemployment and second, higher levels of criminality [what I (Carlen) am calling criminalization] because that is 'youth's speciality'.
>
> (Box, 1983: 215)

It is therefore not surprising that, as has already been noted, more than four times the expected numbers of adult women in prison are from ethnic-minority groups (Home Office, 1986b).

WOMEN, CRIME, POVERTY AND SOCIAL CONTROL

> Box and Hale (1984) considered females convicted of indictable offences over the period 1951–1980 and reported that increases in the rate of female unemployment were significantly related to increases in the *rate*

of conviction for violent crime (assault, and wounding) theft, handling stolen goods, and fraud . . .

(Box, 1987: 73)

Although there is no statistical evidence to indicate that the recent increases in women's criminal convictions are directly linked to increased law-breaking occasioned by increased poverty (and it is difficult to conceive of how any such evidence could ever be obtained!), Stephen Box, having reviewed fifty North American and British studies of unemployment and crime concluded that 'the most plausible reason for [the increase in conventional crimes committed by females] is that more women have become economically marginalized during the recession' (Box, 1987: 43). Going on to quote from the report of his previous researches with Hale, Box further argued that:

> although some upper-middle-class women have made inroads into formerly male professions, the vast bulk of women have become increasingly economically marginalized – that is, they are more likely to be unemployed or unemployable or, if employed, more likely to be in insecure, lower-paid unskilled part-time jobs in which career prospects are minimal. This marginalization, particularly in a consumer-oriented and status-conscious community that is continuously conditioned by aggressive media advertising, is . . . an important cause of increase in female crime rates . . . Furthermore, anxieties concerning their ability to adequately fulfil the social roles of mother, wife and consumer have been heightened during the late 1970s and early 80s because the British Welfare State, on which proportionately more women than men depend, had tightened its definition of who deserves financial assistance and, at the same time, has become increasingly unable to index-link these payments to inflation.

(Box and Hale, 1984: 477)

The effects of such policies are that more young women are to be seen begging on the streets of the capital (Lock, 1987); that more young women either coming out of residential Care or leaving families too poverty-stricken themselves to keep unemployed teenagers are turning to a street life of begging, prostitution or drug abuse; and that more women on social security are making themselves vulnerable to prosecution either by putting forward fraudulent claims to benefits or by engaging in the hidden economy. Furthermore, and contrary to Tory politician Norman Tebbit's assertion that this illegal and hidden economy is based on 'wickedness' (Tebbit, 1985), David Crystal-Kirk has argued that:

> The government *needs* the poverty of the poor to keep inflation down . . .
> The government castigates those on the fiddle yet *connives* to perpetuate their existence. The stark truth is that the government *needs* the safety

valves provided by the black economy in any number of social areas – jobs, housing, credit broking etc. – or it would not be able to contain the wrath of those unable to survive.

(Crystal-Kirk, 1985: 12 and 13)

For example:

Miss A is an unmarried mother. Though performing a useful function within the community, she has neither political nor economic clout and so falls into the poverty trap. To make ends meet and stay sane in her high-rise slum she hires a colour television (by no means a luxury) but fails to buy a television licence – CRIME – she makes spurious claims for social security benefits – CRIME – and she works as a cleaner in a bank for very low pay: because it is part-time work, union rates and conditions do not apply and as a 'moonlighter' she is in no position to complain because she does not declare her earnings to either the Inland Revenue or the DHSS – CRIME and CRIME. This keeps her quiet. The government can now carp hypocritically about 'spongers' generally, but this is exactly how it wants it.

(ibid)

Nevertheless , the fact remains that women *still* constitute only a small proportion of all known law-breakers and at 3 per cent of the total an even smaller proportion of prisoners. To understand the relationships between poverty, women's law-breaking and women's penal-incarceration rates it is necessary to examine the differential modes of social control experienced by women as compared with men and Chapters 4 and 5 of this book do so in some detail. Here, therefore, I will briefly outline what is known about the official response to women who *do* break the law.

Seear and Player, in an analysis of official statistics on women's crime and women's imprisonment, indicate that there is considerable evidence to support the thesis that at least some women are treated more leniently than men by both the police and the courts. For example:

Over one-third (35 per cent) of all women and girls who either admitted or were found guilty of an offence in 1984 did not appear in court but were cautioned by the police, in comparison to 19 per cent of males . . . In 1984, 15 per cent of all sentences were passed on women yet they accounted for only 5 per cent of those sentenced to immediate custody. Furthermore, half of all sentences of imprisonment imposed upon adult women in 1984 were fully suspended as opposed to only 36 per cent for men. Women and girls were more likely than their male counterparts to receive an absolute or conditional discharge or a probation order . . . In

1984, 59 per cent of males found to be in breach of a probation order were given custodial sentences as compared to 36 per cent of females.

(Seear and Player, 1986. Source of statistics: Home Office, 1985)

However, and as the same authors also point out, women are in fact found guilty of less serious crimes than men and, when given a custodial sentence, are more likely to go to prison for a relatively minor crime of theft than for any more serious offence. Conversely, and as Hilary Allen (1986 and 1987) has demonstrated, women found guilty of very serious crimes of violence are much more likely to receive non-custodial sentences than are their male counterparts! How can such sentencing patterns be explained?

The majority of women who go to prison are sentenced not according to the seriousness of their crimes but primarily according to the courts' assessment of them as wives, mothers and daughters (Worrall, 1981; Farrington and Morris, 1983a and b; Carlen, 1983a; Dominelli, 1984). If they are young and their parents or state guardians believe them to be beyond control, if they are homeless, if they are single, divorced or separated from their husbands, or if their children are in residential Care, then they are more likely to go to prison than women who, though their crimes might be more serious, are living more conventional family lives. As the policies of the present Conservative government increase the numbers of families living in poverty, the minority of women who commit easily detectable property crimes (as opposed to middle-class men's organizational or corporate crimes), together with women who as a result of their lifestyles are more likely to be apprehended by the police for other minor crimes, are also those who (again as a result of poverty) are more likely to have their children in residential Care and are less likely to be living in either the idealized conventional nuclear family or the adman's idealized 'family home'.

Furthermore, and despite claims of the New Right that 'permissiveness' and 'women's liberation' have together weakened the family as an inculcator of morality, the rapid increase in the numbers of women passing through the courts and prisons cannot be attributed to 'women's liberation'. The vast majority of women who commit crime have *not* been 'liberated' – either economically or ideologically. On the contrary – and as we shall see in the rest of this book – women criminals are often among the worst casualties of the gender trap. The increase in the numbers of females being prosecuted, convicted and sent to prison, far from indicating that women have been 'liberated', may instead indicate that women's crimes are presently being taken more seriously. For, given the prevailing Tory emphasis on familiness, it may be that increased male alarm at feminist demands has resulted in *any* female deviance – however trivial – being seen as a major threat to a society traditionally centred around home, family, and male-related domesticity. Given, too, that the present Thatcher government is ideologically committed to the celebration of the (dubious) virtues of Victorian family life – including, one must suppose, the actual domestic conditions of the vast majority of Victorian families who lived in squalor and poverty – it is not surprising that the women's prisons are currently filled mainly with poorer women who, in one way or another, have been adjudged as being beyond the control of the conventional (but idealized) nuclear family.

Women, Crime and Poverty is based on the oral histories[2] of thirty-nine women's criminal careers. After the women have been introduced in Chapters 2 and 3, the bulk of the book is an ethnographic analysis of their law-breaking and the official response to it. Chapter 6 examines the study's policy implications.

The ethnographic analysis was informed by 'control theory',[3] a criminological perspective that, instead of posing the question 'Why do people break the law?', asks, 'Why do people conform?' And replies that people are more likely to conform when they perceive that they have a vested interest in so doing, when they have more to lose than gain by law-breaking. This perspective has the virtue of explaining the law-breaking of both rich and poor, though economic factors are not posited as being the only determinants of how people calculate the rewards expected from either law-breaking or conformity. Nor need positive calculation be a prerequisite to law-breaking. A drift into crime, accompanied by the concomitant rewards of friendship, financial gain and excitement, can engender the alternative 'controls' that gradually commit the woman law-breaker to a way of life more satisfying than that offered by conventional labour and marriage markets and/or the meagre (and often uncertain) welfare payments of the Department of Health and Social Security. Thus the inversion of a control theory explaining why the majority of women appear to be law-abiding only partly explains why *some* other women break the law in the first place. It is even less useful in explaining why a few of all women law-breakers go on to become recidivist criminals and prisoners.

Instead therefore of analysing only the processes that condition the conformity of women who are law-abiding, this book will also analyse the particular combinations of circumstances at the specific points in their criminal careers when these thirty-nine women felt that they had absolutely *nothing* to lose (and *maybe* something to gain) by engaging in criminal activity. Marginalized by a combination of class position (the poverty of which denied them adequate material means for alleviating their multiple personal misfortunes such as ill-health, bereavement and isolation), gender, in some cases racism, and in all cases overcriminalization, the women frequently implied that at certain times in their lives they had had neither material nor ideological incentive to be law-abiding. Once they had broken the law (in some cases even *before* they had – see Chapter 4), the inequalities stemming from class, gender and, in some cases, racism, combined to overdetermine their almost certain criminalization. Subsequent institutionalization, outlawing (as far as employment was concerned) and ensuing commitment to a deviant lifestyle ensured that the further they progressed in their criminal careers, the more their options narrowed, the less they had to lose by being 'nicked', and the less they had to gain by conformity. The implicit logic (though not the circumstances and rewards!) of their law-breaking was similar to that of many corporate criminals: that the competitive ethos embodied in Thatcherite capitalism had created conditions implicitly licensing them to get what they could by any means available. For the major differences between white-collar and working-class crime, between men's and women's crimes, and between crimes committed by white and black persons, lie not *primarily* in the reasons, rationales and ideologies associated with the initial law-breaking (though there *are* differences for each group), but in the differential rates and modes of their subsequent criminalization according to class, gender and race.

Cautionary note.   A full analysis of the social and political meanings of crime would explain not only why some people break the law but also why certain groups can continue to do so with impunity. For, while the majority of the economically disadvantaged and the powerless do not become recidivist criminals, many acts of serious law-breaking (most, if we refer only to financial crimes) result neither from poverty nor any other kind of deprivation. It might, therefore, be instructive to readers, as they engage with the stories of these thirty-nine women, to ponder also on the very different economic and political circumstances of that larger group of law-breakers whose crimes are seldom brought to book. I refer, of course, to the crimes of the rich and the powerful.

WOMEN, CRIME AND POVERTY
SUMMARY OF THE ARGUMENTS

Four major factors – poverty, being in residential Care, drug (including alcohol) addiction and the quest for excitement – were explicitly identified by the thirty-nine women as being prime constituents of their law-breaking and criminalization. Ethnographic analysis of the women's oral histories was directed both at finding out *how* and explaining *why* such law-breaking and criminalization had come about. What, therefore, is presented as narrative in Chapters 4 and 5 was originally produced within a theoretical analysis that in turn engendered the argument structuring that narrative. A summary of the general argument is outlined herewith and is partly repeated and then amplified at the beginning of Chapter 4 where it has particular relevance to the Care stage of some women's criminal careers.

1 Whereas for working-class men in employment the major locus of social control is the workplace (Young, 1975), working-class women have traditionally been contained within *two* material and ideological sites of social

control, the workplace and the family. Working-class women have therefore been doubly controlled. They have been expected not only to make the 'class deal' but the 'gender deal' too.

2 Most working-class women make both the class deal and the gender deal because the exploitative nature of those two deals is obscured by ideologies of familiness and consumerism working together to engender within them a commitment to, if not a belief in, the imaginary rewards of respectable working-class womanhood.

3 This commitment to the rewards of 'respectable working-class womanhood' is most likely to be engendered when young women are brought up in families where both psychological and material rewards are represented as emanating from either the labours or the 'love' of a male breadwinner. (Even though many families do not nowadays *have* a male breadwinner, the normative heterosexuality celebrated in women's magazines, pop songs and the predominantly conservative and liberal mass media still represents male-related domesticity coupled with a wage-earning job as the twin ideals to which all (gender-) competent modern women should aspire).

4 Under certain circumstances some women do not acquire the psychological commitments to male-related domesticity, tend not to have their class position occluded by the outward trappings or inner constraints of bourgeois family ideology and yet *do* acquiesce in a commitment to consumerism which is the only space within which they believe they can make their own lives.

5 The majority of women do not become embroiled in criminal careers, even if they do break the law on occasion. This undercriminalization occurs because, while they remain within the family, they are seen to have made the gender deal and to be gender regulated. Conversely, girls in Care, single women living alone and other 'women without men' are often seen as being gender decontrolled. Already seen, therefore, as being *unregulated women*, they are also seen as being potential recidivist law-breakers and the authorities act accordingly.

6 The early imprisonment of young women combines with prevailing economic and ideological conditions to minimalize (or in many cases destroy) the likelihood of their having either future opportunities or inclinations to make either the class deal or the gender deal. They perceive themselves as being marginalized and therefore, having nothing to lose, decide that law-breaking is a preferable alternative to poverty and social isolation.

7 Those women who are rendered marginal by their lack of commitment to both the class deal and the gender deal can also experience a sense of injustice as a result of two major social and political discourses: the 'Christmas card' image of family life and the private/public distinction that celebrates the myth that the governance of family and domesticity should (and indeed does) remain beyond the purview and regulation of the state.

8 The thirty-nine women had in the main committed crime because, in addition

to experiencing poverty and an excess of welfare regulation, they had also sensed that such poverty and welfare regulation violate some of the most fundamental liberal political discourses concerning welfare rights and the rights of private citizens.

9 The women's perceptions of the class and gender deals on offer to them had not been alone in atrophying their capacity to believe in and/or be regulated by either state laws or patriarchal mores. Additionally, the contemporary and competing rhetorics of social welfare and individualistic consumerism had engendered in them a strong commitment to obtaining a decent standard of living and to defending their domestic and personal space by *any* means within their power.

Like all other British women these thirty-nine were born into material conditions structured by two dominant sets of relationships – the class relationships of a capitalist mode of production and the gender relationships of a patriarchal system of social reproduction. Unlike the majority, they had refused to be party to the contract that had been drawn up for them. But their refusals had been neither silent nor polite. The persistence of their nuisances, the violence of their resistances and the audacity of their insouciance before the authorities had gradually marked them, their actions and their files with a criminality that must eventually defy the best jurisprudential attempts to represent them as victims (cf. Allen, 1987). Nor would they wish to be so represented. What follows, therefore, is a theoretical commentary on the women's own vivid accounts of how they set about making their lives within conditions which had certainly not been of their own choosing. Conditions, in fact, that no sane persons *would* choose.

2

WOMEN IN CRIME

> In 1868 Madam Rachel was brought to trial at the Old Bailey for obtaining money on false pretences . . . That she had been a procuress at some time, and that she was a swindler all the time, are not the interesting features of her career. She is extraordinary because she anticipated by more than half a century the most modern methods of advertising. She . . . would have had nothing to learn from courses in salesmanship or the findings of consumer research.
>
> (Jenkins (1949), writing about Madam Sarah Rachel Leverson whose New Bond Street shop 'Beautiful for Ever', was opened in 1863)

While court records and official statistics have always portrayed women as being much more law-abiding than men (Hanawalt, 1979 and 1980; Beattie, 1980), the recent researches of Box (1983) suggest that official statistics most probably do reflect a real difference in the law-breaking activities of men and women. Yet, however meagre women's contribution to the sum total of crime, the relatively small numbers of female criminals have over the ages embraced the whole spectrum of criminal ingenuity and socially injurious behaviour. And they have not always been women in poverty and without power. Indeed, at odd moments in history certain unusually placed and powerful women have demonstrated the will and capacity to be as exploitative, ruthless and contriving as their male rivals. Fourteenth-century Alice Perrers and nineteenth-century Madam Sarah Rachel Leverson are cases in point. Their stories, to be found in E. Jenkins's *Six Criminal Women*, indicate that they were both attuned to the particular economic and cultural conditions of their times and that they could manipulate them to their advantage and with aplomb.

Alice Perrers was a white-collar criminal in the sense that she committed her crimes in the 'normal' course of her occupation – of being mistress to Edward III. Involved in the crimes of 'maintenance' and extortion, Alice let it be known that she would 'use her influence to secure a favourable verdict for a suitor provided she were given a sufficiently large share of the gains' (Jenkins,

1949: 39). But she was no mere closet criminal and her sphere of operation was certainly not confined to the bedroom.

> When a cause in which she was financially interested was being heard Alice would appear in Westminster Hall and seat herself on a bench beside the judge. This example of the insolence of power has never been surpassed. From this vantage ground Alice instructed the judge in what verdict he ought to give . . . She also worked in a combine . . .
>
> (Jenkins, 1949)

After Edward's death most of Alice's ill-gotten gains were forfeited, though, as is usual with white-collar criminals, she never experienced the full rigours of the law and was spared the deprivations and indignities of actual poverty.

In 1863 Madam Sarah Rachel Leverson opened her shop at 47a New Bond Street and called it 'Beautiful for Ever'. To it came the rich but unhappy Victorian women who were ripe for exploitation as they tried to fulfil cruel social demands that they maintain their youthful looks and beauty for ever. Madam Rachel's first prison sentence, however, was for obtaining money by false pretences from a woman who had paid over large sums in the belief that Madam Rachel was arranging her a marriage with a lord. Not so highly placed as Alice Perrers, Madam Rachel eventually died in prison in 1878 while serving a second five-year sentence for again obtaining money by false pretences. Had she been born a century later she would undoubtedly have been able to fulfil a legitimate and powerful position in the pharmaceutical industry (cf. Braithwaite, 1983).

Historical accounts of women in crime together with analyses of the kind of crimes most regularly committed by females do indeed suggest that, on the rare occasions when British women have found themselves in the arms of the law, the majority have been apprehended for committing either minor or impulsive property crimes or personal violence against people already known to them (Hanawalt, 1980; Beattie, 1980; Hartmann, 1977). Yet, at the same time, the rarer but regular emergence of women like extortionist Alice Perrers, pickpocket Jenny Diver (real name Jane Webb) and con-woman Rachel Leverson, indicates that, given both opportunity and the talent to make the most of it, women can and will engage in the more systematic, organized and professional types of law-breaking conventionally assumed to be the prerogative of males. Additionally, the participation of women in anti-clearance revolts (Richards, 1974), rent strikes (Young, 1979) and, more recently, twentieth-century terrorist organizations, testifies to the willingness and capacity of politically outraged women to perpetrate criminal violence in pursuance of political ends. That, conversely, there have always been women prepared to exploit other women – and particularly women as poor as themselves – is instanced by the cases of female racketeers in wartime Britain (Smithies, 1982) and routinely revealed in the records of those lower criminal courts that have predominantly been more concerned to process the crimes of the powerless than the powerful (Hanawalt, 1980; Beattie, 1980). Recent court cases concerning child abuse provide timely reminders to feminists that violence towards other family members is not totally a male phenomenon (cf. Allen, 1987), whilst perusal of fourteenth-century records reveal that it most probably never has been (Hanawalt, 1980).

With the main exceptions of murder, manslaughter, sexual assault and kidnapping (and I talked with women convicted of all these crimes in a previous study: Carlen, 1983a), the women I interviewed had between them committed the whole gamut of more serious crimes including 'granny bashing', 'baby bashing', 'mugging', armed robbery, arson, burglary, pickpocketing, shop-lifting, criminal damage, drug smuggling, fraud, forgery and grievous bodily harm. They had operated in mixed teenage gangs specializing in violence, burglary or sheer hell-raising, in single-sex shoplifting rings, and in organized international drug smuggling; some had engaged in systematic 'mugging' activities, others had involved themselves with professional criminals known to carry firearms. Still others had not scorned the more traditional female crimes of managing or assisting in sophisticated businesses purveying a varied and imaginative range of sexual services. As ex-prisoners many were as well versed in the skills and artifices required for crimes they had never committed as they were confident of their expertise in those they had. Thus, although it will be argued that women's conformity, law-breaking and criminalization are constituted within material and ideological circumstances that are qualitatively different from men's, in this chapter it is argued that, when women *do* break the law:

1 they do so not only because they 'find themselves' outwith conventional class and gender controls but also because they *choose* criminal means in attempts to apply individualistic remedies to the social inequities stemming from class exploitation, sexism and racism;
2 their methods are determined primarily by contemporary modes of criminal organization and operation that (with only a few exceptions) are more class than gender specific.

WOMEN, CRIME, GENDER AND CLASS

A very tan-rig or rumpscuttle she was, and delighted and sported only in boy's play and pastime, not minding or companying with the girls . . . she could not endure their sedentary life of sewing or stitching; a sampler was as grievous as a winding-sheet; her needle, bodkin and thimble she could not think on quietly, wishing them changed into sword or dagger for a bout at cudgels.

(Anonymous pamphlet, *The Life and Death of Mary Frith commonly called Moll Cutpurse*, originally published in 1612 (Salgado, 1977))

> I was a proper little bugger, you know. I used to go out with the boys from
> the housing estate . . . I didn't have sex, nothing like that, but I loved
> being with boys, never with girls.
>
> (Cynthia Payne (Madam Cyn) *c.* 1981 (Bailey, 1982))

A recurrent theme in the relatively few autobiographies and biographies of
women criminals is the women's disdain and active dislike for the constricting
social roles that have been systematically ascribed to women through the ages.
This recorded fact has, moreover, been repeatedly taken up by criminologists
and transformed into a tautological theory: women who engage in those lawless
behaviours, more usually conceived as being the prerogatives of men, do so
because they are, in essence, masculine (Lombroso and Ferrero, 1895; Cowie,
Cowie and Slater, 1968). Yet, as will be seen in Chapter 3, although the majority
of women in this study had committed crimes of a much more serious nature
than those usually committed by women, they had tended to see themselves as
strong *women* rather than surrogate men. Indeed, those who had worn male
garb had done so primarily to protect themselves as *women* from men. 'No',
said one of them to me, 'I certainly didn't see myself as a man. I saw myself as a
woman who was thoroughly pissed-off' (Nadia). But, regardless of how they
had seen themselves, as the women had progressed from participation in
teenage gangs, 'amateur' shoplifting or prostitution, to more serious crimes of
violence or crimes against property, it had undoubtedly become more difficult
for them to enter the conventional labour or marriage markets, and more
difficult, too, even to claim supplementary benefit without becoming objects of
what they had experienced as an excess of official surveillance (cf. Cook, 1987).
However, as the women's choice of presentational style had been as varied as
both their choice of crimes and the progress of their criminal careers, it would be
fruitless for me to attempt to reduce their stories to a uniform explanation of
'typical' women's crimes.[1] What I shall do instead, therefore, is present some of
the 'law-breaking stages' or 'law-breaking syndromes' that I had described to
me either most frequently or in most depth when I asked the women about their
criminal careers.

HELL-RAISING GANGS

One of the sadder admissions of some of the women was that, as teenagers, they
had not realized that the price exacted for nonconformity to conventional
gender roles (what they called 'having fun') or a determination to obtain
consumer goods by criminal means would be so high. In the case of persistent
petty offenders this lack of foresight is readily understandable: they had not
known that sentences are determined not only by the seriousness of the
individual offence but also by the length of the offender's record. But other
women, those found guilty of more serious offences in their teens, had also not

foreseen the effects of their actions. These women had mainly been brought up in Care or in certain neighbourhoods where they had seen their law-breaking as being a bit of conventional fun, 'what everyone in the Children's Home [or 'round there'] did.' This is not to say that these women claimed that they had been *forced* into crime, merely to emphasize that for many of them their youthful law-breaking had been so rewarding *in itself*, that is, so productive of the excitement, friendship and action that they otherwise lacked, that neither its possible financial rewards nor the penal price to be paid if caught had been a prime consideration immediately prior to, or at the time of, crime commission. This insistence on the intrinsic satisfaction gained from law-breaking featured in the accounts of all seventeen women who at an early stage of their careers had been members of what I have called 'hell-raising gangs'.

Della, Daphne, Cynthia, Shirley, Yasmin, Josie, Jill, Bobby, Lisa, Tricia, Anne, Lena, Donna, Hazel, Muriel, Audrey and Mary had, as very young teenagers, all been members of mixed gangs. Their activities had included making 'joke' 999 calls, setting fires, defacing grave-stones, taking and driving away motor vehicles, fighting other gangs, having parties in empty properties, breaking and entering business premises, drinking and drugs bouts, some fairly amateurish burglaries, and, in two cases, the provision of sexual stimulation to elderly men in return for money that was then spent on drinks parties. The main activities of all these groups had, however, centred on a variety of crimes involving property and/or fighting. Shirley's activities had been typical of those who said that their gangs had done 'a bit of everything'; Bobby's typical of the members of fighting gangs.

> It was a mixture of everything. We needed the money and it was exciting. If we didn't do anything we'd be bored, so it was mainly to get money and to keep ourselves occupied. We used to take trips to London, sightseeing, but it always turned out we'd done something. Like we was nicking drink to get the money to buy cannabis. Stuff we'd nicked we'd sell it, electrical goods and things like that. [Shirley, aged 20]

> Best thing is, right? If anybody is ever after us, they daren't touch me because if they did they'd have the other nine to deal with. Like my mate, right? She's got to go to court for hitting this girl. If my mate gets sent down, I'll go and kill the girl if I can. That's the way we are. We're just sort of mental, but it's the best way to be really 'cos you've got a lot of provocative people on to you. But we're not mouthy, we don't go round to someone and say, 'We're going to smack your face', or something like that. We'll go up to 'em, say 'Eh up! How are you?' and all that lot. We'd never class them as one of the gang, but we'd laugh and joke with them. But, if we go to Loughborough, if there's other gangs give us dirty looks, we just go and fight with them. That's the way we are. [Bobby, aged 15]

Fighting was not the only source of excitement. Drug-taking, shoplifting, housebreaking, burglary, taking and driving away and robbery were all described as being productive of the 'buzz' or the 'kick' that the younger women had valued so highly. Unfortunately these buzz-producing activities had also had other by-products; in some cases they had become habit-forming, in all cases they had resulted in a criminal record. By the age of 20 Cynthia had begun to have second thoughts: 'I thought that life was a game, but it ain't, is it? It's a gamble, and I'm gambling with my life.' Others, by the age of 20, had either already chosen to engage in more serious forms of property crime or been involved in more serious crimes of violence. Some had chosen 'to go in with the heavies' after a spell in Borstal or Youth Custody Centre had made them decide that 'next time it would be for something big'. A few had found that, because their 'reputation' had preceded them either to or from Borstal, they had to prove themselves to be as big as their 'rep' or lose face.

VIOLENCE

> Virtually all our ideas of femininity . . . are derived from the middle-class 'lady'. To be pampered, egotistical, passive, nurturous, care-taking requires a certain level of economic security.
>
> (Campbell, 1981: 150)

Although fourteen women had convictions for violence against the person, only three had committed their violent acts in pursuit of gain, i.e. during robberies. Without exception the others had committed their assaults and other crimes of violence when they had felt threatened by other people. Even two of the three who *had* been involved in robberies claimed that their primary satisfaction had derived from the feelings of power or comradeship experienced during the violent episodes.

> I done this robbery with an electric carving knife. I went out to get this money and it was this Paki geezer. I put the knife up to his throat and took the money, but as I was coming out of the shop he started to fight me, and three old women coming past the shop went next door and rang the old Bill. I was just getting away from this geezer with the money when all these [police] cars pulled up. I was their local hero for a day. [Muriel, aged 30]

> She was with another old lady. One went one way and she went that way. I sort of walked in front of her and we had a chain and sort of wrapped that round her head. She got a big cut on her forehead. I've done robberies for quite a long time, see. The highest we ever got was about £50 but, see, there was no need for me to do robberies 'cos I was into my shoplifting.

But then all me mates got into robberies, though we mostly robbed young people. [Tricia, aged 17]

None of the women unreservedly expressed remorse for the injuries they had inflicted. Several said they thought violent behaviour should not be tolerated, that 'violence' in the abstract was undesirable. But then each followed such a statement with an explanation as to why, in her own case, violence had been necessary – to her self-esteem, self-preservation or to protection of her own physical, domestic or psychological space. At least five of the fourteen who had been accused of crimes of violence against the person had themselves been victims of severe domestic violence. Often, too, they indicated that they would not expect me, from my privileged and 'pampered' vantage point, to understand that, for those without privilege and power, violent acts can both provide the kicks that are the spice of life *and* be the currency of morals and status enforcement. Norma, who had caused terrible injuries to her victim, described how she had punished an acquaintance who had grassed on her.

I asked them [the police] how they knew and they said that they had been informed through this girl, Kirsty . . . I picked up a dog chain . . and we got to Kirsty's house and I asked her why the police had come to my door. She said she hadn't said anything and I just laid hell into her . . . She got to the windowsill and said she was going to jump . . . I ran down the stairs and she was lying on the pavement in a pool of blood. She'd broken both her arms, her leg, five ribs, split her mouth open, cut her nose open, broken a bone in her back and half-ripped her tongue off. She went into a coma for two weeks but came out of it; which I'm basically grateful for, otherwise they would have done me for attempted murder – which they were going to but the charge was dropped from attempted murder to grievous bodily harm with intent. [Norma, aged 22]

Carol explained why she had literally taken the law into her own hands in order to collect a debt.

I sold a colour television to a lady over the road there and I couldn't get the money off her. I did phone the police the week before and they said they couldn't do anything. That day when I hit her I said, 'Irene, have you got any money for my telly?' and she just stood there giving me a load of abuse – that's what got my hair off, her mouthing at me. So I hit her. I pasted her and she took me to court for assault. Said she had two broken fingers. [Carol, aged 27]

When I asked them *how* they had learned to fight, most women thought the question a strange one. Jill said her dad had taught her and Carol that her fighting had begun in response to teasing at school:

How did I learn to fight? Well, since I was a kid, since I was about 12, I'm covered from head to foot in psoriasis, and when the kids used to say 'Look at her, scabby,' I used to turn round and hit 'em one . . . [Carol, aged 27]

But most shrugged off my question by stating that they had been forced either to fight or threaten violence in order to survive family life, street life, Care, welfare surveillance, Borstal , police station and prison.

I'm not hard really. It's just that when people get me going – if they push me and push me, that's when the punches will swing out. But if I am having a fight with someone, I won't stop until I've done bad to him. [Lena, aged 21]

If I was threatened in any way, I would hit out. I wouldn't let anyone get away with pushing me around or talking to me like a piece of shit. I would fight to my death. And it was like a sort of status thing and I got off on that, a bit, I suppose. But I remember once consciously thinking 'Oh Christ, it's like I've got to keep it up', when there were times when I didn't really want to fight but still carried on. [Nadia, aged 35]

I've hit many a copper but they don't charge you because they know you're hitting them back in defence. In here [Bullwood Hall] no one has took liberties with me because they've heard my mouth. First day I come in here, this officer says, 'Get to your room'. I said. 'Listen, don't get rash because you're a screw. Because this mouth and this fist can work untold times faster than you could ever do.' And she just looked at me and must have thought, 'Oh! Gotta be careful.' [Cynthia, aged 19]

It was when they talked about violence that the women were most ill at ease or impatient with me. They knew that I 'wouldn't understand'. They thought that I was making too much of what for them had been a fact of life as they had known it. Bobby expressed the generally held view when she simply stated:

I can't say I like fighting and I can't say I don't. I mean, if someone gives me a dirty look, I'll smack 'em one. So I can't say I don't like it and I can't say I do. I just do it if anyone does owt wrong to me. [Bobby, aged 15]

Josie finally silenced me with:

You've never been in a situation where you've had to hit someone before they hit you, have you? If you had, I think you'd understand it more. [Josie, aged 30]

TABLE 2.1   Nature of drug-related offences committed

Name (age) at interview	Drug-related offence	Drug involved	Nature of relationship between drug and offence
Della (15)	Assault	Glue	Offence committed when in her own words she was 'high'
Yasmin (16)	Criminal damage	Glue	Offence committed after she had been sniffing glue
Shirley (20)	1 Possessing drugs	1 Cannabis/other	1 Possession for own use
	2 Arson	2 Alcohol and cannabis	2 'Drunk' and 'stoned' at time of offence
Jessie (20)	Deception (in relation to forged prescriptions); possession of drugs; conspiracy to supply	Heroin and other	Offences committed to finance own heroin habit
Anne (20)	Shoplifting; fraud; burglary	Heroin and other	Offences committed to finance own heroin habit
Jill (21)	Burglary; assault	Alcohol	Offences committed always after heavy alcohol consumption
Lisa (21)	Fraud	Heroin	Later offences committed to finance own heroin habit
Kay (21)	Fraud	Heroin	Offences committed to finance own heroin habit
Lena (21)	Arson	Glue	Committed when, in her own words, she was 'glued up'
Dawn (23)	Attempting to supply heroin	Heroin	Offences committed to finance her own heroin habit
Mary (27)	1 Arson	1 Alcohol	1 Dropped cigarette when in drunken stupor
	2 Forgery (prescriptions)	2 Unknown	2 Unknown
Nicky (27)	Burglary; shoplifting; fraud; deception	Heroin	Offences committed to finance own heroin habit
Zoë (28)	Forgery (prescriptions)	Unknown	Unknown
Hazel (29)	Arson and carrying firearm with intent to endanger life	Alcohol	Fire accidentally started whilst in drunken stupor
Jeanette (30)	Customs evasion	Cannabis	Offence committed for financial gain
Nadia (35)	Forgery (prescriptions); shoplifting	Heroin	To supply/finance own heroin habit
Sally (35)	Soliciting; possession of drugs	Heroin	To finance/supply own heroin habit
Yvonne (37)	Evasion of customs	Cannabis	Offence committed for financial gain
Queenie (43)	1 Shoplifting	1 Alcohol	1 Later offences committed when drunk
	2 Forgery (prescriptions)	2 Unknown	2 Unknown
Monica (44)	Shoplifting	Alcohol	Offences committed to finance purchase of alcohol for own consumption

DRUGS, DRINK, POVERTY
AND POWERLESSNESS

As we will see in Chapter 3, seventeen of the women claimed that at some time they had had an addiction to either glue, heroin or alcohol, and both they and many of the others who had never had an addiction also said that they had taken amphetamines, cannabis and other drugs whenever they had had easy access to them. In fact, all thirty-nine said that on occasion they had used illicitly obtained drugs. Six had convictions for forging doctors' prescriptions. Two women who had neither had an addiction nor ever been heavily involved in drug-taking had convictions for drug-smuggling. Altogether, twenty of the thirty-nine had committed drug-related offences, though, as Table 2.1 indicates, the nature of the relationship between offence and drug had varied. In the cases of two women (cited above) the factor relating drug to offence had been profit motive: they had been motivated to commit the offence because of the high financial gain to be had from trafficking in illegal drugs. Nine had committed offences in order to finance or supply their own addictive habits; eight had committed at least some of the crimes when they had been either drunk, 'glued-up' or 'high' on a variety of drugs; one had been convicted of being in possession (for her own use); and one, Zoë, could not remember exactly why she had forged prescriptions!

It was with reference to crimes committed to finance drug addictions that the women had appeared to be most conscious of their choice of offence. Sally, for instance, said that, whereas she did not regard prostitution as morally wrong, she was pleased that she had never financed her heroin habit by committing crimes of dishonesty. Conversely, all the other addicts said that they would rather commit any crime of dishonesty than fund their habit through prostitution. Yet, whatever the relationship between drug and criminal offence, it was mainly in relation to drugs-related offences that women mentioned 'depression', isolation, boredom and poverty, as being associated factors – even in those two cases where the prime motive for committing the offence had been directly related to profit rather than any need to fund an addiction.

This is not to argue that only the poor take drugs or that drug-taking (legal or not) is either directly or indirectly only caused by poverty. It *is* to assert that, whilst drugs (including alcohol) are easily available, then those already living on the margins have a higher likelihood than others of being both casualties of drug abuse and/or victims of the state's attempts to regulate it by criminal sanctions. In examining just four dimensions of the 'crime and drugs' problem as it was exemplified in the lives of these twenty marginalized women, it will be seen how, at least in the short term, drug usage and drug-related crimes either gave relief, or at least promised to give relief, from living situations that were being experienced at the best as being bleak or at the worst as being unendurable (cf. Messerschmidt, 1986: 78).

Evasion of Customs (cannabis)

Jeanette, aged 30 and Yvonne, aged 37, were both given their first prison sentences for evasion of customs when illegally attempting to bring cannabis into the country. Jeanette was a single parent who worked in a night club and who had three previous convictions for (police) assault (of a minor nature). She had been approached and recruited for the crime at a time when she was depressed and out of work after having a major abdominal operation. She said that, although her apparent reason for agreeing to the deal was economic, in retrospect she thought that she had also regarded it as a 'test', something to brighten up her life. Her description of the crime was brief.

> I was guilty. I had been introduced to somebody. I had just had my operation. I wasn't really in need of the money. I had friends who would lend me money. But because I wasn't working at that time I was tempted. It sounded okay, to go away for a few days to Zurich for £2,000. I was assured that everything would be 100 per cent good for me to get through. I took a gamble and I lost it. [Jeanette, aged 30]

Jeanette was arrested in Customs and eventually sentenced to twelve months' imprisonment. She was of the opinion that the following facts had gone against her in court: that she was a single parent; that she was already 'known' to social services (having been in dispute with them about the welfare of her child); that she was already 'known' to the police as a result of being forced to give evidence against the procuring activities of a male customer at the night club where she worked as a receptionist; and that she already had convictions for assault, all of which had involved disputes with the police at her place of work.

Yvonne had also committed her crime when depressed, physically ill (cervical cancer was diagnosed during her six-month term of imprisonment), mentally disturbed (she was, at the time, waiting for a psychiatric appointment at a leading London hospital) and recently out of work. She had never been in criminal trouble before, but, as had happened with Jeanette, Yvonne's previous work in night clubs and restaurants (as a singer) had brought her into contact with people who had interests in a variety of criminal enterprises, including the illegal importation of cannabis. To those on the lookout for recruits to drug-smuggling Jeanette and Yvonne would have appeared ideal candidates: both were articulate, very presentable, and had 'been around' long enough to be able to keep cool in a crisis. Most importantly, because they were out of work, it could also be assumed that they might be very much tempted by a promise of a relatively large financial reward. Yvonne's story is best told in her own words.

> Maybe I should start off by telling you a bit basically about myself. I was depressed for quite some time and a situation came up where I could perhaps get myself out of the major problems that I had, which were: I wasn't working – I'm a singer – song-writer and I had a few years of

success and then all of a sudden just nothing happened; I was living in bed-and-breakfast accommodation . . . and you got drug addicts and alcoholics in there which was making me depressed; and emotionally there was a big gap in my life. I didn't have a boyfriend and so everything at the same time seemed to get on top of me. My doctor had made me an appointment for a psychiatrist, saying he'd like an emergency appointment, and he prescribed me tablets. My whole world was upside down when a friend suggested I take a trip to the West Indies. I'd saved up some money from the time I was a croupier and I decided I'd go because I really felt like committing suicide. I thought, 'I might as well go on this trip and then if I feel like committing suicide when I get back,' you know, when you get so depressed you think about illogical things in a very logical fashion. (It frightens you afterwards when you pull yourself out of it – you know, 'How could I be thinking like that?')

Anyway, I arrived over in the West Indies and I was approached while I was over there . . . and it just seemed that this was an ideal opportunity to get myself out of my situation. I just felt, you know, if it doesn't work I can always commit suicide. It was stupid. Anyway, I did the thing; I got caught at Heathrow . . .

I mean, we weren't talking about thousands, just a couple of thousand, just to give me a start, to put down a deposit on a decent flat, to make me push forward and get some work. But after I'd said, 'Yes' to the deal, to be honest with you, my bottle went. But I was too far into it by that time. My suitcase had been taken away, the stuff was being pressed into it, and obviously if you've got the facilities to do all this pressing business you're talking about the big boys . . . It was just too late and I had to swallow my fears and go ahead. My arm hadn't been twisted, I hadn't felt any pressure but, you see, because I'd agreed to it, I didn't know what the repercussions would be if I backed out later. I had been told that the way they were handling this thing was that somebody was going to travel on the aeroplane with me. I wouldn't know them but they would know me and I would be contacted in London. Half the money would be put up front when I arrived – £1000 – and once the stuff had been sold I would get another £1000. At Heathrow I was in the middle of the Green and Red Section and I thought, 'Well, the best thing I can do' – I mean, I had no rule-book for smuggling you know, 'is just do what I would do if I was coming back from any place.' . . . I was then aware of this very big chap following me . . . [Yvonne, aged 37]

Yvonne was stopped. Her suitcase was searched. She was arrested, charged and sent for trial. She pleaded guilty and was sentenced to six months' imprisonment.

Glue-sniffing

Glue-sniffing and other solvent abuse had been limited to the younger women interviewed. Della, Yasmin, Shirley, Jill and Lena all admitted to having had an addiction to glue-sniffing while still in Care, though all claimed that they had already given up the habit by the time of commencing their current Youth Custody sentences. Three of them, Lena, Yasmin and Della, attributed some of their offences to their 'glued-up' state at the time of crime commission.

Pat: Why did you set fire to the carpet?
Lena: 'Cos I was 'glued-up' – I used to glue-sniff. Plus I didn't like it there, the warden was a bit too strict.

I used to glue-sniff for a long time but then I gave it up. You're more aggressive on glue I think. I just go crazy on it, I just freak out. [Yasmin, aged 16]

All five women (unlike the users of other drugs) made almost totally negative remarks about glue, as well as comparing it unfavourably with the other drugs they had used. However, though all said that they had found it relatively easy to stop glue-sniffing, they had all subsequently engaged in other drug usage. Della spoke at length about the attractions and effects of glue.

There'd be certain places you'd go to sniff and you'd see loads of people doing it. I just started it because my friends did it. First of all, we used to nick it and sometimes we used to buy it. But then they started putting it behind the counters and you weren't allowed to buy it unless you were over sixteen. So that was one of the other reasons why we tried to give it up. When you're high, you don't care what you're doing – stealing or fighting. I mean, if you see people you get really paranoid about it, you think they're looking at you, and you just go up and hit them and the Old Bill gets called in. Glue just closes your head, and you don't know what you're doing. You just do anything. First of all, I did it because you get a buzz and then after a while you're just getting hallucinations. Some are jolly good but some get bad and so in the end I got really scared, because I kept getting bad hallucinations and had all rashes on my face. I just couldn't be bothered to eat or nothing. I'd just get up, get ready to go out, fix glue, sniff it all day, get glued and do it until about 12 o'clock at night. You look a mess, you've got scabs and sores all over you mouth and you get it all over your clothes and hands. [Della, aged 15]

And Yasmin agreed. 'I just couldn't handle it any more,' she said. 'Stuff reeks.' According to these five, therefore, solvent abuse had been initially engaged in as a communal activity promising relief from bleak lives (see Chapters 4 and 5 on the early experiences of each of these young women). Once, however, they had become frightened by hallucinations, their own aggressive behaviour or the sickening physical effects of 'sniffing', it had been, they claimed, relatively easy to abandon glue in favour of alcohol (Jill, Lena, Della), cannabis (Shirley, Yasmin) and LSD (Yasmin).

Alcohol-related crimes

Alcohol consumption is so deeply imbricated within British culture that it is not surprising that a majority of women referred to times in their lives when they had been drinking heavily. Conversely, a few said that, because they had seen the domestic violence that had ensued after their father or other men had been drinking, they had 'always been against drink'. However, only five (Jill, Mary, Hazel, Queenie and Monica) of the thirty-nine said that they had ever had an addiction to alcohol. Those five and Shirley were the only ones, too, who said that some of their more serious crimes had been alcohol related, though there were several others who mentioned that they had often been in trouble with the police as a result of teenage drinking bouts, and who told of states of mind similar to Anne's when she said, 'From the age of fourteen, whenever I went out, I always had to be drunk.'

Shirley, Hazel and Mary had not intended to cause fires but had both been convicted for arson after they had 'endangered life', when they had carelessly dropped matches whilst drunk. Shirley's and Hazel's offences had been relatively minor, Mary's more serious.

> I was in the police station one day and I'd been picked up on the bus with my friend and we were drunk and had had a bit, you know. And I was in the cell and I was smoking a fag. I lit a match and I lit the fag and threw the match on the floor. It caught light to a blanket, so I picked up the mattress to put it out. I was stamping on the mattress but it burnt the mattress too . . . [Shirley, aged 20]

> I had no electricity or gas at my flat so I had candles. I came home drunk and knocked the candles over, so I got done for arson. It wasn't actually arson as such, but they call it arson when you endanger life. [Hazel, aged 29]

When Mary had accidentally set fire to the flat in which her baby was sleeping, she had been crying drunk.

> All I remember was, I was sat at the bar and there's only about five of us there, including the landlord. I'd just been having a drink and just sat at the bar. I don't even know who was there. I had an argument with the landlord over something and I punched him. I can remember standing outside the pub and I was crying 'cos I couldn't walk and I don't remember going home at all. Tony said he let me in and that I was in a right state – couldn't even stand up, so I don't know how I got home. I remember

sitting on the settee, I remember kicking my shoes off and I remember getting a fag out. Next minute I was woken up and the settee next to me was on fire. [Mary, aged 27]

It was as a consequence of this fire that Mary was serving a three-year sentence for arson.

Four of the five, who admitted to either having or having had in the past, an addiction to alcohol, linked their drinking and their alcohol-related crimes to severe depression engendered by their bleak living circumstances. Of these four, both Mary and Hazel had made several suicide attempts, whilst one of Jill's most serious bouts of drinking (the one that had eventually climaxed with her being involved in a stabbing incident) had begun after she had come out of Styal prison with her baby and the social worker had attempted to settle her in a Homeless Families' Unit. Monica, unlike the other four, had not experienced much hardship in her life until, in her mid-thirties, she had had three miscarriages and also started having epileptic fits. Hazel and Monica had both tried to assuage the pain of losing their babies by turning to alcohol.

When I lost my other child I was taking overdoses. I was having a nervous breakdown. Then they took him [her child] into Care and it just sort of cracked me up. My mate had this Hurricane air pistol – it wasn't really a bad sort of gun – you can only put pellets in it – and this policewoman came round. I'd had a few drinks and I started shooting. [Hazel, aged 29]

By this time I had lost my third baby. And then I was depressed and, when I was depressed, I wanted a drink. I used to do my housework and then sit and have my drink. And then I thought, 'I haven't been shoplifting in Hanley.' So I shoplifted in Hanley and got caught. [Monica, aged 44]

Heroin

It is nowadays well known that heroin addiction is to be found in all social classes and that its use can be as much lauded by the rich for giving a sense of meaning and power to their lives (cf. Picardie and Wade, 1985: 45) as it can by the poor for 'blanking off' the grim realities of theirs (Pearson et al., 1986: 75). However, as not one of the women in this study was even reasonably well-off, it is not surprising that all eight past and present heroin addicts emphasized the drug's 'blanking-off' powers as being its major attraction. All eight of them had had plenty to blank off. The four who had been in Care, i.e. Anne, Dawn, Nadia and Sally, had, together with Nicky, been on the run since their early teens. Of the others, Lisa had led a 'street life' from the age of 6 (see page 111), and Kay and Jessie were both recorded as having had such chronic depression that they had not been able to attend school but instead had been provided with home tutors. All seven, who had experimented with some kind of illegal drug before the age of 12 (Kay was the only heroin user who had not), claimed that the 'cocooning' effects of heroin had made it the most pleasurable drug that they had ever experienced.

Unlike the glue and alcohol users, the heroin addicts had not committed their crimes when experiencing either the immediate stimulus or stupefying effects of the drug. Rather they had knowingly committed their offences to ensure that their habit could be maintained at a level that would make it forever pleasurable. As a result, several of them distinguished between the drug addiction and the crimes committed to finance it and, though they regretted the latter, could not unambiguously denounce the heroin usage itself. Sally, who had been addicted for twenty years, was quite adamant that she would always choose to use at least some heroin. The three who at the time of interview were confident that their heroin usage was a thing of the past could still remember the pleasurable as well as the 'diabolical' effects of the drug. Not surprisingly, it was Sally who had the most well-developed position about the relationship between the law, heroin usage and crime (in her own case, prostitution) and, though Anne and Kay also gave vivid accounts of their crime careers as addicts, it should be noted that all eight heroin users in this study had had at least one conviction prior to the time of their addiction (cf. Auld, Dorn and South, 1986). Thus I am not claiming that poverty *causes* people to take heroin and that heroin then *causes* them to commit crime. Rather (and following Pearson *et al.*, 1986) I am suggesting that, once people experience the pleasure of heroin, whether or not they continue taking it will depend upon the incentives they have to come off and *stay off* it. For as Pearson *et al.* (1986: 75) put it:

> What 'keeps' people into heroin is what matters. For some it is the pleasure – the 'buzz'; the sense of power, the 'wrecked feeling' of gouching out. For others it is the ability of heroin to 'solve' their problems and to cushion them either from the world or from themselves.

Listen now to Anne, Kay and Sally as they talk about their addiction, their crimes and their general social circumstances. (Anne is talking as an ex-addict; Kay is talking as an imprisoned addict who doubts her ability to 'keep off' once she is released from prison; and Sally is talking as a committed addict, resentful of the laws relating to the regulation of heroin and other dangerous drugs.)

> The first time I fixed smack I was sixteen. It was with a girl I knew from Borstal. We met up outside and she was using smack. I wanted to try it because it sounded nice and a lot of girls inside were junkies and they were all talking about it . . . But I didn't get a habit until I was seventeen . . . The first time I came out [of Borstal] I was going to college and I enrolled for all these O levels, but I started dropping out of 'em one by one. I was getting more and more into smack. I used to think, 'Oh, even if I do get a habit, I can get off. It can't be that bad coming off.' But it really is, it really is.
>
> The first time we knew we had a habit, we were staying at my mother's,

and we'd had the last hit the day before. By the next day, when we were at my Mum's, I started to feel a bit ill and then I was really, really ill. I couldn't sleep at all. Anyway we went home the next morning and we had a little bit at home. We both had a fix and we were perfectly okay till the next morning, and that's when we realized we had a habit . . .

So I had a habit for three years. To finance it, first of all, we used to run for people, that's scoring for other people, and you get a bit out of it. Then I was shoplifting again, doing refunds, going getting loads of things and taking them round to this woman who got rid of it all for us and getting money. I was always running about scoring or running down the West End shoplifting. I was always saying I'd gotta come off it 'cos I was getting really depressed. I just couldn't see an end to all the shoplifting and getting money together.

It cost us £210 a week, sometimes more. At one point we were using a gramme a day. At another point we were using about £400 worth a week but that's when we were selling it. We were getting it laid on us by these guys who didn't use it at all and they just used to come round with loads of gear and dump it on us and we used to sell it for them.

You can't really blame it on anybody, like your friends or your dealer. I mean there are always circumstances, but once you've actually got a taste for it, if you want it, you'll get it. The physical part [of coming off] is one part of it, but then you've got the mental part which never leaves you. It never leaves you. You're always thinking about it. [Anne, aged 20]

What first happened was I started going out with him and he always had a lot of money and I was infatuated by him. He used to take me out to night clubs. He used to always be sniffing this line and one day he said to me, 'Have a sniff at that.' I said 'What is it?' and he told me it was sulphate, like speed. He didn't tell me it was heroin. I sniffed it and it made me feel really lovely and after that he used to say, 'Go on, have a little sniff,' and I didn't even know that it was heroin I was taking. For about nine months I just thought it was speed 'cos I've never seen speed so I didn't know the difference. I've never smoked weed and I don't even drink, nothing at all, and I was taking it for about nine months till I got up one morning and I was really sick. I thought 'God, why am I so ill?' and my friend said, 'Have you been taking the powder?' and I said 'yeh', and she said, 'It's smack – heroin – that you've been taking, not sulphate.' But I didn't know.

I was really ill. He was out all day and I didn't know where to go to buy it, so I had to wait for him to come home. And he said, 'Oh, give us your money then, I'll go and get you some.' He went and got me some but, where as he'd been giving it to me all the time, as soon as I had a habit, he stopped giving it to me. He said, 'Well, if you want it, you've gotta get your money to get it,' and that's when he started bringing the cheque books home. He said to me, 'It's really easy.' He got the cheque card and he put it in brake fluid and he shook it and he took the signature off. All I had to do was sign the card, exactly the same like my signature. So I went out and done a cheque and it seemed such easy, easy money. We'd just go in the bank and draw £150. It seemed really easy. I was doing it for about four, five months, and then I got caught. I was at a friend's house and I was staying the night and we had this cheque book and we were going out the next day to do it, when they raided her house for drugs and found me with the cheque book. They arrested me for it and that's when I went to court and got twelve months.

It's a wicked drug, that. I really wanna come off, but I don't think it's coming off, it's staying off that's the problem really, ain't it? [Kay, aged 21]

I went straight on to heroin. It was just available then [1960s], you know. I didn't realize how dangerous it was. You could get it from any doctor and I just used to get registered with different doctors. *Now* it takes you three months to get on the clinic. They tend to take younger people who, they think, have got a chance. I've tried every doctor in the area. My clinic – the one that covers my area – will only take you on for seven weeks of methadone. You have to produce urine specimens so that, if they find any heroin, that's it, you're out. I don't wanna be controlled like that. I'd like to take methadone and then have a fix if I want one. It's really annoying when they spend so much money keeping you in prison . . . They all know I have to do prostitution to keep that habit. It's just part of that life, isn't it, going to prison? I mean, drugs are illegal and that's that, isn't it? I don't think it's right that you go to prison for it; but that's the way it is, so in there you go. [Sally, aged 35]

POVERTY, PROPERTY AND CRIME

So deplorable is the state of affairs in most slum districts that many men, and probably more women, turn criminal for no better reason than they can no longer endure the conditions in which the chance of birth has cast their lot . . . . People who live in a hell on earth cannot be expected to endure indefinitely without protest.

(Bishop, 1931: 81)

The majority of the crimes committed by the women were property offences. Some were organized or pursued in what I have called a 'professional' way (see next section), the majority were committed as part of what, in Chapter 5, I call the 'sod it syndrome' – at those times when women on the margins saw crime as the best method of both solving their financial problems *and* getting some control over their lives.

> I wasn't doing it, you know for the sake of doing it. I was doing it to sell because I was on the dole and not getting much money. [Queenie, aged 43]

> They [DHSS] kept saying they were sending a giro [cheque], but the giros were not coming so that made me start doing their books too. [Kim, aged 28]

> It was when we were short of money that we first started forging those giros. It seemed the easiest way to get some money. [Zoë, aged 28]

Property crime was chosen because certain types (e.g. shoplifting and cheque fraud) were seen to be so 'easy' and because most women expressed inhibitions about engaging in prostitution. For, although several claimed that their only realistic choice of crime was between shoplifting, cheque fraud and prostitution, the latter was rejected by most: first, because they would not risk the loss of character involved in being known as 'a common prostitute' and secondly because they believed that all prostitutes have pimps and were adamant that they themselves were 'not prepared to do *that* for any man to live off'. Kim was most explicit about her choice of crimes.

> I'd always been one of these people who think, 'Oh well, a girl mustn't do this and a girl mustn't do that because she will receive a bad name for herself. I didn't mind them calling me a thief but any kind of name to do with sex, I think I would have done myself in. Most of the people I knew were thieves but to say I was a slag . . . . I couldn't bear those sorts of names. I knew I had to do this [commit crime] to survive and there were four things I could have become in Clapton. I could have become a prostitute, but I was shy with my body so I ruled that out. I could have become a pickpocket, but I can't go and steal off a person, my conscience wouldn't let me. Shoplifting is fine but it's a lot of work. Or I could do the cheques and cheque books which were just nice for me because it wasn't interfering with anybody and to me it was the easiest thing in the world. I got up in the morning, went out and I signed all my cheques and I came back in the evening to a full-up house. It was like a job. The rewards are good and it's easy. I still think cheques are the easiest things to do. [Kim, aged 28]

It was frequently claimed that property crime is without stigma in many sectors of society and that the very same people (both working-class and middle-class) who pronounce most loudly against the rising crime rate are also those who, when given the chance, always buy stolen goods, are always game for a fiddle.

I was doing it just for the money really, but then people said, 'We'll give you so much if you get us such and such a thing and then we got to where we could get loads of things and didn't get caught. [Sadie, aged 20]

They knew we'd nicked 'em [leather jackets] but where I live people didn't care. They'd buy owt, doesn't bother them if it's nicked. We sold fifteen of them to a market stall and he didn't care 'cos he was going to sell them at D— market anyway. So there's no harm on his back is there? I mean, the police didn't go round and check his stores. [Bobby, aged 15]

We used to say, 'If you want anything, you say, and we'll nick it.' We used to take it to my sister's. She worked in an office, in a big typing pool. She used to sell it there for us. [Lisa, aged 21]

When I was doing cheques I had crooked people who knew what I was doing. I'd go in, write a cheque for £50 and they'd give me £25 cash and they were keeping the other £25 cash (because even if a cheque bounces, they still have to pay you out if you've got a card number on it). So, really, all these respectable businessmen (that I *thought* were straight business people) were as crooked as me. [Kay, aged 21]

I'd say to my mates, 'What do you want from the shop? I'll get you this, I'll get you that – shoes, jumpers, dresses. No trouble.' [Jean, aged 26]

Some of our friends even used to take it home to their mothers and they'd buy it. So it was quite easy to get rid of. [Shirley, aged 20]

Thus it was that the women's individualistic and crimogenic solutions to their problems often blossomed into skilful businesses with relatively high profits in the short term. Without the collusion of the 'respectable' of all classes (either as receivers of stolen property, customers for illegal drugs or clients of illegal sex transactions) none of the 'professional' types of crime discussed in the next section could flourish. However, the selective operation of the criminal law, together with the snowballing effects of penal policy on those whose poverty has already thrust them to the margins of society, ensure that again and again the price of crime is paid not primarily by those who most benefit from it. Instead, it is paid by those who, because of their impoverished circumstances, are not only frequent *victims* of crime but also prepared to take the greatest risks when they themselves commit the most visible crimes. The *profits* of crime, like all other profits, are enjoyed primarily by middle-and-upper-class men.

'PROFESSIONAL' AND SYSTEMATIC CRIME

Only Dee actually admitted to being a 'professional'. The others were, in the main, amused by the notion that they could even be considered as such. 'If I'd been a professional, I wouldn't have been caught, would I?' was the most

TABLE 2.2   Professional aspects of women's criminal careers

Name (age) at interview	Type of activity/offence	Mode of operation
Bobby (15)	Burglary	With small mixed group. Car journeys made with specific aim of engaging in burglary. Network of informal receivers for stolen goods
Audrey (18)	Shoplifting	Worked by self. Hired rooms to store stolen goods in
Cynthia (19)	Burglary	Worked with group. Used car for goods stolen. Used known receivers
Anne (20)	Shoplifting	Worked by self. Used one 'professional' receiver of stolen goods
Shirley (20)	Burglary and shoplifting	Worked with small mixed group. Network of informal receivers
Lisa (21)	Cheque fraud	Worked with all female group. Recruited and employed others
Tara (21)	Cheque fraud/shoplifting	Worked alone or with boy-friend
Kay (21)	Cheque fraud	Worked with boy-friend and other males. Organized cheque fraud. Cheques supplied by 'professional' pickpockets
Donna (22)	Prostitution/soliciting	Worked alone but lived in houses hired out only to prostitutes
Sheila (22)	Cheque fraud	Worked alone. Cheques obtained from pickpockets and other thieves
Nicky (27)	Burglary	Worked with mixed groups
Zoë (28)	Prostitution/soliciting	Worked from flat with other women
Kim (28)	Cheque fraud	Worked daily. Bought cheque books from 'professional' pickpockets
Queenie (43)	Shoplifting	Worked with two others. Linked into local 'professional' receiving network
Dee (46)	Sexual services/keeping a brothel	Specially equipped flat hired specifically to use for clients requiring sexual services. Maid employed. Business advertised in shop windows

frequent comment when I raised the question of 'professionalism'. Yet several acknowledged that they knew criminals (both women and men) to whom the term would be applicable, and four replied that, though not 'professional' themselves, they had worked with or for 'professionals'. Reluctance to define themselves as 'professional' criminals seemed mainly to stem from their definition of the 'professional' as not only being someone who had made a good living through well-planned and efficiently executed crimes, but also as one who had high status and power in the criminal underworld.

My own definition (as given in Chapter 3, page 59) is wider: 'lawbreaking

pursued in an organized way (either alone or with others) for the primary purpose of providing the woman's major source of income during an extended
period of time (even though arrest might cut short the projected time span)[1]. On
this definition, fifteen of the women were categorized as 'professional' as Table
2.2 indicates, though often the term refers only to one period in their criminal
careers. (For example, by the age of 15 Bobby could describe her short career
both in terms of the 'hell-raising gang' to which she had belonged *and* in terms
of the systematic burglary and break-ins which the gang had engaged in just
prior to her arrest.)

Excluded from this categorization are the 'systematic' lawbreakers who, for a
variety of reasons, argued that they were not professional: for example, heroin
addicts like Sally, who insisted that they were not professional because they
committed their crimes only when they desperately needed money for a 'fix';
those like Jill who did burglary only when they had been drinking; and those
like Jean and Mary who claimed that they were not professional because their
law-breaking had been mainly opportunistic rather than planned or that the
goods they had stolen had been 'practically given away'.

However, many judges and magistrates would have defined at least some of
these systematic law-breakers as professional in terms of the scale of their
criminal activity – if not in terms of its mode of organization. So, in addition to
the fifteen women categorized here as 'professional', most probably another
seven could be so defined if the term were to be used merely to refer to the scale,
rather than the mode of organization, of their criminal operations. These systematic but only semi- professionals, who might be seen as wholly professional by
judges, magistrates and many others were Tricia, Jill, Dawn, Jean, Mary, Prue
and Sally. Interestingly, several women claimed that once judges had decided to
imprison them, they often then attempted to justify the sentence by referring to
them (erroneously, according to my informants) as 'professional' criminals.

Yet, regardless of how they formally defined themselves, all who had engaged systematically in some type of criminal activity spoke spontaneously at
other points in the interviews about how they had learned the requisite criminal
skills; how they saw themselves as having acquired a specific competence; and
about the drawbacks and pleasures of particular criminal occupations. Dee, per-
haps the most 'professional' of them all, was also very conscious of the simi-
larity between the professional – client relationship in the provision of an illicit
service and the professional – client relationship in the professional provision of
more legitimate services.

Learning the trade

When I asked how the women had got into or chosen their particular criminal
specialism, the most frequent reply was that they had either learned it from a
group of friends or that they had learned about it in Borstal, Youth Custody

Centre or prison. Sally, however, had chosen prostitution because she did not see it as a 'real crime' but rather as a necessity thrust upon her by a law that prevented her getting cheaply and legitimately the amount of heroin she needed.

> I started soliciting when the government made it illegal for clinics to carry on giving us heroin. From the age I first started to when I was 23, I was always registered, which meant I got it on the National Health. I used to get three grammes a day, which is a lot and it was pure – I couldn't get any infections – and it was legal. Then the law changed and they could only give you methadone which is what you drink and I didn't want that. And that's when I had to start soliciting. Like I've always told the magistrates, if they fine me I will only have to go back on the streets to earn money. I don't like to steal. I mean, it's ripping-off. I can't steal. I can't shoplift. I feel prostitution – well, it's not all right – but at least I'm not ripping anybody off that way. [Sally, aged 35]

The majority had chosen a particular crime because it had appeared to them that they could commit it easily and with impunity. Of the 'easy' crimes, cheque fraud was seen to be both the easiest and the least risky. Shoplifting was also seen to be easy but with the drawbacks of being both risky and tiring, whilst burglary was by and large favoured for its adventure element. As to a popular notion that all women are introduced to crime by men, when in the following accounts women mention that their teacher and/or partner in crime was male, it should be noted that each speaker had committed crimes on her own prior to instruction in a particular crime by a male associate.

> I just learned everything I could about cheques and then went out to earn money, so that I wouldn't be caught. I just learned from other people. [Sheila, aged 22]

> I just went in the bank one day and I asked them about cheques. They told me how you apply for your book, and how you fill in the cheque. I knew a lot of people who were pickpockets then, so to get cheque books wasn't a problem. One of my friends came with a book and I pretended that I'd done it all before and I hadn't. Then you learn as you go on. I started in the West End and began to get to know more people. I learned how to forge cheques easier. I used to get the pickpockets things. When you're doing things like cheques, you make lots and lots of friends – and I was still shoplifting! (Laughs.) [Kim, aged 28]

> He used to take about six leather jackets at a time, and I used to watch out. He went into the British Home Stores once and they'd got a big steam-cooker thing in one of them boxes, and he just picked it up and walked out with it. I thought, 'My God!' He said, 'Go on. Now you do it.'

He always said to me, 'You have a go'. So I went and done it and I says, 'That's easy.' [Mary, aged 27]

He used to say to me, 'Oh, I'm going on the move.' I used to say, 'What's "the move", what's "on the move" mean?' He said, 'Do you want to come with us?' I said, 'No, I wanna know what you mean first.' He said, 'Burglary.' So I went with him and his three mates and they parked the car. He said, 'Right! Sit in the driver's seat, we'll be back in ten minutes.' Sat there for half an hour and and I see them coming down the road with a video and other things. Simon said, 'All right, start the car up.' I said, 'What? You can't . . .' He said, 'Shut up and start the car up.' Started the car up and drove round the corner. He said, 'Right, let's swop seats.' Got home, they give me twenty-five pound. I goes, 'Where did you get all that stuff from?' He says, 'Shut up.' Then they started using me as decoy, me knock on the door. 'No one there', I'd tell 'em, then sit in the car with the engine running and tell them if anything was going to happen. Anyway I started going with my mate. I went round for her early one morning and said, 'Come on we're going on the move.' So, like, in the morning, when everybody's gone to work you think you stand a better chance. Because you've gotta be out by four o'clock when the kids come home from school. You can't go through a house beating them up 'cos then you'd be done for aggravated [burglary]. [Cynthia, aged 19]

I call myself a professional. I do it for the money. There's no game in it because if you get caught you can go to prison. If you're doing it, you have to be serious about it. To me it's like a job, a full-time job. I'm only learning how to make more money each time. I *love* every minute of it. I didn't know what I was doing when I started, then I got wiser. I'd sit down and forge signatures that would agree. To me it's just a lesson every time I get nicked. I just go in there [prison] and take it and say, 'Well, you've learned your lesson, it's your own silly fault.' It's a tiny little mistake, maybe; you know that you've done wrong. I know next time not to do that. [Tara, aged 21]

Competence

Once the women had learned a particular criminal skill, they took pride in increasing their competence. Being 'professional' meant that you did not drink or take drugs when you went to work, that you 'looked the part', that you kept your criminal life as separate from your private life as possible and that you worked with people whom you could trust. In practice, this ideal type of professionalism was seldom realized. Criminal and non-criminal worlds overlapped and often merged; colleagues could let each other down by turning up drunk, or even worse, losing their bottle [nerve]; and several of the women admitted to having been 'grassed-up'. Nonetheless, between them they could articulate a very definite code of professional criminal practice and ethics.

At that point the people I was working with, they *were* professional and they didn't drink. The saying was then that you didn't trust a drinker and you didn't trust a junkie. Either one you didn't work with because they weren't trusted in court. I had to prove myself by doing silly little things like percenting and stuff like that because the main concern for men on those sort of crimes [armed robbery] is that when you're actually nicked you can keep your mouth shut. Also that your bottle won't go. [Josie, aged 30]

I wanted to become more professional, be a professional thief going to the top. It was my business, it was my life. I had to get up very early in the morning, about six, get prepared so that I looked the part and I had to use my brain. I couldn't just sort of do it casually like an odd job. I was working my brain all the time. I had to work out my plans and my moves. I never used to come home with the stuff I got. I used to lock it in lockers and collect it another day. I used to cover every trace. I had to have a few bedsits to keep the stuff; I couldn't just take it back to where I was living. [Audrey, aged 18]

They [cheque forgers] have gotta know how to act like the person whose cheque book and card it is. One girl I knew went to the shop with an Access card and she didn't know how to do the signature. Next thing I knew she was in Harrow police station. She said to me, 'Oh Cynthia, it's all your fault, you were talking about cheque cards.' And I said to her, 'I never told you to get into it.' I said, 'You've gotta know what you're doing.' And I for one won't go in and shoplift because I don't look the part. [Cynthia, aged 19]

I seem to have a little in-built radar. It makes me say 'No' if I don't like the look of them [clients]. And I always take them to a flat where there's someone else there. I wouldn't want them to know where I live 'cos they're a bloody nuisance most of the time. [Sally, aged 35]

We knew the way to get into that house 'cos we'd been planning it for ages. We nicked £250 that was in this vase thing. If we were nicking, right? Someone used to keep guard and we used to know all the store detectives. If there's a woman who never leaves the shop, you know she's a store detective. So we go back in, walk around and watch that woman specially and I will make sure she sees us go and buy something so she doesn't think we're nicking. [Bobby, aged 15]

And, if arrested, the real professional should also know how to behave in the police station.

> If they catch me, I just go with them. No use fighting. When I get to the police station, that's when I do the fighting, 'cos I give a bogus name, play the innocent. You know, that's when you fight, 'cos that's when you have to get *out* of it. [Tara, aged 21]

The *measure* of their professionalism was to be calculated according to the number of crimes they had got away with.

> I used to get more money than the others because they used to be a bit scared. I used to go in first and smash the window, make sure everything was all right. I was really doing the dirty work by breaking and entering. We took risks. We did this one house and the people came home and I was upstairs at the time and the only way out was through the window. So I went through the window, went down the drainpipe, fell and dislocated my knee. I didn't get caught 'cos the others came to rescue me. We always used to get away. Never been caught by the police in actually doing the jobs. [Jill, aged 21]

> I'd been doing it [shoplifting] for two years, I'd had a really good run and got away with it. Twelve months' imprisonment and I came out . . . and then started burglary. And we were having a good run at that. We were doing that for a good while and selling it at antique shops. We used go knock on doors and, if there was nobody in, we'd get through a window. I got two years' imprisonment for that and came out and started shoplifting. Got community work for that – which I really enjoyed doing. God, what did I do next? Did I start going shoplifting again? Oh no, I fiddled social security and I nicked some prescriptions. Oh yes, and I did next door. I even broke into next door's. [Queenie, aged 43]

> I got away with loads before they caught me. I'm pretty good. I've got away with it loads and loads and loads of times. [Tara, aged 21]

> We used to do night-time or day-time jobs [burglary]. But I only used to work with two people, one woman, one man, because I knew if anything came on top they wouldn't grass me up. If you're good at something, you're good at it. I was good at it, that's why I only got caught once. [Nicky, aged 27]

Dee – a classical professional

Dee, like many professional women (and men) criminals before her, has been able to make a reasonable living by providing for the illicit sexual fantasies of men in a society sadly hypocritical about both the regulation of sexuality and the relationships between sexual fantasy and social structure. She is a professional in the 'classic' sense to the extent that she has mastered a particular expertise in providing for her clients' requirements, developed a set of ethics to govern the professional–client relationship and formulated a coherent ideology to justify her practices. Listen:

How I got into it in the first place was I was living with this girl in Bournemouth and she was working in a flat above the factory where I worked. All these men were going upstairs and all of a sudden she just left and disappeared. The man I was working for downstairs owned the flat upstairs as well. He said to me one day, 'You're a bloody fool, Dee. Why don't you go upstairs?,' he says 'And give 'em a couple of smacks with the cane. You'll earn yourself a little bit of extra money.' I said, 'No, I couldn't do that.' I really thought it was disgusting and also I thought you actually had to go with them, that they wouldn't just stand for being hit, that you'd actually have to sort of go with them later. But he said, 'No, you'll be all right. Look at him with the Rolls Royce pressing the door bell, they've all got money that come here.' So I thought, 'Well, I'll try it,' and I did. The ones that I didn't want to deal with, like personal service [sexual intercourse], I used to refuse. I used to do what we call the kinks. And that's how I started. They were all upper class. Then I moved back to London and I had a fully equipped torture chamber, a lot of rubber stuff, leather hoods, whips, canes, handcuffs, boxing gloves, everything. It was just like going to a factory. I mean, I used to go to work, get there by 11.30 in the morning, have my bath at 7.30 at night and leave at 8. It's like *you* going to work. You go to work and, when you clock off, you go home. It's the same with the girls in flats, it's the same with me. You have to make some divide, otherwise you'd go absolutely barmy. It was just like going to an everyday job. As far as clients were concerned, it was like being on a conveyor belt.

I was very surprised how easy the money was. I had one man who was a slave and he had about £700 or £800 on him and he just stayed and stayed. Every time he told a lie, I took another £20 off him. I had all his money.

They always got a good service. I mean, they get the service they want. A lot of girls they go to, they pay, but then don't get the service. And this is when girls start getting into trouble. I mean, clients come in and say, 'Please don't mark me.' Okay, if they don't want to be marked, they don't have to be marked but, if they *do* want to be marked, then they have to be marked, otherwise they won't come back. They come in and I say, 'What can I do for you?' and then they start telling you. You've got to sort of pick their brains, be a bit of an actress, a bit of a psychiatrist. Some of them are so funny – I mean one wanted to be a horse, another wanted to be a baby and I had to put his nappy on him – but I can't laugh because I'm not supposed to laugh.

Clients need to go somewhere. I mean, let's face it, businessmen, television stars – I could mention names but I will not because I'd *never* do that – they have a hard day at work and they can't go home to their wives and say, 'Oh, I feel like dressing up like a woman tonight,' or 'Go and get the cane and give me a dozen whacks on my backside, because that's what I feel like.' Their wives would turn round and think, 'He's bloody barmy.' But they're not barmy. It's a need. At least it stops them going out and raping little kids. If they can't go to somebody and get it out of their system, it's like a worry and it nags them. It all stems from their schools and I think it's a relief to them that they can find someone that understands them. Because it's not just the money; you actually can make a good friendship with these people. You sit and talk to them while they're getting dressed and they tell you about their child's going to this school 'because it's a very good school' and problems about work. They know that they can talk to somebody like myself. They know I understand, and won't just turn round and say, 'Oh, don't talk a lot of bloody rubbish, I'm not interested.' [Since the beginning of the court case and the subsequent temporary abandonment of the business] friends of mine have phoned me and said, 'Your clients are still looking for you.' But I would never bring a client here to my home. It's a thing I've never done. And if I've gone away on holiday I've never let anybody else use my flat, never. I've always stuck to my rules: this is my flat and nobody else will work here. I'll tell you for why: one, it's against the law; number two, they steal your clients; and number three is they wouldn't just do what I was doing, they would do everything and by the time I got back from my holiday I'd find all these people that wanted other things that I don't do – so that would ruin my business, anyway. So, I tell my clients in advance that I'm going away and they wait while I come back. It's as simple as that. [Dee, aged 46]

Rewards and costs

The three main attractions of 'professional' law-breaking were described as being: the prospect (and, at least in the short term, the reality) of easy money; the sense of purpose thereby given to unemployed young people, otherwise denied purposeful occupation; and the sense of 'belonging', otherwise denied to unemployed working-class women living outside family and domesticity. Those who had committed their crimes to fund an addiction said that the law-breaking in itself had held no attractions for them. The most 'professional' law-breakers like Tara were adamant that, because their criminal activities had been undertaken purely for financial gain, they had experienced them as being very hard work and nothing else. However, before listening to descriptions of the less obvious and more psychological rewards of law-breaking, it is worth taking a closer look at the oft invoked notion of 'easy money'.

More often than not, it is the well-off who sneer at those wanting 'easy money' and this is ironic when the 'easiest' money nowadays comes via inheritance, the stock market and other gambling tables of the rich. Irony apart, it is also to be noted that the more sober magisterial disapprobation of 'easy money' usually refers to that money which people obtain by illegal rather than legal means – the legal means in the case of working-class women being wage labour or (and) unwaged domestic labour. Yet, when in this study women explained why cheque fraud, etc., produced 'easy money', they were not in the majority of cases juxtaposing the 'easiness' of crime to the hard work of wage labour. More frequently, they were comparing the 'easiness' of crime with the difficulties of getting their legitimate entitlements from the Department of Health and Social Security (cf. Cook, 1987 and pages 114–115 of this book). Indeed the humiliations, delays and frustrations involved in getting DHSS cheques owing to them were often uppermost in the minds of women explaining why, at certain times in their lives, law-breaking had been such an attractive option. 'Helping themselves' to what they wanted had given a tremendous boost of confidence (as well as an illusion of power) to women who had become angry at, and embittered by, the indignities they had suffered as claimants. Additionally, and at least whilst they were young, the excitement of more organized crime could often override every other emotion.

> I was working cheque books, earning a lot of money. Going to Holland and places and getting girls to do it. We were organizing them, getting the books and sorting them out. I used to get this feeling inside me – the adrenalin was going – and it was good, especially to see a girl walk out of a shop with a bag and think 'Great! More money!'. It was fun. [Lisa, aged 21]

Nineteen-year-old Cynthia described how telling tales of past crimes could cement feelings of cameraderie amongst prisoners and recreate the laughs and excitement commonly experienced by those who engage in adventurous or deviant pursuits – whether legal or illegal.

> We all talk about the funny things. Like creeping at night. I've done burglary when people are in bed sleeping and you creep round their house quietly unplugging their things and take them out. We all have a laugh . . . Like my first experience of creeping at night in someone's house was really funny 'cos I went in the bedroom and I see people asleep. I creeped to the floor . . . and I went to get her bag . . . . The geezer slept but his arm fell on my back and I thought, 'Oh, what am I gonna do?' But, when we talk, we laugh about it, 'cos it's all a big joke now. [Cynthia, aged 19]

Yet, despite the money, the laughs and the excitement, the women did not romanticize themselves, their crimes or their lives. Those who took their criminal occupation seriously told of the constant tension and the usual physical tiredness that comes from a day's work. Audrey recalled, 'It *was* exciting but it was so tiring as well. I was on my feet all day and by the end of the day I used to be so tired and worn out.' Other crimes had become deadly boring through constant repetition and it was often boredom that had led to the carelessness resulting in detection and arrest. To earn their money, women engaged in prostitution had had to contend not only with police harassment but also with the increase in danger that the police regulation of streetwalkers at present entails.

> The police call us toms and they never leave you alone, you know. I can't walk through King's Cross because, if I'm walking down the street, I get arrested for prostitution even if I don't speak to anybody. I said to a magistrate once, 'Does this mean I can't go outside my front door?' And he said, 'You should move to a different area.' You can't plead Not Guilty because [then] the police either make sure you don't get bail and you get remanded in custody or they just nick you every time they see you. It's very hard now, very hard 'cos you haven't got time to spend five minutes talking to the guy to find out what he's like. You've gotta be straight into the car and it could be any maniac. [Sally, aged 35]

Alternatively, if a prostitute woman chooses to work from a flat with the additional protection of a maid, then, under the present law, she is likely to be accused of keeping a brothel.

> The police said to a friend of mine, 'If you don't move out of this flat by tonight, we'll come back and nick you again.' So she had to find another flat which she's worked on her own since with an answer phone. It's very dodgy, that, very dodgy. But she daren't have anybody else 'cos, if they find she's got a maid, they'll go and nick her again. You see, the thing is, if you haven't got a maid and you're there on your own, on your back, what chance have you got if he decides to go the other way and strangle you? [Dee, aged 46]

For these marginalized women the financial benefits of their crimes had always been transient – spent on the immediate needs of children, used to pay ever recurring bills and other debts, or lost to the expensive demands of destructive lifestyles involving heroin, alcohol and other drugs. With the exception of Dee, none could claim that they had been lifted out of poverty by the proceeds of their crimes. Kim, for instance, was derisive of prosecution claims that she had made a fortune.

The cheques had gone but it wasn't £15,000 to me, even though he was telling them it was £15,000 because the cheques change from £50 to £30. The prosecutor said that it was like Aladdin's cave at home. It wasn't. It was a shithouse. I'd never had any furniture in the front room; I'd just decorated up a bit. [Kim, aged 28]

Not only had crime failed to deliver the financial rewards, the women's crimes had sometimes led to lifestyles and self-concepts with which they were far from happy. Being 'wanted' for crime, or 'on the run' from Care or Youth Custody Centre had in all cases resulted in a round of 'ducking and diving' that had left them physically, mentally and emotionally exhausted. Relationships (with men and/or women) had become 'heavy', drug-taking had increased, and what the young teenagers had seen as a criminal roundabout of fun and excitement the older women had increasingly experienced as a tawdry syndrome of cheap lodgings, constant emotional and financial crises and wasteful periods of imprisonment. Some, too, nowadays worry about their reasons for committing crime. Have they become 'hooked' on shoplifting or forgery? What about if, in the future, a husband, a girl-friend or a child finds out about their prostitution? Are they now so 'far out' that it is not even worth trying to lead a law-abiding life?

Unlike white-collar business crime, which more often than not increases its perpetrator's status and implicates him even more securely in the social power structures, crime by already marginalized people increases their powerlessness and puts them even further beyond the pale. When it is a marginalized woman who commits crime, then the individual costs are likely to be significantly greater. Crime is still considered to be a masculine prerogative and women who engage in it are usually made to carry a bigger load of guilt and bear a heavier burden of shame than male criminals. The latter, because criminal activity is supposed to come 'naturally' to them, often escape social stigmatization altogether.

Of the thirty-nine women who took part in this study, twelve had already turned their backs on crime by the time of interview, while another twelve said that they intended to continue with their criminal activities in the foreseeable future. The remaining fifteen claimed that, although they wanted to abandon their life of crime, they doubted their ability to keep out of trouble. In the rest of this book, therefore, we shall investigate the decisions, conditions and processes that enmesh and keep women in crime as well as the decisions, conditions and processes that have helped some to renounce their criminal careers for good. By way of policies based on an informed understanding of some of the relationships between identity and social structure we might be able to prevent today's wayward girls becoming tomorrow's criminal women.

__ 3 __

THIRTY-NINE WOMEN

Women have been pushed back twenty years since there came a Tory government.

(Zoë, aged 28)

In 1985 I conducted taped interviews with thirty-nine women between the ages of 15 and 46. Each had at least one criminal conviction and the main aims of the research were, first, to discover what they themselves saw as being major influences on, and turning-points in their criminal careers; and, second, to explain both the sources of those self-perceptions and their effects.

I was singularly lucky in my contacts. The Governor of Bullwood Hall (HM Prison and Youth Custody Centre) supported my application to the Home Office for interviewing facilities at Bullwood and I was allowed to interview twenty women there (the Bullwood Group). The other nineteen (the Contact Group) were contacted through four intermediaries: six women through a probation officer, five through Josie O'Dwyer; four through Jenny Hicks of the ex-prisoners' theatre company, Clean Break; and four through the warden of Stockdale House (ex-prisoners' hostel) in North London. As a result of this pattern of contacts the majority of the women (twenty-one) were either London-based at the time of interview or (in the case of the Bullwood Group) had been living in London immediately prior to their imprisonment. The remaining eighteen either resided at the time of interview or (when not in prison) normally resided: in Staffordshire (six), Surrey (two), Essex (two), Lancashire (one), Leicestershire (one), Sussex (one), Cardiff (one), North-ampton (one), Suffolk (one), Birmingham (one) and Middlesex (one).

With the exception of Josie, I refer to all of them by fictitious names.

Anne, aged 20, was interviewed in her home in London. Since the age of 15 she had spent twenty-two months in Bullwood Hall and three months in Holloway prison, her crimes included burglary, shoplifting, fraud and obtaining money by deception. Since the age of 9 she had lived variously with foster parents, in a

Community Home with Education, and in a Secure Adolescent Unit. After absconding from the latter Anne had lived rough for several months. In Care since the age of 14, most of her early crimes had been *incidental* to attempts to free herself of social services control. The later crimes, however, had been *incidental* to the need to fund her heroin addiction. At the time of interview Anne had broken with the heroin habit and felt that, so long as she kept off heroin, she would not commit crime in the future.

Audrey, aged 18, was interviewed in Bullwood Hall and was serving twelve months for theft and breach of a Community Service Order. She had previously had a conditional discharge for taking and driving away as well as several fines and suspended prison sentence for theft. In Care since the age of 2, she had been in a variety of Children's Homes, a Community Home with Education, a Secure Adolescent Unit and a therapeutic community. Audrey's criminal activities seem to have been *incidental* to the authorities' response to the trouble she had caused in the various Children's Homes to which she had been sent. Audrey felt that her prospects upon release were good, first because she had both employment and accommodation (the latter in what she described as a 'luxury hostel') to go to, and second, because now that she was 'out of Care', she felt that she would be able to settle down in one place.

Bobby, aged 15, was interviewed in Bullwood Hall and was serving six months for burglary, breach of the peace, grievous bodily harm and criminal damage. In trouble since the age of 12, she had previously been found guilty of burglary, breaking and entering, shoplifting and assault. Her best friend, brother (also in prison) and mother had all been aware of, and to some extent involved in, Bobby's law-breaking activities which for a time had certainly been pursued in a *professional* way and which Bobby had *opted* for as providing an exciting lifestyle. However, although she claimed that she wanted to 'behave' in future, Bobby also doubted her ability to keep out of trouble once she returned home. Perceived thus, her law-breaking also appeared to have become *incidental* to her whole lifestyle.

Carol, aged 27, was interviewed in her home in Staffordshire. She had been taken into Care at the age of 12 when her mother died. After misbehaving in a Children's Home, she had been sent to Rampton Special Hospital at the age of 13 and stayed there until she was 19. She had shoplifted as a child and, since leaving Rampton, had had several convictions for shoplifting and five for assault. Most of her crimes seemed to be *incidental* to her belief that someone from her poor background had no legitimate means of either acquiring goods or of obtaining legal protection. In fact, like many other women I interviewed, Carol believed in the punning proverb that 'God helps those who help themselves'.

Cindy, aged 22, was interviewed at Bullwood Hall and was serving her third custodial sentence (fifteen months) for shoplifting. In trouble with the police since the age of 14, she said that she had had so many findings of guilt and convictions for theft and burglary that she could not remember them all. Unmarried and with two children, Cindy had *opted* for theft and burglary as a way of solving her financial difficulties (according to her Social Enquiry Report 'at the time of the last offence she had been receiving £27 from the DHSS'). She said that she now felt that she *must* stop breaking the law (and coming to prison) as she did not wish to be parted again from her two children.

Cynthia, aged 19, was interviewed at Bullwood Hall and was serving six months for actual bodily harm and burglary. Put into Care by her grandmother at the age of 13, Cynthia had been placed on probation on three separate occasions and had been fined several times for theft. At 17 she had given birth to a baby boy and she was anxious to have him adopted. Everything she said suggested that her law-breaking was a chosen lifestyle (*optional*). Finally, she made it quite clear that she intended to commit crimes whenever she found herself to be in need in the future and she also fully expected to serve further prison sentences.

Daphne, aged 15, was interviewed in Bullwood Hall and was serving four months and one day for theft, deception and burglary. She had previously been cautioned for smashing a caravan, ordered to attend an Attendance Centre for being found guilty of deception and arson and had also been fined several times for theft. After smashing the caravan she had been taken into Care at the age of 13 and had first begun stealing when she had absconded from the Community Home with Education to which she had eventually been sent. Daphne said that she did not think that her pattern of law-breaking would change in the near future as she thought that it was *incidental* to the fact that she was mentally ill.

Dawn, aged 23, was interviewed at Bullwood Hall. She was serving three years for attempting to supply heroin and had previously been fined for shoplifting. Expelled from school at the age of 12, Dawn had spent a short time in an Approved School after running away from home and thereafter, she claimed, had spent most of what should have been her schooldays 'on the run'. All her crimes had been *incidental* to funding her heroin habit and, at the time of her last arrest, she had been involved with professional (criminal) heroin dealers. Dawn expressed a desire to give up heroin for the sake of her small daughter who had always lived at home with her, but she was not optimistic about her chances of breaking the heroin habit.

Dee, aged 46, was interviewed at her home in London. She had been providing 'special services' (not sexual intercourse) for men for several years. Two years prior to interview, she had served four months in prison after a conviction for keeping a brothel (a charge she still vehemently denies) and had also had fines after convictions on two similar charges (also denied). Dee saw herself as a *professional* person providing services, which although illegal, fulfil a social need. At the time of interview Dee had stopped work because of police harassment.

Della, aged 15, was interviewed in Bullwood Hall and was serving nine months for actual bodily harm. Since the age of 12, when she had been taken into Care as a result of truanting, she had been fined several times for theft and once for burglary. Tenth child in a travelling family with thirteen children, Della had nine brothers who had all been in prison. At the time of interview Della was confident that she had given up glue-sniffing well before she had commenced her Youth Custody sentence. Her previous law-breaking and poor school record seemed to be *incidental* to her family's lifestyle and certainly Della had seen the Care Order as a punishment. She said that she would hope to keep out of trouble when released.

Donna, aged 22, was interviewed at her home in London. In Care since the age of two months, she had lived in various Children's Homes, a Community Home with Education, an Adolescent Unit, a therapeutic community, a special school, and in hostels and hotels. For a period of several months she had lived rough. Donna had been committing burglary and shoplifting since the age of 13 but her many convictions and several prison sentences had all (but one) been for soliciting. She had once spent twelve months on remand in Holloway charged with burglary, a charge to which she pleaded guilty and for which she was put on probation when, after twelve months, the case came to court. At the time of interview Donna had been out of trouble for two years. All her law-breaking appears to have been *incidental* to the severe social and economic problems she encountered on being put into a bedsitter on her own whilst still a teenager in Care.

Hazel, aged 29, was interviewed at her home in London. She had served four months in Borstal for criminal damage (breaking a window) and thirteen months' imprisonment for arson (knocking over a candle and starting a fire when drunk). In Care since the age of 6, most of her crimes seemed to have been *incidental* to a complex of economic and health problems that she had encountered early in life. At the time I met her she was living with her son in her own self-contained accommodation and did not expect to be in any more criminal trouble.

Jean, aged 26, was interviewed at her home in Staffordshire. She had never been to prison but had had several convictions for shoplifting and receiving stolen goods. She thought that she ought to give up thieving because she did not want to be separated from her two children by a prison sentence. At the same time her hand-to-mouth existence as a single parent made her feel that she would continue to take any 'safe' opportunity to 'nick' stuff. All her law-breaking had been *opted* for as a solution to her very poor economic circumstances.

Jeanette, aged 30, was interviewed in Bullwood Hall where she was serving twelve months for evasion of customs. She had previously been fined three times for assault and once for criminal damage. Although she had *opted* to commit the crime for which she was serving her present sentence, her other convictions appeared to have been *incidental* to her employment (working in a nightclub). She did not expect to be in further trouble with the police.

Jessie, aged 20, was interviewed in Bullwood Hall and was serving an eighteen-month Youth Custody sentence for conspiracy to supply drugs. She had previously served a six-month Youth Custody sentence and had convictions for shoplifting, deception and possession of drugs. Her initial law-breaking could be classified as optional but since the age of 14, when she became addicted to heroin, all her crimes had been undertaken to finance the purchase of the drug. She therefore did not think she could stop committing crime as it was *incidental* to her heroin addiction. In order to give up crime she would have to give up heroin first and she did not feel that she could realistically make such a commitment whilst in prison.

Jill, aged 21, was interviewed in her home in London. In Care since the age of 4, she had served a thirteen-month Borstal sentence for assault and burglary and an eighteen-month one for assault. She claimed that she had enjoyed doing burglaries and had *opted* to commit crime just as, well before the time of interview, she had then chosen to 'go straight'. As she had obtained a full-time job and had moved into her own flat, she was convinced that her future would be crime free.

Josie, aged 30, was interviewed at her home in London, She had previously written of her experiences of imprisonment in the book, *Criminal Women* (Carlen *et al.*, 1985). In Care since the age of 11, she had been in trouble for breaking and entering, malicious wounding and armed robbery. Most of her early law-breaking appeared to have been *incidental* to her early induction into the custodial system and her consequent isolation from family and friends. Later involvement in crime appeared to have been *opted* for as an antidote to boredom with life on the dole.

Kay, aged 21, was interviewed in Bullwood Hall and was serving twelve months for her first conviction for fraud. Prior to her conviction she had engaged in many fraudulent acts, all *incidental* to her addiction to heroin. She stated that she wanted to kick the habit but was not optimistic about doing so in the near future.

Kim, aged 28, was interviewed at my home in London. She had recently served six months' imprisonment for shoplifting and prior to that sentence had served terms of three years' imprisonment and four months' Borstal training for fraud. She had also had a variety of non-custodial penalties. *Opting* for shoplifting and cheque fraud as ways to obtain goods that she could otherwise not have afforded, Kim had rapidly become professionally organized in her cheque frauds. At the time of interview she said that she intended to continue thieving.

Lena, aged 21, was interviewed in Bullwood Hall where she was serving three years for burglary. She had previously served seven months for arson and robbery and prior to that had had several fines and twice been put on probation. In Care since the age of 7 (as a result of being 'battered' by her mother), Lena's law-breaking appeared to be *incidental* to her family's lifestyle and, although Lena stated that she did not intend to engage in further crimes of dishonesty when she was released, she said that she would most likely still engage in fighting. She therefore fully expected to serve another custodial sentence at a future date.

Lisa, aged 21, was interviewed at a London rendezvous. In trouble with the police before the age of 10, and since then convicted of assault, she had served several sentences for *professionally* organized cheque fraud. Although she had first opted for cheque fraud as a *professional*, at the time of interview she thought that her future law-breaking might be *incidental* to her heroin habit. Since the interview Lisa has faced further fraud charges.

Mary, aged 27, was interviewed at Bullwood Hall, where she was serving three years for arson (starting a fire accidentally by dropping a cigarette when drunk). Prior to this, her first prison sentence, she had had several convictions for shoplifting and forgery, and many more for breach of the peace. Asked to leave home at the age of 16, Mary had spent months at a time living rough, though for the last few years she had cohabited with the same man. Throughout her adult life Mary had suffered from depression and had made several suicide attempts involving slitting her wrists and taking overdoses of valium. Her 4-year-old daughter had lived with her until Mary had been sent to prison. Although Mary had been hospitalized several times for alcoholism and although, too, she recognized that most of her recent troubles (including the accidentally started fire that had resulted in the arson conviction) had been *incidental* to her heavy drinking, she told me that she had no intention of giving up alcohol.

Monica, aged 44, was interviewed at her home in Staffordshire. She committed her first crimes of shoplifting at the age of 36 when she turned to alcohol after having two miscarriages in quick succession. At her first appearance in court she was fined, at her second she was placed on probation and at her third (which occurred after a divorce, remarriage and third miscarriage) was given three months' imprisonment, two months of which were suspended. Her crimes had been *incidental* to her belief that alcohol was the best antidote to depression. At the time of interview she had obtained a good job, come to terms with the fact that she would not have a second child and, as she had competely given up alcohol, foresaw no likelihood of engaging again in shoplifting.

Muriel, aged 30, was interviewed at a London rendezvous. In Care since the age of six weeks, she had spent her childhood in several Children's Homes and with many different foster parents. Expelled from three schools, Muriel then went on to Approved School, Borstal and prison. She had convictions for burglary, housebreaking, robbery and shoplifting. Although she had *opted* for law-breaking as an exciting and independent alternative to the bleakness of her life in Care, her involvement in crime also appeared to have been *incidental* to her estrangement from adults both whilst she was in Care and during the years immediately following. At the time of interview she had acquired both a good job and her own accommodation. She had not been in criminal trouble for several years.

Nadia, aged 35, was interviewed at her home in London. In Care from birth to 9 years' old and from 12 to 18, Nadia's main troubles began after the death of her adoptive parents when she was 12 years old. Sent to an Approved School, she spent much of her time 'on the run' and engaging in a variety of criminal activities in order to live. Although she had at various times opted for crime as a way of introducing more interest into a life made bleak by poverty, much of Nadia's law-breaking activity seemed to have been *incidental*, first to her need to survive after absconding from Approved School, and secondly to the maintenance of a heroin habit. At the time of interview she had been out of prison for two years and, as she was no longer addicted to heroin, did not expect to commit further crimes.

Nicky, aged 27, was interviewed at Bullwood Hall where she was serving four months for theft. Although it was her first prison sentence, she had previously had convictions for burglary, fraud and deception. All of her crimes had been *incidental* to her heroin addiction which she had mastered two years before being arrested for crimes committed when she had still been addicted. She therefore expected to be crime free in the future.

Norma, aged 22, was interviewed at Bullwood Hall where she was serving three years for grievous bodily harm. She had previously been fined several times for theft and deception. Taken into care in 1978 after severe physical abuse by her mother, Norma had lived in several Children's Homes before giving birth to her own child in 1981. This child was taken into Care after being physically abused by Norma who in 1982 was convicted of causing him grievous bodily harm (an offence which she still denied at the time of interview). Her second child was also taken into Care. Her crimes of dishonesty appeared to have been opted for as an easy way of earning a living. At the time of interview Norma's husband was in prison, her elder son had been adopted and her younger son was with foster parents. Norma expressed a hope that she would not get into further trouble but also the feeling that she had very little control over a lifestyle of feuding with others, a lifestyle which she thought would continue to involve her in acts of violence.

Prue, aged 46, was interviewed in Bullwood Hall. Same age as me, she had attended the same grammar school, gaining seven O levels and three A levels. After a brief spell in the Civil Service she was convicted of fraud and forgery in 1960 and since then had had fourteen other convictions for the same offence (fraudulently drawing from Post Office saving accounts). Altogether she had spent twelve and a half years in prison, though, when outside, she did not mix with anyone engaged in crime. A loner, Prue told me that she had always been worried about money and that, after *opting* to commit the first offence, she had 'just gone on'. Her later crimes appeared to have been almost *incidental* to a *compulsion* to get money by repeating the one crime that she knew she could do. She said that she ought to stop because 'she couldn't keep coming to prison' but also appeared doubtful of her own ability to break the fraud 'habit'.

Queenie, aged 43, was interviewed at her home in Staffordshire. During the last twenty years she had had many convictions for theft and burglary and had served two prison sentences of twelve months and fifteen months each. Although she had earlier *opted* to commit crime as a more interesting way of earning a living, her later crimes appeared to have been incidental to her heavy drinking. At the time of interview she had been out of prison for two years and wanted to keep out of trouble for the sake of her teenage daughter. However, she was totally depressed about her failure to get help with the alcohol problem and thought that she might get into further trouble as a result of heavy drinking.

Sadie, aged 20, was interviewed in her home in Staffordshire and had just come out of prison, having served three months for burglary. Since the age of 13 she had had several convictions for shoplifting and, although her early crimes could be classified as *optional*, the later ones appeared to have been *incidental* to her chosen lifestyle. Her husband was in prison at the time of interview and therefore, although Sadie thought that economic need might tempt her to steal again in the future, she also hoped that she would resist temptation for the sake of her two small children who lived with her.

Sally, aged 35, was interviewed at her home in London. Addicted to heroin for twenty years, Sally engages in prostitution to fund her habit which she acquired whilst repeatedly absconding from the Approved School to which she had been sent after 'staying out too late at night'. She has been to prison many times for soliciting. As her prostitution is *incidental* to her need to obtain heroin, at the time of interview Sally saw no alternative to her present lifestyle other than being able to obtain heroin legally by prescription.

Sheila, aged 22, was interviewed at Bullwood Hall whilst she was serving a three-year sentence for passing stolen cheques and obtaining a vehicle by deception. She had previously served three years for conspiracy to defraud the clearing banks, had been fined twice for deception (relating to stolen cheques) and had been put on probation for causing actual bodily harm. She had *opted* for crime as a way of solving her financial problems and, although she denied that she was a professional criminal, she had been operating with a professional group at the time of her last arrest. Sheila expressed a wish to give up crime and thought she ought to be able to as her boyfriend, who had never been in any kind of criminal trouble, had stood by her, as had a previous employer who was willing to re-employ her upon her release.

Shirley, aged 20, was interviewed in Bullwood Hall and was serving six months for arson, burglary and theft. She had previously served Borstal sentences for assaults on police officers. In Care since birth, she had intermittently been 'on the run' (and/or living rough) since she had been put into a hostel for much older women at the age of 15. In all, she had had fourteen findings of guilt and ten previous convictions consisting of offences of burglary, possessing drugs, insulting behaviour, assault and criminal damage. The law-breaking which had at first been *incidental* to her lifestyle had for a period become full-time shoplifting, organized with others and with a network of 'customers' to whom goods were being sold (*professional*). Shirley was *desperate* to change her lifestyle but, like Yasmin, could envisage nothing positive in her life upon release. She expressed no wish to continue law-breaking but obviously despaired of ever having the material, social and emotional wherewithal which she perceived to be a necessary prerequisite to a law-abiding life.

Stephanie, aged 22, was interviewed at Bullwood Hall where she was serving nine months for theft (shoplifting). Prior to this, her first prison sentence, she had had several fines, a community service order and a suspended sentence for shoplifting. She had *opted* to commit crime as a solution to her financial difficulties and thought that she would most likely steal again in the future for the same reason.

Tara, aged 21, was interviewed at her home in London. At the time of interview she had been out of prison eight months, having served three short custodial sentences in all. She had had innumerable convictions for fraud, forgery, shoplifting and other theft. Tara had *opted* for crime as a way of earning a living. She saw herself as a *professional* criminal and fully intended to continue as such.

Tricia, aged 17, was interviewed in Bullwood Hall and was serving two years for robbery ('granny-bashing'). She had already served a Youth Custody sentence for taking and driving away and prior to that had been fined for a variety of crimes including fraud, deception and shoplifting. Tricia said that, although the robbery for which she had been convicted had been but one in a series of similar robberies, she considered that her main criminal activity had been shoplifting. She perceived all her law-breaking as being *optional* although she stated that she had wanted to become a 'full-time *professional* criminal'. Upon release she intended to try to find a job. In the event of not obtaining employment she would return to shoplifting.

Yasmin, aged 16, was interviewed in Bullwood Hall and was serving six months for grievous bodily harm. She had previously served four months for arson, and, prior to that, had been fined for criminal damage. In Care since the age of 2 Yasmin had lived in various Children's Homes, a Community Home with Education, three special schools, and an Adolescent Unit. At one stage she had engaged in regular glue-sniffing. Prior to her first Youth Custody sentence she had been placed in a bedsitter on her own. Alone and 'filled with despair' (Social Inquiry Report) she had then engaged in a number of criminal acts. In Bullwood Hall she was moved continuously between segregation block, hospital and cell and, at the time of interview, was waiting to go for trial on a charge relating to assault of a prison officer. She had several times embedded needles in her arms and told me that life in Bullwood Hall was preferable to life outside. Her law-breaking seemed to be totally *incidental* to her isolation and emotional deprivation. She fully expected to serve yet another custodial sentence in the near future.

Yvonne, aged 37, was interviewed at her home in London. She had committed her first crime at the age of 34 and subsequently served six months' imprisonment for a customs offence relating to the importation of cannabis. She had *opted* to commit the crime at a time when she was ill and depressed and at the time of interview had no intention of committing further offences.

Zoë, aged 28, was interviewed at her home in Staffordshire. Taken into Care for being beyond parental control at the age of 12, she had remained in a Children's Home until she was 18. She had then gone to a residential domestic science college which she left after one term. Out of Care and with nowhere else to go, Zoë next drifted to London. There she became involved in prostitution and was variously convicted on charges relating to theft, fraud, forgery and drugs. She had served two short prison sentences. At the time of interview Zoë expressed a determination to lead a law-abiding life for the sake of her young daughter. However, although she felt that in her younger days she had *opted* for a criminal lifestyle, she believed that her most recent crimes (shoplifting and receiving) had been *incidental* to the poverty in which she lived as a single parent. Furthermore, because of her criminal record, she felt pessimistic about her chances of ever earning a decent wage. In these circumstances she felt that she had little inducement to remain law-abiding.

TABLE 3.1   Numbers and percentages of thirty-nine women with one or more convictions for specific offences

Type of offence	No. of women	%
Theft and handling stolen goods	26	67
Fraud/forgery/deception	16	41
Burglary/breaking and entering	15	38
Violence against the person	14	35
Arson	8	20
Criminal damage	8	20
Importing/supplying/possessing drugs	6	15
Soliciting/brothel-keeping, etc.	4	10

THE CRIMES

At the time of interview twenty-six (67 per cent) of the thirty-nine women had convictions for theft and/or handling stolen goods (see Table 3.1). All twenty-six had at least one conviction involving shoplifting and six of the same group had convictions for theft other than shoplifting. The next most frequently cited convictions were for fraud, forgery and deception (mainly in relation to cheques, post office books, and doctors' prescriptions) and sixteen women (41 per cent) had convictions for those offences. When these figures are compared with those for all women found guilty of indictable offences in England and Wales in 1983, it is seen that in that year approximately 80 per cent of women were found guilty of theft and handling stolen goods and only approximately 8 per cent (the next largest group) found guilty of fraud and forgery. So, although the largest number of convictions of the thirty-nine women reflects the most prominent feature of women's law-breaking – that it is mainly comprised of relatively minor acts of theft – their other convictions indicate that disproportionate numbers of them had at some time been convicted of more serious crimes. For example, whereas the figures for the total number of women found guilty of indictable offences in 1983 indicate that only 3 per cent had been convicted for burglary and 6 per cent for violence against the person, 38 per cent of the interviewees had had convictions for burglary and 35 per cent for violence against the person.

The disproportionate numbers of interviewees with convictions for more serious crimes was, of course, determined by the research topic. Investigating women's criminal *careers* (as opposed to studying one-off acts of delinquency) necessarily involved seeking out women with longer records. Interviewing in Bullwood Hall ensured access to at least some women who either had longer records or who had been convicted of serious crimes (even though it still has to be remembered that the majority of women's individual sentences are for minor acts of theft). As for the Contact Group, once it was known that I was investigating criminal *careers*, it was correctly assumed that, by definition, the topic entailed contacting law-breakers who had substantial 'form'.

WOMEN'S PERCEPTIONS OF THEIR CRIMES

Once the tapes had been transcribed, the women's lawbreaking acts were categorized as being 'professional', 'optional' and/or 'incidental' (see table 3.2). These categories are not mutually exclusive and only serve the purpose of loosely categorizing the women's own views of their responses to situations in which they found themselves at various stages of their criminal careers. The categories have, moreover, been used to denote *dominant* processual features of acts or sequences of law-breaking; secondary features of the same act might fall under another category. For example, if a women in effect said that she had had no intention of remaining relatively poor whilst she could earn money by thieving, but that she also felt that she had no *need* to steal, then such law-breaking was categorized as having been predominantly *optional*. If, however the same woman in effect said that she had engaged in certain acts of stealing because she felt at the time that there was no alternative, then such law-breaking was categorized as having been *incidental*. Several women's perceptions of their crime (and/or its actual organization) had also changed over time. The woman in the foregoing example who began engaging in optional (non-professional) law-breaking might later have turned to *professional* law-breaking and then, finally, perceived her most recent law-breaking as being *incidental* (i.e. secondary) to the need to fund an addiction; a criminal record not *allowing* her 'to go straight'; a feeling of hopelessness/helplessness, etc. Thus the categories of law-breaking apply to law-breaking acts which in effect the women described as having the following features:

Optional law-breaking (professional or non-professional)

1 At the time of committing the acts the woman weighed-up the options and then chose to break the law.
2 After the act or sequence of acts, the woman felt that whether or not she reoffended, depended entirely upon herself – not upon either circumstances or need.

Incidental law-breaking (professional or non-professional)

1 At the time of committing the acts the woman cither did not know she was breaking the law (e.g. as with kids playing/trespassing in empty houses) or knew that she was breaking the law but felt that under the circumstances she had no option.

2 After the act or sequence of acts the woman felt that, whether or not she engaged in further law-breaking depended entirely on whether or not her situation changed, either partly through her own agency, e.g. giving up heroin, or through that of 'others' (individuals or official agencies, e.g. if she were provided with accommodation, if she were offered a job, etc.).

Professional law-breaking (optional or incidental)

Law-breaking pursued in a systematic and organized way (either alone or with others) for the primary purpose of providing the woman's major source of income during an extended period of time (even though arrest might cut short the projected time-span).

ENTRY INTO, PROGRESS OF AND TURNING-POINTS IN THE WOMEN'S CRIMINAL CAREERS

The concept of criminal career has been central to symbolic-interactionist perspectives on crime. The basic assumption is that each act of law-breaking and its judicial and penal consequences have either joint or independent effects on subsequent acts or sequences of law-breaking and/or criminalization. These effects can be either subjective and include the various interpretations that people might put on the meanings of previous acts of law-breaking and criminalization or objective and include the social consequences of conviction and imprisonment – such as inability to obtain employment and loss of accommodation. The objective effects exist independently of a person's awareness of them and therefore can be the cause of subsequent imprisonment independently of a defendant's interpretation or agency. For example, when a judge decides that, because a female defendant's children are already in Care (as a direct result of a previous sentence of imprisonment), he need have no qualms about imposing a custodial sentence (see Carlen, 1983a: 70).

A difficulty impeding the charting of symbolic-interactionist sequences of law-breaking and criminalization in this research was that some criminal careers had been so complex that the women could not always recall the order of events. Or they insisted that the circumstances in which the events had occurred were more important than their temporal order. Women found it particularly difficult to remember which non-custodial penalties had been imposed for which crimes. (This was sometimes because the charges had borne little relationship to the crimes in which the women had been engaged prior to their court appearances and sometimes because their other problems had been so overwhelming that at the time they had not taken much notice of a non-custodial penalty.) All of them could remember their first acts of law-breaking and/or their first contacts with the police and courts. Except for Donna and Sally (who had both received many

TABLE 3.2   Criminal careers of thirty-nine women

Name (age) at interview	First accusation of law-breaking[1]	First criminal offence(s) for which found guilty, convicted or cautioned[2]	Subsequent convictions of findings of guilt[3]	Supervision Orders, Cautions, Care Orders or non-custodial sentences[4]	Custodial sentences[5]
Daphne (15)	13	Criminal damage (smashing up a caravan)	Deception, arson (1), theft (several), burglary	Care order, caution, attendance centre, several fines	14 months, 1 day YC
Della (15)	12	Stealing, asault	Theft, burglary, ABH	Care order, Conditional discharge (1), fines (several)	9 months YC
Bobby (15)	12	Assault	Breaking and entering, breach of peace, burglary (several), theft, GBH, shoplifting (several), criminal damage	Caution, fines, IT	6 months YC
Yasmin (16)	15	TDA	Criminal damage, arson, GBH	Deferred sentence, fine	4 months, 1 day YC, 6 months YC
Tricia (17)	14	Shoplifting	TDA, deception, theft (from mother), shoplifting, fraud (cheques), robbery with violence	Care order, several fines	4 months, 1 day YC 2 years imprisonment YC
Audrey (18)	11	TDA	TDA, criminal damage, shoplifting	Conditional discharge, suspended prison sentence, CSO	12 months YC
Cynthia (19)	9	Shoplifting	Deception/handling, assault on police, common assault, criminal damage, theft, burglary, ABH	Care order, probation (3), fines (several)	6 months YC

Notes

1 Many of the women reported that they had been in trouble with the police for status offences well before the age at which they had first been taken to a police station or court.

2 The description of the offences duplicates neither the categories used in the official crime statistics nor the exact wording of the charge; they are those which best indicate what the woman had done (or was supposed to have done). The numbers in brackets in this column indicate when the woman knew how many times she had been charged with a particular offence. Unless indicated otherwise, 'shoplifting' and 'burglary' always refer to more than one charge. Often the women could say only that they had gone to court for 'a whole lot of things', and other times they could tell me what they had done but not what they were charged with. This column and the one immediately to the right of it therefore give only a rough guide to the *range* (rather than the number) of offences that women had been charged with.

3 ABH: actual bodily harm; BOP: breach of peace; GBH: grievous bodily harm.

Categories of lawbreaking"			Has given up law-breaking	Wanted to give up law-breaking but doubtful about keeping out of trouble	Definitely expected to continue law-breaking
Optional law-breaking	Incidental	Professional			
—	1	—	—	√	—
—	1	—	—	√	—
1	2	√	—	√	—
—	1	—	—	—	√
1	—	Aspiring	—	—	√
—	1	√	√	—	—
1	—	√	—	—	√

4 The numbers in brackets indicate when a woman could actually remember how many times she had received a particular sentence.
5 CSO: Community Service Order; IT: Intermediate Treatment; YC: youth custody; YP: young prisoner sentence.
6 The categories 'optional' and 'incidental' refer to the degree of choice which a woman perceived herself as having at the time of crime commission. For example, if a woman said that she had chosen to break the law because she had thought that her poverty justified her crime, then her lawbreaking is categorized as 'optional'. If, on the other hand, she said that at the time she felt that in the circumstances she had no option but to commit crime, then the law-breaking is categorized as 'incidental'. The main difference between optional and incidental law-breaking is that 'optional' refers to that lawbreaking perceived as being *primarily* determined by the choice of the law-breaker; whereas 'incidental' refers to the law-breaking perceived by a woman as being *primarily* determined by circumstances beyond her control.

TABLE 3.2—continued

Name (age) at interview	First accusation of law-breaking[1]	First criminal offence(s) for which found guilty, convicted or cautioned[2]	Subsequent convictions of findings of guilt[3]	Supervision Orders, Cautions, Care Orders or non-custodial sentences[4]	Custodial sentences[5]
Shirley (20)	15	4 assaults on police	Total 24 previous burglary, possessing drugs, assault, insulting behaviour, criminal damage, arson, shoplifting	Cautions, fines	Borstal, Borstal recall, 6 months YC
Jessie (20)	11	Shoplifting	Deception (prescriptions), possession of drugs, conspiracy to supply drugs (1)	Supervision order, fine (1)	6 months YC, 18 months YC
Sadie (20)	13	Shoplifting	Shoplifting, burglary	Probation, several fines	3 months YC
Anne (20)	13	Shoplifting	Shoplifting (several), fraud (prescriptions), burglary	Care order, several fines	Borstal, Borstal recall
Jill (21)	9	Shoplifting	Burglary (many), arson, assault, shoplifting	Probation	Borstal, 13 months and 18 months
Lisa (21)	12	Shoplifting	Assault, fraud (cheques – several)	Supervision order, fines	6 months YP imprisonment, 6 months and 3½ years
Kay (21)	20	Fraud (cheques)	First conviction	—	12 months imprisonment
Lena (21)	16	Shoplifting	Shoplifting, arson, robbery with violence, burglary	Probation (2), several fines	7 months Borstal, 3 years imprisonment
Tara (21)	16	Forgery and fraud (Giro)	Fraud, forgery, shoplifting	Care order, several fines	3 short custodial sentences
Cindy (22)	16	Shoplifting	Shoplifting, burglary	Several fines	3 months YP, 21 days YC, 15 months imprisonment
Stephanie (22)	14	Shoplifting	Shoplifting	Several fines, CSO, suspended prison sentence	9 months imprisonment
Sheila (22)	17	Fraud (cheques)	Conspiracy to defraud, deception (cheques)	Probation, fines (2)	3 years Borstal, 3 years imprisonment
Norma (22)	13	Shoplifting	Theft, deception (cheques), GBH (2)	Caution, probation, several fines	3 years imprisonment
Donna (22)	16	Soliciting	Soliciting, burglary	Fines	Several short prison sentences

Categories of lawbreaking"			Has given up law-breaking	Wanted to give up law-breaking but doubtful about keeping out of trouble	Definitely expected to continue law-breaking
Optional law-breaking	Incidental	Professional			
—	1	√	—	√	—
1	2	—	—	√	—
1	2	—	—	√	—
—	1	√	—	√	—
1	—	—	√	—	—
2	1 and 3	√	—	—	√
—	1	√	—	√	—
—	1	—	—	—	√
1	—	√	—	—	√
1	—	—	—	·√	—
1	—	—	—	—	√
1	—	√	√	—	—
1	2	—	—	√	—
—	1	√	√	—	—

TABLE 3.2—continued

Name (age) at interview	First accusation of law-breaking[1]	First criminal offence(s) for which found guilty, convicted or cautioned[2]	Subsequent convictions of findings of guilt[3]	Supervision Orders, Cautions, Care Orders or non-custodial sentences[4]	Custodial sentences[5]
Dawn (23)	12	Shoplifting	Shoplifting, attempting to supply heroin (1)	Fines, probation	3 years imprisonment
Jean (26)	19	Shoplifting	Shoplifting, receiving (1)	Probation, several fines	None
Mary (27)	16	Shoplifting	Shoplifting, BOP, arson (1), forgery (prescriptions)	Probation, several fines	3 years imprisonment
Nicky (27)	14	Shoplifting	Burglary, deception, fraud (cheques), shoplifting	Probation, several fines	4 months
Carol (27)	23	Assault	Assault (5), shoplifting (2)	Probation, fines	None
Zoë (28)	18	Soliciting	Shoplifting, forgery (prescriptions), receiving	Probation, fines	4 months imprisonment, 7 days imprisonment
Kim (28)	14	Stealing apples	Shoplifting, fraud (cheques)	Caution, probation, fines	4 months Borstal, 3 years imprisonment, 6 months imprisonment
Hazel (29)	14	Abstracting electricity	Carrying a firearm, deception/ forgery, criminal damage (3), arson (1)	Probation, fines	4 months Borstal, 13 months imprisonment
Muriel (30)	18	Burglary	Burglary, housebreaking, robbery with violence, shoplifting	Probation, fines	Borstal, 3 prison sentences
Jeannette (30)	22	Assault	Assault (2), criminal damage (1), customs evasion (1), (cannabis)	Fines	12 months imprisonment
Josie (30)	11	Arson – burning down a row of cottages (with others	Burglary, malicious wounding (1), armed robbery (1)	Caution, Care Order, probation	Borstal, Borstal recall, imprisonment 6 months, 3 years (reduced on appeal)
Nadia (35)	17	Receiving stolen goods	TDA, forgery, deception (several relating to prescriptions), shoplifting	Probation, fines, 6 months imprisonment (suspended)	Borstal, 7 months imprisonment
Sally (35)	17	Possession of drugs	Soliciting, possession of drugs	Probation, fines	Many short terms of imprisonment

Categories of lawbreaking[a]			Has given up law-breaking	Wanted to give up law-breaking but doubtful about keeping out of trouble	Definitely expected to continue law-breaking
Optional law-breaking	Incidental	Professional			
—	1	Involved with professional heroin dealers	—	√	—
1	—	—	—	—	√
—	1	—	—	—	√
—	1	√	√	—	—
—	1	—	—	√	—
1	2	√	—	√	—
1	—	√	—	—	√
—	1	—	√	—	—
2	1	—	√	—	—
2	1	Worked for professionals	√	—	—
2	1	Worked with professionals	√	—	—
2	1 & 3	—	√	—	—
—	1	—	—	—	√

TABLE 3.2—continued

Name (age) at interview	First accusation of law-breaking[1]	First criminal offence(s) for which found guilty, convicted or cautioned[2]	Subsequent convictions of findings of guilt[3]	Supervision Orders, Cautions, Care Orders or non-custodial sentences[4]	Custodial sentences[5]
Yvonne (37)	35	Evasion of customs (cannabis)	None	None	6 months imprisonment
Queenie (43)	21	Shoplifting	Shoplifting, burglary (1), forgery (prescriptions) (1)	Fines, probation	12 months imprisonment, 15 months imprisonment
Monica (44)	36	Shoplifting	Shoplifting (2)	Fines, probation	2 months imprisonment (2 suspended)
Prue (46)	21	Fraud and forgery	Fraud and forgery (13)	Fines, probation	Several terms imprisonment totalling 12½ years
Dee (46)	Late 30s	Keeping a brothel	Controlling prostitutes (1), keeping a brothel (1)	Fines (2)	4 months imprisonment

short prison sentences for soliciting), they could also remember their custodial sentences (though again, not always the actual minor crimes for which the sentences had been imposed). Yet, although many could not remember the details like 'whether that six months was for doing shoplifting or cheques – I was doing both at the same time', all of them appeared (to a greater or lesser extent) to be interested in discussing the ways in which they had thought about (or in some cases not thought about!) their involvement in law-breaking. It was according to these retrospective descriptions of the circumstances, reasons, justifications or motivations preconditional to their crimes, that their views on the meanings of their law-breaking were categorized. (See Table 3.2 for summary of the range of crimes committed, sentences imposed and categorizations of a range of subjective meanings given to the acts of law-breaking. See Table 3.3 for the actual range of substantive circumstances, reasons, justifications or motivations thought to be preconditional to the crimes.)

Every woman was asked about the turning-points (for good or bad) in her life. From many the question provoked a bitter laugh and an incredulous, 'Good! What *good* has ever happened to me? I can tell you the *bad* right enough, but *good*! You must be joking.' More than once the question was flung back at me with a sardonic 'Well, you've heard it all. What would *you* say was good about it? Nothing, right?' Yet in further discussion many could remember when things had 'begun to get worse' (see Table 3.5), whilst others (particularly those who had

Categories of lawbreaking[a]			Has given up law-breaking	Wanted to give up law-breaking but doubtful about keeping out of trouble	Definitely expected to continue law-breaking
Optional law-breaking	Incidental	Professional			
1	—	Worked for professionals	V	—	—
1	2	V	—	V	—
—	1	—	V	—	—
1	2	—	—	V	—
1	—	V	—	—	V

given up crime) could identify points at which things had taken a turn for the better. Additionally, many who were not able (or did not think it relevant or appropriate) to identify specific turning-points were nonetheless prepared to describe social processes, social conditions, ideologies or specific situations which they thought had had significance both for their lives in general and for their criminal careers.

Four major factors – poverty, being in residential Care, drug (including alcohol) addiction and the quest for excitement – were explicitly identified as being prime constituents of women's law-breaking and criminalization. Although all women had committed at least some crimes for financial gain, eleven women claimed that they would never have developed criminal careers at all, had they either not been brought up in residential Care or not been taken into residential Care for some trivial offence in adolescence. Thirteen knew that at least some of their crimes had been related to their heroin addiction or alcohol abuse. Seven said that the prospect of excitement had been a major inducement to break the law, whilst several others admitted to 'getting a buzz' from crimes demanding skill, courage or bravado.

At the time of interview twelve women said that they had given up law-breaking, and twelve that they were still involved in crime (or would be when they left prison). Fifteen stated that, although they would try to keep out of trouble in future, if they were to be honest (with me) and realistic (about their chances),

TABLE 3.3   Material circumstances preconditional to the law-breaking of thirty-nine women

Name (age) at time of interview	Circumstances, reasons, motivations and justifications	Category
Daphne (15)	Said that she often felt that she didn't know what she was doing. She wondered if she were mentally ill	Incidental
Della (15)	Family's lifestyle involving much travel and law-breaking	Incidental
Bobby (15)	Desire for financial gain and excitement	Optional (professional)
Yasmin (16)	Isolation, loneliness and poverty after being placed in bedsitter whilst still in Care	Incidental
Tricia (17)	To get away from home and to have an exciting lifestyle. Desire for financial gain	Optional (aspiring professional)
Audrey (18)	Constant trouble in a variety of residential institutions whilst in Care. Desire for financial gain	Incidental (professional)
Cynthia (19)	Desire for financial gain (in situation where labour market not seen to offer adequate wage)	Optional
Shirley (20)	Isolation and loneliness after being placed in hostel 'for much older people' whilst still in Care	Incidental (professional)
Jessie (20)	1 Desire for financial gain 2 Heroin addiction	1 Optional 2 Incidental
Sadie (20)	1 Desire for financial gain 2 Mixing with known criminals	1 Optional 2 Incidental
Anne (20)	1 Attempts to free herself of social services control – being 'on run' from residential institutions 2 Heroin addiction – desire for financial gain	1 Incidental 2 Incidental
Jill (21)	1 Desire for excitement 2 Desire for financial gain	Optional
Lisa (21)	1 Desire for exciting lifestyle and financial gain 2 Heroin addiction	1 Optional (professional) 2 Incidental
Kay (21)	Heroin addiction – desire for financial gain	Incidental
Lena (21)	Family's lifestyle – always quarrelling with neighbours	Incidental
Tara (21)	Desire for financial gain (in situation where labour market perceived as offering nothing in way of living wage)	Optional (professional)
Cindy (22)	Desire for financial gain (in situation where labour market perceived as offering nothing in way of living wage)	Optional
Stephanie (22)	Desire for financial gain (in situation where labour market perceived as offering nothing in way of living wage)	Optional
Sheila (22)	Desire for financial gain (extra money)	Optional (worked with professionals)
Norma (22)	1 Desire for financial gain 2 Pre-existent violent lifestyle	1 Optional 2 Incidental
Donna (22)	1 Being on run from residential institutions, desire for financial gain 2 Isolation, loneliness and poverty after being placed in a bedsitter whilst still in Care	1 and 2: incidental (professional)
Dawn (23)	Heroin addiction, desire for financial gain	Incidental involved with professionals

TABLE 3.3—continued

Name (age) at time of interview	Circumstances, reasons, motivations and justifications	Category
Jean (26)	Desire for financial gain (in situation where neither labour market nor social security seen to offer solution to poverty for single parent)	Optional
Mary (27)	Alcohol problem – desire for financial gain	Incidental
Nicky (27)	Heroin addiction – desire for financial gain	Incidental
Carol (27)	Belief that, unless a person in her circumstances took the law into her own hands, she would be 'kicked about' by others – desire for financial gain	Incidental
Zoë (28)	1 For financial gain after leaving Care	1 Optional (professional)
	2 For financial gain after criminal record resulted in only low-paid jobs	2 Incidental
Kim (28)	For financial gain (in situation where neither labour market nor social security seen to offer solution to poverty of single parent)	Optional (professional)
Hazel (29)	1 Response of social services to her behaviour whilst in Care.	Incidental
	2 Being 'on run' from residental institutions (economic necessity)	
	3 Health problems (mental and physical)	
Muriel (30)	1 For excitement and financial gain	1 Optional
	2 Constant movements between residential placements whilst in Care	2 Incidental
Jeanette (30)	1 Lifestyle – worked in nightclub, mixed with criminals	1 Incidental
	2 For financial gain (extra money)	2 Optional
Josie (30)	1 Early institutionalization/isolation upon release from Care	1 Incidental
	2 Excitement, for financial gain	2 Optional (with professionals)
Nadia (35)	1 Need to survive whilst on run from approved school, financial gain	1 Incidental
	2 Excitement	2 Optional
	3 Heroin addiction	3 Incidental
Sally (35)	1 'On run' from Approved School	
	2 Heroin addiction – for financial gain	Incidental
Yvonne (37)	For financial gain	Optional (for professionals)
Queenie (43)	1 Excitement	1 Optional
	2 Alcohol problem – for financial gain	2 Incidental
Monica (44)	Alcohol problem – for financial gain	Incidental
Prue (46)	1 For financial gain (extra money)	1 Optional
	2 Compulsion	2 Incidental
Dee (46)	For financial gain	Optional (professional)

they could not hold out much hope of succeeding in the attempt. This latter fifteen had all indicated that their law-breaking had been (or become) incidental to circumstances over which they felt they had little control (see Table 3.2).

Yet, although desire for more money, problems associated with being in

TABLE 3.4   Immediate and sufficient circumstantial reasons for law-breaking and/or criminalization

Immediate circumstantial reasons for law-breaking and/or criminalization	No. of women describing these circumstances/reasons as being operative in their criminal careers
Desire for more money	32
Problems associated with being in residential Care	11
Desire for excitement	7
Heroin addiction	7
Alcohol problem	3
Family's lifestyle	2
Mental illness	2
Mixing with people involved in crime	2

TABLE 3.5   Pre-emptive conditions or pre-emptive life events affecting women's lives so adversely, prior to the time of crime commission, that it could be claimed that they were in part responsible for their law-breaking/criminalization

Pre-emptive condition/life event	No. of women describing these conditions/events as affecting their lives adversely
Poverty	12
Going into residential Care	12
Acquiring a dependency on drugs or alcohol	9
Death of one or both parents whilst woman under age of 16	5
Leaving home under age 18 due to father's physical and/or sexual abuse	5
Inability to obtain employment/becoming unemployed	4
Isolation upon leaving Care	4
Leaving home because of physical abuse by mother	3
Parents' separation whilst woman under age 16	3
Emotional involvement with man involved in crime	3
Truancy from school	3

residential Care, drugs (including alcohol) problems, plus the quest for excitement, were most often mentioned as being immediate circumstantial reasons for law-breaking and criminalization, the women were reluctant to attribute the shape of their criminal careers to any one cause. At different times different factors had predominated. Even though they could recall the immediate circumstantial reasons for law-breaking and/or criminalization, women often insisted that the crimes had been related not only to immediate circumstances but to pre-emptive conditions of longer standing. Thus Table 3.4 lists the main circumstances or reasons recalled by the thirty-nine women as having been immediately preconditional to some of their crimes, whilst Table 3.5 lists the pre-emptive conditions or pre-emptive life events that had affected their lives adversely even prior to the time of crime commission.

Some of the difficulties in developing a symbolic-interactionist perspective on women's criminal careers should by now be apparent. The extraordinary complexity of the task can be illustrated by discussion of the multifarious ways in which women saw the relationship between poverty and law-breaking.

THIRTY-NINE WOMEN, POVERTY AND LAW-BREAKING

'People are poor in Britain in the 1980s . . . in the sense that their incomes are too low in comparison with the living standards enjoyed by most of the population' (Field, 1981: 46). In terms of their membership of one or more of three groups – the unemployed, single-parent families and the poor in institutions – that Field identifies as being amongst the seven major groups in poverty, thirty-two of the thirty-nine women had been poor all their lives. Of the seven others, four were unemployed at the time of interview and, because of their criminal records, did not expect ever again to obtain employment. Two had never been poor and, when I met them still had good jobs, though, as Monica's employer did not know about her criminal record, she feared dismissal if he ever found out. Finally, Dee had years before rescued herself from the poverty of a low wage by engaging in a lucrative but illegal occupation. Apart from Dee, none of the others had achieved any long-term financial prosperity from their crimes though some had managed to achieve a reasonable standard of living for relatively short periods. Yet, although it can confidently be asserted on objective criteria that thirty-seven (95 per cent) of the thirty-nine women had been in poverty at some time in their lives and that, of their own admission thirty-two (82 per cent) had committed at least some of their crimes primarily for financial gain, only twelve (30 per cent) saw poverty as having been even part cause of their criminal activities. So why did twenty-five of the thirty-seven women who had at some time been poor either fail to mention or explicitly reject poverty as a pre-emptive condition partly responsible for their law-breaking?

Eleven did so because they believed that, their poverty notwithstanding, they would never have been in trouble with the criminal courts, had they either not been brought up, or not spent considerable parts of their childhood, in Care. Four others had committed crime *only* because they had needed the extra money to buy either heroin (three women) or alcohol (one woman) (yet as was suggested in Chapter Two there *are* links between poverty and heroin usage). The remaining ten had each offered a variety of reasons as to why their poverty had been unrelated to their crimes: that, because they had spent most of their lives in institutions, at the time of crime commission they had not yet realized how poor they were; that their only motivation had been the desire for excitement; that they had 'drifted' into crime without really thinking about it; that *poverty could not* have been a reason for their law-breaking because they had known other poor people who had always 'managed' without breaking the law – and so on.

The foregoing catalogue of varying perceptions that women held of poverty as a cause of law-breaking exemplifies the two major criticisms that have been levelled against oral histories and symbolic-interactionist studies; that they can only describe, not explain, social and psychological phenomena; that there is no end to the multiplicity of meanings that can be attributed to life events. Furthermore, if thirty-nine women hold such differing views on the connections between their law-breaking and a fundamental social condition like poverty – a condition experienced by 95 per cent of them at some time or other – whatever is the point of trying to incorporate those wildly differing perceptions into any general statements about the causes of women's law-breaking and criminalization? The point is that, by taking seriously women's own accounts of their criminal careers, there is, first, a refusal to reduce those lives to a sociology that erases the uniqueness of individual female experience; and secondly, a commitment to deconstructing those careers into the elemental ideological and political components which many of them share, albeit in the different combination that renders each unique.

4

OUT OF CARE, INTO CUSTODY: dimensions and deconstructions of the state's regulation of twenty-two young working-class women

> Ever since the sixteenth-century custom of chopping off the ears of vagabonds, rogues and beggars, the British have always had some difficulty in distinguishing between poverty and crime.
>
> (Booth, 1985: 7)

This perennial difficulty was exacerbated in the nineteenth century when the discovery of childhood (Aries, 1973) coincided with the transformation of the 'lower orders' into the 'dangerous classes' (Briggs, 1967; Radzinowitz, 1966). Concern about the poor was thereafter inseminated by a bourgeois missionary zeal to save working-class children from the moral degeneracy assumed to be associated with poverty and squalid living conditions.

Young working-class women were seen to be at especial risk of moral contamination, and the ensuing state regulation of young women's sexuality and the development of conventional femininity have persisted (Smart, 1981). For, although only a small minority of children in the Care of local authorities have been in trouble with the law prior to the imposition of their Care Orders (House of Commons, 1984: xiii), of the 3–4 per cent of young persons in Care on the grounds of 'moral danger' about 80 per cent are young women (Campbell, 1981: 7; Hudson, A., 1983: 9). In fact, girls are disproportionately admitted to residential Care for what are called 'status offences' – like running away from home, staying out late at night or being aggressive – behaviours which would not be punishable at law if engaged in by an adult 'and which would not justify a Care Order under criminal proceedings' (Hudson, B.,

TABLE 4.1   Research groupings of the women by place of interview

Bullwood Group		Contact Group	
Name	Age at interview	Name	Age at interview
Daphne	15	Anne	20
Della	15	Jill	21
Yasmin	16	Tara	21
Tricia	17	Donna	22
Audrey	18	Carol	27
Cynthia	19	Zoë	28
Shirley	20	Kim	28
Lena	21	Hazel	29
Norma	22	Muriel	30
Dawn	23	Josie	35
		Nadia	35
		Sally	35
Total: 10		Total: 12	

Note
The Bullwood Group were interviewed in Bullwood Hall Prison and Youth Custody Centre. The Contact Group were interviewed in private houses – mostly in their own homes.

1984: 41). Yet, whatever the official or actual reason for the Care Order, studies indicating that maybe half the population of young offender institutions have previously been in residential Care (e.g. Home Office, 1977) suggest, too, that disproportionate numbers of young people either go directly out of Care into penal custody – or, in some cases, into penal custody whilst still in Care. The majority of young people in Care do not, of course, acquire criminal records; but, because twenty-two of the thirty-nine interviewed about their law-breaking and criminalization had also been through the Care/custody mangle,[1] an urgent task in the deconstruction of their socio-biographies was analysis of the Care factor in criminal careers.

All twenty-two who had been (or were still) in residential Care (see Table 4.1) were from working-class backgrounds. Six were black. In terms of their membership of three groups – the unemployed, single-parent families and the poor in institutions – identified by Field (1981) as being amongst the major groups in poverty, the twenty-two had been poor all their lives. Consequently this chapter will not only try to indicate how ideologies of family and femininity pave the paths from Care to penal custody. It will also attempt to show how class-biased and racist inequities in the administration of welfare and criminal law are intertwined with discriminatory typifications of gender-competence. Together they have a complex but malign influence on the mode and degree of criminalization experienced by young women in Care who break the law and/or step out of place.

TABLE 4.2   Research groupings of the women by age of entry into Residential Care

Pre-11 entry		Post-11 entry	
Name	Age at interview	Name	Age at interview
Yasmin	16	Daphne	15
Audrey	18	Della	15
Shirley	20	Tricia	17
Jill	21	Cynthia	19
Lena	21	Anne	20
Donna	22	Tara	21
Hazel	29	Norma	22
Muriel	30	Dawn	23
Nadia	35	Carol	27
		Zoë	28
		Kim	28
		Josie	30
		Sally	35
Total: 9		Total: 13	

STRUCTURE OF THE ARGUMENT

What is presented in this chapter is an ethnographic analysis of a 'slice of life' – or, more precisely, a deconstruction of a sequence of events that occurred in the early lives of young women who went into penal custody, either whilst they were still in or very soon after leaving Care. The interplay of class, racism, gender and Care factors is presented in sequential mode, a descriptive procedure entailed by a project taking 'careers' as the focus of investigation.

To facilitate understanding of the complex interplay of class, racism, gender and Care factors and their diverse material, ideological and psychological preconditions and effects, a summary presentation of the ethnographic analyses is given in Table 4.3. A summary of the general argument is outlined herewith.

Argument

1 The dynamics of the process whereby a small section of working-class women are translated from Care to Custody are partly explained by that perspective in criminology known as 'control theory'.

2 The version of 'control theory' used here is based on the assumption that people outwardly conform whilst they perceive it to be worth their while (psychologically and materially) to do so. (However, the subjective calculation also takes into account the likelihood of apprehension and criminalization; the white-collar criminal can rationally calculate that it is not worth his

TABLE 4.3 Out of Care, into custody: dimensions, deconstructions and dynamics

Career Stage[1]	Economic and ideological conditions			Deviant or law-breaking activities	Consequences
	Class	Gender	Racism		
Entry into Care	*Pre-11* – parents lack money and access to other material goods and therefore cannot meet extra financial demands.	*Post-11* 1 Self referral owing to restrictions at home. 2 Referred by parents or guardians who fear that girl's behaviour is gender deviant.	Disproportionate removal of ethnic-minority children from their homes because of 'Euro-centric' views on child-rearing.	*Post-11* – status offences – like staying out too late at night, truancy, general 'unfeminine' behaviour.	1 Excessive assessment and categorizing, leading to feelings of self- and social estrangement. 2 Attempts to escape Care through drugs or absconding. 3 Quest for 'care' through development of non-institutional relationships.
'Trouble' in residential institutions	1 Developing sense of deprivation and difference – sense of being in the 'Care' class. 2 Developing sense of lack of control over life chances. 3 But class position often not perceived because immediate material needs well-provided for.	1 Castigation of women via talk. Developing feelings of guilt (about being outside 'the family') and abnormality. 2 Higher standards of behaviour expected of adolescent girls than of adolescent boys. 3 Insensitive response to girls' physical development. 4 No discussion of women and sex.	1 Children brought up as 'white'. 2 Racist presumption that black children in Children's Homes cause problems. 3 Racist assumption that young black women are likely to be promiscuous. 4 Isolated in Children's Home from other black people.	1 Drug-taking. 2 Absconding. 3 Various petty crimes.	1 Increased sense of difference and isolation. 2 Movement from 'placement' to 'placement' and eventually to a Secure Unit. 3 Increased determination to 'escape' – absconding. 4 Drugs administered to control behaviour. 5 Placing most troublesome young women in 'independent' accommodation whilst still in Care.

Into crime	1 Increased poverty once girl has absconded. 2 Once apprehended by police, no 'friendly' adults to intervene – only social workers who have run out of 'placements' for them.	1 Girls in Care are likely to be viewed by Court as already being out of their 'proper' place and - therefore are dealt with more harshly. 2 Fewer non-custodial facilities for law-breaking women. 3 Knowledge that they will be approached by male predators whilst on the run results in many women carrying a knife and then being arrested for carrying an offensive weapon. 4 Escalation of young women up sentencing tariff for a variety of reasons.	1 Racism operative when young girl comes to attention of the police. Reports of verbal abuse with sexual connotations. 2 Likely to be under greater surveillance in shops and public places. Greater likelihood of arrest if they do break the law.	1 Crimes committed for survival whilst on the run. 2 Drugs – to provide non-institutional network of friends. 3 Entry into some types of more organized crime.	1 Deviant/lawbreaking activities more likely to come to attention of police because children are in Children's Home. 2 Magistrates look doubly askance at law-breaking *women* who are already in *residential Care*, not living with a family. 3 Custodial sentence likely if social workers say that the troublesome young women had already been through every 'placement' (Care and penal systems merge at this point). 4 Young women placed in independent accommodation – bedsitter or hostel.
Out of residential Care	1 Extreme poverty encountered upon leaving institution. 2 Difficulties with DHSS or supplementary benefits payments. 3 Living in hostels that do not allow residents to remain indoors during day. 4 Growing awareness of stigma and economic deprivation.	1 Women suffer disproportionately from shortage of rented housing for single people. 2 Through loneliness or hostel policies, women forced to seek company in public places and are likely to be seen as violating appropriate gender behaviour by so doing. 3 Growing awareness of gender ideologies – especially 'deviance' of being apart from nuclear family.	Affects housing and employment opportunities.	1 Unauthorized removal of personal file from institution. 2 Prostitution and theft and other minor crimes both for economic survival and to carve out an independent way of life.	1 Some choose to 'live rough' rather than in unwelcoming and exploitative hostels. 2 Some become pregnant in order to acquire both family and home. 3 Institutional living has left them ill-equipped to look after themselves. 4 Once apprehended for crime, their institutional record and gender deviance goes against them in Court. 5 Increase in belief that law-breaking is the only way of making a decent living.

TABLE 4.3—continued

Career Stage[1]	Economic and ideological conditions		Racism	Deviant or law-breaking activities	Consequences
	Class	Gender			
Into custody	2 Material circumstances outside prison by now so bad that prison viewed as a refuge from men, money – problems and isolation. 2 Nothing in their past histories leads them to believe that they have any chance now of making the 'class deal' and gaining even the meanest rewards for class conformity.	1 Once they have completed their sentences very few after-care facilities for women. 2 Housing situation worse for women ex-prisoners. 3 Nothing in their past histories leads them to believe that they have much chance of making the 'gender deal' and gaining even the meanest rewards for gender conformity.	Varies from institution to institution[2] but more than 4 times the expected number of adult women in prison are from ethnic minority groups.	1 With nothing going for them on the outside, they create trouble in Youth Custody Centres in order to stay there. 2 Some invoke 'hard' girl status by tattooing; determination to gain prison reputation. 3 Some experience despair and guilt and engage in self-mutilation.	1 Custodial sentence results in loss of accommodation and in loss of few possessions they have. 2 Custodial sentence results in loss of embryo family through children going into Care. 3 Women begin to fear the cumulative effects of institutionalization but 4 find it difficult to conceive that they have much to gain in the future by conformity.

Notes
1 The stages are not numbered as their ordering is different for individual career patterns.
2 See Reports of the Chief Inspector of Prisons 1983–85 and also *Breaking the Silence*, GLC, 1986.
3 *The Guardian*, 19 June 1986, reporting Home Office figures published on 18 June 1986 (Home Office 1986b).

or her while to conform because, even if the crime is detected, the gains accruing from the fraud, etc., would most likely far outweigh the disabilities arising from the punishment.)

3 For working-class men in employment the major locus of social control is the workplace (Young, 1975). Thus, while men can continue to calculate that the rewards from employment outweigh those from crime, employed men are unlikely to engage in the more easily criminalized forms of law-breaking. Through employment and trade unions they can make the economic and political 'class deal'.

4 Working-class women on the other hand have traditionally been contained within *two* material and ideological sites of social control, the workplace and the family – though it can be argued that both sites have provided women with fewer rewards than they have men. Working-class women have therefore been doubly controlled. They have been expected not only to make the class deal but the 'gender deal' too. (True, feminists have persistently constructed 'alternative' reward sites, but when women in institutions do this – and especially if they choose other women as sexual partners – it is usually taken as evidence of their essential gender deviance and is punished by the authorities.)

5 Most working-class women make both the class deal and the gender deal because the exploitative nature of those two deals is obscured by the ideologies of familiness and consumerism working together to engender within the women a commitment to, if not a belief in, the imaginary rewards of respectable working-class womanhood.

6 This commitment to the rewards of 'respectable' working-class womanhood is most likely to be engendered when young women are brought up in families where both psychological and material rewards are represented as emanating from either the labours or the 'love' of a male breadwinner. (Even though many households do not nowadays *have* a male breadwinner, the normative heterosexuality celebrated in women's magazines, pop songs and the predominantly conservative and liberal mass media still represents male-related domesticity coupled with a wage-earning job as the twin ideals to which (gender-) competent modern women should aspire.)

7 Women brought up in Care since birth or early childhood, together with those put into Care by seemingly rejecting families in adolescence, tend not to acquire the psychological commitments to male-related domesticity, tend not to have their class position occluded by the forms and outward trappings of bourgeois family ideology, and yet *do* acquiesce in a commitment to consumerism which is often the only space within which, they believe, they can make their own lives. (There is also often a commitment to an imaginary family form. See Chapter 5.)

8 The majority of women are *not* criminalized, even if they do break the law, because while they remain within the family they are seen to have made the

gender-deal and to be gender regulated. Conversely, girls in Care (by definition beyond family control in at least the physical and sometimes also in the disciplinary sense) are often seen as being gender decontrolled. Already seen, therefore, as being *unregulated women*, they are also seen as being potential recidivist law-breakers. Their 'files' become 'records' and the authorities act accordingly.

9 The official responses to young women in Care who get into trouble combine with prevailing economic and ideological conditions to minimalize (or in many cases destroy) the likelihood of their having either future opportunities or inclinations to make either the class deal or the gender deal. They perceive themselves to be marginalized and therefore, having nothing to lose, decide that law-breaking is a preferable alternative to poverty and social isolation.

In this chapter it is argued that, when certain economic, ideological and regulatory/penal practices combine as constituents of individual life histories, they overdetermine both the law-breaking and the criminalization of a small section of working-class women. The narrative describes how these conditions repeatedly combine to effect the belief (held for different reasons by both the young women in Care themselves and by their state guardians) that life outside the Care/penal custody complex has nothing to offer that might either *induce* the women to conform or *enable* them to keep out of trouble in the future.

INTO CARE

The majority of young people in Care are there because their families are too poor to pay for alternative ways of coping with illness, bereavement, single-parenthood, homelessness, etc. (cf. Freeman, 1983: 148; House of Commons, 1984). Further biases are accounted for by race and gender.

In 1984 the *Second Report from The Social Services Committee Children in Care* (Volume I House of Commons, 1984: cxix) observed that 'ethnic minority children are disproportionately represented in the Care population.' Summarizing views put to it by a number of organizations, the Committee reported that 'the unnecessary removal of black children from their families' (ibid.: cxx) was 'said to spring from "Eurocentric" views held by social workers about ideal family patterns and ideal family behaviour'. Idealizations of femininity are also operative in Care proceedings.

Department of Health and Social Security statistics (1984), together with a number of research studies (e.g. Casburn, 1979; Hudson, B., 1984; Webb, 1984) support the view that:

the majority of girls do not get drawn into the complex web of the personal social services because they have committed offences. It is more likely to be because of concerns about their perceived sexual behaviour and/or

because they are seen to be 'at risk' of 'offending' against social codes of
adolescent femininity . . .

(Hudson, A., 1985)

So with the twenty-two women interviewed, thirteen had been taken into
residential Care after the age of 11 (the post-11 group) and 'status offences'
accounted for the Orders imposed on eight of them (even though three of the
eight had been taken to court after admitting criminal offences). Two orders had
been occasioned by 'family circumstances' and three by acts of law-breaking.
Yet, whatever the official reasons for the Orders, it is an ironical fact that, whilst
all those admitted to residential Care before the age of 11 (the pre-11 group)
held inaccurate views on the normal form of the modern family (cf. Barrett and
McIntosh,1982; Segal, 1983), together with romantic idealizations of its
functions, the majority of the post-11 group claimed that their own experiences
of family life had made them initially welcome the removal from home (cf.
Hudson, A., 1985: 8).

Once they had reached puberty, many of the women had found that
previously permissive parents suddenly became unduly restrictive (cf.
Christina and Carlen, 1985). Indeed, several had been glad to get away from the
beatings suffered at the hands of relatives. Except for Sally (who at 15 had
already chosen her own 'way out' by 'being into drink and drugs'), all of the
post-11 group had seen 'going into [residential] Care' as an escape from difficult
family situations. Their families appeared to have held similar views. Tricia's
and Zoë's mothers had been the first to report their daughters to the police.
(Tricia for theft from her mother's purse, Zoë for running away from home).
The fathers of Carol and Josie, Daphne's mother and Cynthia's grandmother
had made repeated requests for the girls to be taken into Care. Sally had already
been turned out of home before being sent to Approved School. Kim had
'cleared off' in response to her grandmother's unjust accusations of prostitution.

Certainly none of the post-11 group had been 'typical girls' (Griffin, 1985) in
terms of being 'muted' (Ardener, 1978; Stanworth, 1985), limiting their
activities to the private spaces of their homes (McRobbie and Garber, 1976)
and/or engaging in only those pursuits allowed by the conventional discourses
of femininity. And, as Barbara Hudson (1984) has argued, whereas much
behaviour seen to be peculiar to teenage boys is legitimized by discourses of
adolescence that allow adolescent males a developmental space for behavioural
experimentation prior to their emergence into adulthood, no such discursive
leeway is allowed to girls who engage in the same behaviours. Discourses of
femininity are seen to be subverted by discourses of adolescence. The young
female is always an embryo woman, never a developing person (cf. Sachs and
Wilson, 1978). If, therefore, the discourse of femininity does indeed supersede
that of adolescence, then from the accounts they gave me of their teenage

TABLE 4.4 Institutional and other residential experiences of twenty-two convicted women who had spent part of their lives in Care

Name (age)	Age of entry into residential Care Order and duration	Summary reason for Care Order as explained by interviewee	Reason given for Care Order as explained by interviewee	Institutions experienced – excluding assessment and remand centres
Daphne (15)	13 years – time of interview	Criminal offence	With others, set fire to, and destroyed, a school	CH, CHE* foster-parents, YCC
Della (15)	13 years – time of interview	Status offence	Poor school attendance (but taken to court for theft)	CHE, YCC
Yasmin (16)	2 years – present	Family circumstances	Unknown to Yasmin	CH,* CHE, Adolescent Unit, Special School,* YCC (2), own single accommodation whilst still in Care
Tricia (17)	13 years – time of interview	Status offence	Truancy (but taken to court for theft)	CH, CHE, Adolescent Unit, YCC (2), hostel*
Audrey (18)	2–18 years	Family circumstances	Unknown to Audrey	CH*, CHE, Adolescent Unit, Therapeutic Community, hostel, single accommodation whilst still in Care, YCC
Cynthia (19)	13–18 years	Family circumstances	Mother (single parent) unable to care for her	CH,* CHE, Special School, hostel, YCC
Shirley (20)	birth – 18 years	Family circumstances	Unknown to Shirley	CH,* foster-parents, hostel, own single accommodation whilst still in Care, living rough/on the run, YCC
Anne (20)	14–18 years	Status offence	Out of mother's control (but taken to court for stealing a book)	CHE,* Adolescent Unit, foster-parents, hostel, own single accommodation whilst still in Care, living rough/on the run, YCC
Jill (21)	4–18 years	Family circumstances	Mother's illness and death (father living elsewhere)	CH,* Adolescent unit, foster-parents,* Special School, living rough* or hostel, YCC
Lena (21)	7–18 years	Family circumstances	Physical abuse by mother	CH,* CHE, hostel, YCC

Name (age)	Age	Offence type	Circumstances	Placements
Tara (21)	14–18 years	Criminal offences	Fraud, forgery, theft	CHE, living rough/on the run, YCC
Norma (22)	14–18 years	Family circumstances	Physical abuse by mother	Special School, YCC
Donna (22)	2 months – 18 years	Family circumstances	Mother (single parent) unable to look after her	CH,* Adolescent Unit, therapeutic community, special school, own single accommodation whilst still in care, living rough/on the run, YCC
Dawn (23)	13–18 years	Status offence	Running away from home	Approved school, living rough, prison
Carol (27)	12–18 years	Status offence	Father unable to cope with daughter after death of wife	CH, mental hospital, hostel
Zoë (28)	12–18 years	Status offence	Staying out late, running away from home	CH, living rough/on the run, prison
Kim (28)	12–18 years	Status offence	Running away from home	CH,* Borstal, prison
Hazel (29)	6–18 years	Family circumstances	Mother (single parent) unable to care for her	Approved school, Borstal, prison
Muriel (30)	6 weeks – 18 years	Family circumstances	Unknown to Muriel who was found abandoned on Waterloo Station, 6 weeks old	CH,* mental hospital, foster-parents,* approved school, hostel, living rough/on the run, Borstal, prison
Josie (30)	11–18 years	Criminal offence	With others, accidentally setting fire to a row of cottages	CH*, Approved school, living rough/on the run, hostel, borstal, prison
Nadia (35)	birth to 9 / 12–18 years	Family circumstances	Original reason for being in Care unknown – adopted at 9 – returned to care 3 years later after death of both adoptive parents	Approved school, living rough/on the run, Borstal
Sally (35)	14–18 years	Status offence	Staying out late at night, drinking alcohol	Mental hospital, approved school, hostel,* living rough, on the run, Borstal, prison

CH: Children's Home
CHE: Community Home with Education
YCC: Youth Custody Centre
* indicates several placements

activities it can clearly be seen that Zoë and the others had definitely slipped their ideological moorings.

Refusal to stay within oppressive families, schools, and, later, institutions was a distinguishing feature of the twenty-two women's careers. All said that they had truanted from day schools and/or absconded on more than one occasion from residential Care. As far as school was concerned hostility was directed less against the teachers and more against the system of 'schooling' itself. Repeatedly women made remarks like, 'I just couldn't bear sitting down all day being told what to do', though two had provoked expulsions rather than submit to corporal punishment.

By the time they reached secondary school many young women were already feeling overconstrained by the combined disciplines of family or residential institution and school. Those still at home often felt devalued in comparison with brothers, and with nothing on offer at home or school some of the youngsters had sought fun in public spaces outside the domestic, educational and institutional spheres. For as Hagan, Simpson and Gillis (1979:29) have stressed: 'delinquency frequently is *fun* – even more importantly, a type of fun infrequently allowed to females.'

Because every one of the post-11 group had run away from home at least once, and most had roamed the town when truanting from school, they had also spent much of their time in the company of young men who, unlike young women, are seen as natural occupiers of public space. Yet only three of the post-11 group admitted to having had sexual intercourse in their early teens. The others either claimed to have had no interest in men at all at that age or, more often, merely to have wanted a share in the greater degree of freedom accorded to males (cf. Christina and Carlen, 1985; Tchaikovsky, 1985). Questioned about their early teenage ambitions, the most frequent reply was the deceptively simple (and as things turned out, movingly innocent) 'I just wanted to lead my own life, that was all.' With their working-class situation limiting their options on alternatives to life in the family home, entry into residential Care was in prospect seen as being at least a step on the road to independence. In reality the opposite was true. Sooner or later each of those thirteen women discovered that, in terms of developing independence, life in residential Care was no life at all.

TOO MUCH CARE: TOO LITTLE CARE

'All children coming into Care need some degree of planned, professional diagnosis' (Home Office, 1970). So reported the Advisory Council on Child Care in 1970, and, given the range of residential facilities used by local authorities, it is not surprising that strenuous attempts are made to 'fit' child to Children's Home or other 'placement' (see Richardson, 1969). Yet, as Foucault (1977) has indicated, assessment, categorization and 'placing' also have hidden disciplinary functions, coercive and, ultimately, exclusionary effects that the women in this study had certainly sensed and rebelled against.

Psychological assessment had been a major element in construction of the 'outsider' status frequently invoked by the women as being partly responsible for their rebellious reactions to Care. Constant assessment, categorization and recategorization had led to a sense of essential difference, otherness and deviance. This, in conjunction with continual movement from placement to placement (the implication being that for every normal child there *is* an appropriate placement) had finally resulted in their envelopment in a tenacious isolationary matrix. Psychologically manacled to their files (and the 'outsider' identities constructed therein), physically filed away behind the bars of Secure Units and Youth Custody Centres, it had seemed to many of the women that too much Care had pushed them into a disciplinary space where no one cared at all. The complex social problems that had precipitated them into Care in the first place had Carefully been translated and redistributed as the individual problems of yet another batch of gender-careless, delinquent girls.

Filing, assessment, categorization, 'placing'

Morris *et al.* (1980) have pointed out that many children in Care 'believe that they have done wrong, especially when they later meet young offenders at the Children's Home and find that they are on the same kind of order – a Care Order'. Yet, even when they accept that they were taken into Care solely for 'family reasons' beyond their control, young women desperately want to know what those reasons were. It is then that 'the file' takes on such importance. What is in it? Is the record accurate?

Young people in Care who do eventually read their files are frequently surprised at the inaccuracies and prejudices they contain (see Denton, 1984; Wakerley, 1984). Many of the women interviewed thought that at least some of the absurder assessments stem from the pressure put on young women in Care to define and share their 'problems' (cf. Ackland, 1982: 145).

> If they'd nothing to write about you, then you didn't stay there long. Sometimes they used to make things up and write them about you. I think they read these books and it doesn't really matter what you say, as long as it's got a slight link with the book. If you've got nothing to say at all, or if you have great difficulty in expressing yourself, then they're fucked. [Muriel, aged 30]

Talking about why she had always been 'on the run' from her various placements, Anne remarked that 'It's too hard to explain but they were always trying to get at you mentally.' Other stated more tersely that 'Case conferences and reviews just do people's heads in.' The most constant complaint concerned the 'pressure to have problems', the coercive assumption of difference. What the women were talking about, in effect, was the psychiatrization of women's deviant behaviour (cf. Carlen, 1985, 1986) and the way in which attempts are made to regulate women through redefining them and castigating them by talk (cf. Okely, 1978; Carlen, 1983a). For although only three of the interviewees had spent time in a mental hospital, the majority mentioned that they had frequently been made to feel that they were 'not quite right in the head'.

> I always felt that, being in Care, they sort of put things into your mind and make you feel as if you're all mixed up, when really you haven't got a problem. It's *very* hard to explain, but they make you feel that you're very special because you're in Care and that you've got problems. Really, they're just messing up with your head. [Audrey, aged 18]

Donna's account of being sent to an Adolescent Unit reveals not only her own sense of violation at the clumsy 'therapeutic' intervention but also the sexist and racist assumptions incorporated into the 'assessment' that had occasioned the move.

> They were definitely a lot stricter with girls than boys. I found out *why* because I took my file out of the office. It said how I was an attractive 13-year-old West Indian girl and that, if I kept on like I was, I'd soon have a couple of babies. So they sent me to an Adolescent Unit. There were bars on the window, we were all locked up and they wanted you to join in all kinds of games. Like they wanted me to hold on to this pillow and imagine it was my mother. It was embarrassing; that wasn't my problem, my mother. They were saying I wasn't relaxing myself. I did try but it was like lying. I think that affected my life really. 'Cos I keep thinking back on it and I think, 'Oh, my God! How embarrassing.' I ran away from there. [Donna, aged 22]

Difference

'Care's' emphasis on individual assessment and problem-solving was not the only cause of the overwhelming sense of difference that had assailed so many of the young women. Growing awareness of the dominance of the 'normal nuclear family' myth had also depressed several of the pre-11 group at some stage in their childhood.

> I always felt that I wanted to be with a proper family, be the same as everyone else. I didn't want to be different. But they do try to make you feel different. That's why I was against them. [Yasmin, aged 16]

A sense of difference permeated other spheres, too (cf. Page and Clark, 1977: chap. 3).

> Like at the school I went to, no one wore uniform. But I had to because we came from the Children's Home. [Shirley, aged 20]

> I felt I had no control over anything at all. I had to get the social worker to sign a bit of paper even before I could go on a school outing. [Muriel, aged 30]

> 'Cos I was in Care a lot I couldn't mix with the others. I had to go home on a special bus. There was a definite difference. [Nadia, aged 35]

> We were always special cases at school. We were never told off if we didn't have our PE kit or if our uniform was imperfect. But, if we were missing from the lesson, the headmaster would straightway ring the Children's Home. You used to get some people say, 'Why are you in a Children's Home?' and then there would be the other ones who would say 'What are you in a Children's Home for' [Zoë, aged 28]

> When you go out, it seems as if you've got a name tag. People say 'Where do you live?' and you say 'High Street', and they say, 'Oh, I know that, that's the Children's Home'. You try and forget it, but it always comes up. You try and start anew, but it's always there. [Shirley, aged 20]

It was in Care that Donna learned about racism; Josie about class differences – including the 'Care class' and poverty.

> I was brought up the white way. I was only aware of colour when a kid called me a wog and I beat the hell out of him. I asked the children at the Home what it was and Uncle told me. I was bitter, angry and upset, and eventually I was proud of it. [Donna, aged 20 (cf. House of Commons, 1984)]

> I can remember going to Marks and Spencer with a social worker to buy clothes and, because we had a welfare grant form, we had to wait while they served all the other customers. You were really made to feel small. It came to the stage where I felt I'd rather go out and thieve it off someone's line. I didn't . . . but you know . . . This is when you realize that you're being given charity handouts, being written off as poor, put in a low bracket. And suddenly you become aware that there's people that are well off, people that are reasonably well off, and then, that you're working class. And then it's as if there's another class of people having to live on charity. That is probably when I started to become aware of class barriers. [Josie, aged 30 (cf. Stein, 1983: 90, NAYPIC, 1983: 24, on clothing books and voucher systems)]

ISOLATION

Many of the women said that, independently of their actual experiences in Children's Homes, the very fact of being in Care had made them feel guilty, had made them believe that they must have done something wrong to be so 'unwanted'. Local authority social-work practices such as moving them from placement to placement and separating them from their brothers and sisters had aggravated that loneliness.

> I didn't like it when they used to push you about from one kids' home to another. You got attached to one kids' home and then the next minute you'd be moving somewhere else, leaving your mates. [Lena, aged 21]

For Shirley and Kim, young black women, the sense of isolation was even worse.

> The staff changed a lot so it took time to build up another relationship with another member of staff. After I'd been separated from my brother – that hurt me a lot, he was the only one I had – and moved backwards and forwards in Children's Homes, there wasn't anyone I could relate to, you know. [Shirley, aged 20]

> So I thought I was white until I went to junior school. Then the black children kept asking me why I lived with white people. So I got it both ends. Then the social workers kept having these meetings about me but, as I was the only black person there, I couldn't relate to any of them. [Kim, aged 28]

Jill, also black, had had no one to whom she could turn when sexually assaulted by her white foster-father.

> My foster-dad put me off men because when I was a little girl he tried to attack me – sexually, you know. When that happened I couldn't tell anyone. I had no one to turn to. I was too scared. I liked my foster-parents and I didn't want to be taken away from them. After that I closed myself in a little bit. [Jill, aged 21]

Fostering that 'didn't work' had made other women feel guilty (even abnormal) for not, as Muriel put it, 'being grateful for breathing the same air as them'. With each new move the sense of difference and isolation had increased, though Muriel (with good reason – she had been found abandoned on Waterloo Station at 6 weeks old) thought that Providence had marked her card from birth.

> I think it was sort of stamped on me from when I was a baby, you know. They could do exactly what they liked cos there was no one there to stand up for me. I had so many foster-parents, it was like being reconditioned

every few weeks, like a car engine. Oh . . . I don't know. I felt such an outcast. [Muriel, aged 30]

For some of the women the sense of 'otherness' had gradually developed into a sense of nothingness, a void that they had to fill by building up a life amongst people who would *not* cast them out.

On top of everything else, the black women had had imposed on them a 'white' upbringing which some of them were later to question. All twenty-two women, however, complained (though for varying reasons) that in Care they had been denied opportunities to develop any modes of control over their lives, especially over their own sexuality.

In my first kids' home I didn't go out with boys because I didn't realize that growing up *meant* I was to go out and have a good time. That wasn't what I was allowed to do. So when I met Jack things just happened [she became pregnant] between us. [Norma, aged 22]

I knew nothing about sex. They never tell you anything. You know what? When I first started growing tits, I didn't even ask for a bra. That's how much I knew. When I came on with my period, I didn't know who to tell. I was petrified. What made it worse was that when I did tell the woman, she only went in the office and told the man that I'd come on with my periods. They never told me nothing. I didn't even know what pregnancy was. The doctor said to me, 'Haven't you been told about these things?' I said, 'No.' He sat and explained it all to me. And I cried because I didn't know what had happened. They persuaded me to have a termination. [Donna, aged 22]

'In Care,' said Zoë, 'you just don't get a chance to be your own person,' and most of the women echoed that sentiment, claiming that the peripatetic life, the lack of time, space and opportunity in which to learn to make and sustain relationships based on reciprocated trust had had lasting and painful effects. For, however much they had previously felt constrained within family relationships, *all* the women (the pre-11 group and the post-11 group) expressed views on Care that suggested that they had nonetheless sensed a real distinction between imaginary relationships based on notions of familial reciprocity and relationships in Care. In their relationships with their state guardians (social workers and social work departments) they had sensed themselves as being constituted as debtors within an imaginary debtor–creditor relationship (cf. Wilden, 1972). One result of this objectification was that, instead of gaining an independence in personal relationships, the young women had come to fear relationships as always *threatening* independence and inducing dependency. Zoë and Jill described the effects as they were experiencing them.

Nowadays if people help me or do something for me because they want something back, they needn't bother because if I've got to be grateful I don't want to know. If social workers do it, it's my right, they're paid for it, they're obliged to. I've been rejected by so many people that now I always break the relationship myself before they can do it. [Zoë, aged 28]

I've been very lucky with social workers and probation officers. I've really got on with them people. But sometimes, still to this day, I am still scared of grown-ups even though I'm a grown-up woman myself. [Jill, aged 20]

Thus, at every over-assessed step in the journey from Care to custody, the twenty-two women had experienced an interplay of emergent difference and increasing isolation. Sensing that the whirlwind round of placements might eventually lead to their own psychological *displacement*, the women had resisted Care's proprietary manoeuvres by engaging in the series of escapes that had eventually (and ironically) landed them in penal custody.

INTO CRIME

Eleven of the twenty-two women claimed that their minor (and often non-criminal) early misbehaviours would never have escalated into 'criminal careers' at all, had they not been in Care. Others, though reluctant to attribute their crimes to any one factor, thought that 'being in Care' had been an important influence on their law-breaking and/or criminalization.

As far as their juvenile misconduct or teenage law-breaking was concerned most of what the women said supports a formal explanation based on control theory.[3] The elements of the argument, therefore, are:

1 That the women's passage through Care had increasingly loosened those informal controls that primarily regulate by inducing conformity without recourse to the criminal law.
2 That, specifically, Care had broken their attachments to family and friends; failed to equip them with a whole range of knowledge (sexual, educational and life skills) necessary to independent adult living; stripped them of the rights, privacy and individuality constitutive of adult identity; and reared and regulated them as female public property rather than as private citizens.
3 That the women had responded by engaging in deviant behaviours born either of a desire to establish ties or contact with some person or group or of a sense that they had always/already been knocked out of the race to obtain the rewards of social respectability.

As for their criminalization? The argument is that once they had misbehaved, their progress through the welfare and criminal control apparatuses had been escalated both because they were in Care *and* because they were female. For though it is *power* that engenders the most serious forms of *crime*, it is *powerlessness* that produces the most persistent patterns of *criminalization*. The following ethnography of their journeys from Care to Crime will demonstrate how the complex interplay between the survival strategies of young females in Care and the discriminatory social policies and ideologies constitutive of their increasing institutionalization swiftly translated gender-deviant working-class girls into criminal women.

FROM CARE TO CRIME

Analysis of the interview transcripts suggested that one or more of three main types of situation had usually triggered off, or contributed to, the passage from Care to Crime:

1 Situations in which a young woman's *quest for care* had resulted in behaviour that the authorities had responded to by the imposition of further restrictions.
2 Situations in which a young woman's *flight from Care* had almost inevitably resulted in law-breaking behaviour.
3 Situations in which a young woman's *departure from Care* had precipitated her into a series of crises involving poverty, homelessness, and unemployment. In each of these situations, too, discriminatory factors emanating from gender ideologies, plus the fact that the range of facilities for troublesome girls in Care is narrower than that for boys, operated to ensure that the young women were processed through the so-called 'alternatives' to penal custody at a reprehensible speed.

THE QUEST FOR CARE

As can be seen from Table 4.3, most of the women had experienced several moves of residence whilst in Care. When asked about this, they all gave a reply similar to Yasmin's: 'I kept getting in trouble and they couldn't cope. So I had to move on.' When questioned about their reasons for 'creating hell' in Children's Homes, etc., the answers were more varied. Some referred to their resentment at being placed with people who had already committed crimes; others referred to an awareness of more basic injustice. Some said that they had been bored by lack of attention, were searching for friends who would appreciate them or that they had felt so derelict they had needed to make their mark upon someone or something. In short, their answers were variations on the same theme: that to create or maintain identity they had had to provoke a specific response to themselves as *individuals* rather than as clients of welfare.

I didn't have a lot of respect for the people who brought me up. Instead of parents I had social workers and I wanted parents to run my life, not social workers.' [Yasmin, aged 16]

Audrey and Muriel (amongst others) claimed that deviant behaviour had been a demanded response in all types of 'Care' institutions.

I used to do really stupid things to get attention, make them think that I was a bit mad. But I do honestly feel that the staff used to encourage it by making you think that you did have a problem [Audrey, aged 18]

The worse rogue you were at Approved School the better time you had of it. They didn't take any notice of anyone who did everything correctly. It was a sort of prep. school for prison. [Muriel, aged 30]

Shirley thought that she had had particular difficulties to overcome and maybe part of her isolation *had* stemmed from the following type of racist policy towards young black people in Care.

It seems that the presence of a large number of black children in an institution creates problems for staff and other residents . . . . It has been suggested that as a result of such difficulties some institutions operate an informal quota system to ensure that no more than 20–25 per cent of their population consists of black children.

(NACRO, 1977: 21)

In the Home I was in there wasn't many blacks or half-castes, just mainly white, and you were trying to get your own friends, you wanted to get your own identity. So, you know, you tried to do something different. [Shirley, aged 20]

Getting into trouble in Children's Homes was mentioned most frequently by the pre-11 group. The post-11 group (and the pre-11 group in adolescence) had more usually responded to Care by fleeing from it, that is, by absconding. However, when absconding was made difficult, other means of escape were tried and it was incarceration in closed or secure accommodation that had provoked several first major encounters with the police.

I had to go to an Adolescent Unit, a sort of closed one. It was like a hospital, surrounded by trees and woods. It was boredom most of all, boredom. We set fire to the woods because we knew that was the only way we could get help, for them to transfer us somewhere else. The police came in and took my fingerprints and took me down the police station. [Jill, aged 21. See Blumenthal, 1985 and Freeman, 1983: 176–7, on secure accommodation.]

TABLE 4.5   Women admitting to illicit drug usage or heavy consumption of alcohol whilst in Care

Name	Age at interview	Age + duration of usage	Drug involved
Della	15	14–15	Glue
Yasmin	16	15–16	Glue + other drugs
Audrey	18	15–18	Cannabis + other drugs
Shirley	20	13–17	Glue + other solvents
Anne	20	16–19	Heroin + other drugs
Jill	21	12–13	Glue
		16–19	Alcohol
Lena	21	15–18	Glue
Donna	22	15–20	Alcohol
Dawn	23	13–15	Various drugs
Nadia	35	16–18	Various drugs
Sally	35	14–16	Various drugs
		16 – time of interview	Heroin

THE FLIGHT FROM CARE

By the time they had reached their teens the pre-11 group had realized that, although bizarre behaviour would always gain them attention, 'It was the wrong kind of attention' (Audrey) and that they would have to look beyond Care for the space in which to develop as secure but independent adults. All of the post-11 group had absconded from the institutions to which they had been sent. Yet, before discussing the important part that absconding had played in their criminal careers, it is appropriate to look first at a less spectacular mode of escape, an activity often undetected by the authorities but one that nonetheless had also had consequences for some of the women. I refer to drug-taking.

Eleven of the women volunteered information that they had either taken illicit drugs or had started drinking heavily whilst in Care. Only one (Della) had begun her habit prior to her removal from home. Others said that drugs had been administered to control their behaviour (see Taylor, Lacey and Bracken, 1979: 80 and Freeman, 1983: 172 on the drugging of children in Care).

> I was on largactyl and I remember being on a lot at one point and feeling like a zombie. Yet we were only allowed to have one cigarette a day! [Nadia, aged 35]

> I went to this secure place. It was meant to help you sort out your life a bit better. I threw a fit the first time I went in there. Got a needle right up the bum. (Laughs.) I was out flat. [Yasmin, aged 16]

Given that the young people most likely to be drugged by the authorities were also those who were themselves seeking ways to assuage their gnawing sense of futility, it is not surprising that outside the institution they should have sought the 'fix' that they had already experienced (or heard of) within it. And, in the short term, at least, drugs *had* eased their pain.

> All along the line I'd got this thing that I was a waste of time and that I was in the way. When I started taking drugs, like deksies and bombers, it was bloody wonderful, you know. [Nadia, aged 35]

> I was taking speed and I started getting into smack [heroin] when I was 16. It was very nice. [Anne, aged 20]

> When I take drugs, I enjoy myself. Acid calms me down and makes me feel good. When I'm taking acid, tripping like mad, that's the only time I enjoy myself. [Yasmin, aged 16]

In the longer term several had found that drug usage just added to their problems:

> I had nobody really. I was a very lonely person, and because I was lonely I found myself mixing with a crowd of really heavy people who dealt in drugs. I was never on heroin – other things, you know – and I was turning into a complete and utter junkie. I thought I was dying. [Audrey, aged 18]

> I was sniffing glue from the age of 13. A little section of us out of the Children's Home got glue and Bostik and then we started drinking cider, and then got on to spirits. I gave up the glue when I was 17 because it *was* a problem. I wasn't eating, I used to get the shakes and at the end, when I was 17, it had done nothing for me so I just give it up. [Shirley, aged 20]

Only three women said at interview that they still had a drug problem, though all eleven thought that some of their crimes had been drug or alcohol related. It is likely that their drug-taking in Care had also had an indirect effect on their careers. For it was frequently after official detection of illicit drug or alcohol consumption that they had been moved to securer accommodation or even locked up in a Secure Unit.

Whether the misbehaviour in Care involved violence, drug-taking, staying out late or whatever – the official response had always seemed to involve the young women in a move of residence – to more of the same but worse! Small wonder that Muriel's characterization of the care she received in Care was echoed (though less graphically) by so many of the others interviewed.

> As far as they were concerned, I was the devil itself. If I'd have been a dog, they would have put me to sleep. In fact they just tried to put a muzzle on. [Muriel, aged 30]

To escape the 'muzzle' the young women repeatedly absconded.

Absconding

> The majority of absconders are like everyone else and the absconding problem is created by the institutions through which the children pass.
>
> (Milham, Bullock and Hosie, 1978: 76)

Except for Zoë, all the women had absconded at least once and eleven had 'lived rough, on the run' for considerable periods during their time in Care. Anne's and Nadia's experiences were similar to those of the eleven other girls who had been almost continuously 'on the run' and who had committed crimes in order to keep themselves (Christina and Carlen, 1985).

> *Anne*: When I was 14 I ran away. I was in a squat at King's Cross but I couldn't stay there, so I went up to Oxford. I really liked it and made a lot of friends. I stayed for about five months until I was caught – and then that was my TDA [taking and driving away] with being in a stolen car. I was taken back to Middlesex Lodge again – and then – it's really confusing because I've been in Middlesex Lodge five times, Cumberlow Lodge, Lytton House (I've been so many different places, I forget the times I've been). Well, it went on and on, I was running and being caught and running – I did a cheque book, and when I was 15 there was a burglary as well . . . . I did it for survival, I was pretty desperate and I didn't have any money. Then I got done for the cheque books and, when I was 15, I ended up in Borstal – after going to Holloway.
> *Pat*: But why did you keep running away from CHEs?
> *Anne*: I didn't think they had a right to keep me there.
> *Nadia*: I always used to finish up down the Dilly – at Playland.[3] When I went there I felt that I *did* belong. People were like me, talked like me, behaved like me. I felt accepted. The women there were strong. I mean, they were prostitutes and that as well, and doing kinky punters – and I did that myself for quite a while as years went on. Anyhow, I got picked up and had my sixteenth birthday in Holloway.
> *Pat*: They sent you there straightway?
> *Nadia*: I got sent to the only place that would have me. The police said nowhere else would have me and I remember saying to 'em, 'If I had people of my own you wouldn't treat me like this.'

Other young women had absconded for short periods and then returned, but they had still risked trouble of one kind or another.

When I absconded from school I needed food, so I kept nicking things so I could sell them. 'Cos I had no money, see? [Daphne, aged 15]

Yasmin: I used to do a lot of absconding. I'd go up to London, I've a lot of friends up there. If I hitch it to somewhere and I don't get to their house that night, I sleep in a bus shelter. I always carry a knife on me but I want to be careful in case the police stop me one day and they found it. But I would kill anyone who comes near me.

Pat: How do they get you back when you abscond?

Yasmin: They don't get me back. I go back. Because I get fed up running you know, all the time. All my life I've been running and running and I just get fed up and feel it's doing me no good. I just go back. Then I pack my bags and go off again. And come back!

Whatever the reasons for absconding – and most were related to the way in which trouble in institutions had been responded to by the imposition of even further restrictions – once they *had* absconded, the young women were frequently treated like dangerous and wanted criminals.

I ran away and got done for carrying an offensive weapon. I had a knife, 'cos I used to hitch-hike. It was just to carry around with me just in case . . . you can get some weirdos. Especially 'cos of my height, they think they can be clever. Especially these lorry drivers . . . it was just for my own protection. I got picked up in Birmingham and ended up getting Borstal, Borstal re-call. [Hazel, aged 29. Note: Hazel's first Borstal sentence had been for 'criminal damage', i.e. breaking a window.]

I ran away when I was in there [Adolescent Unit]. With some girls I went to Brighton and we slept on the beach. We phoned them because we wanted to see what they had done and in five seconds, as soon as we put that phone up, there was a police car there. [Donna, aged 22]

I was strip-searched when I was 14 years old in the police-station. I was picked up and I was on my period at the time and I was really – you know – and I had to bend over, take my Tampax out. And I was sort of like that, with my clothes on, and the policewoman said, 'I don't know what you're being bashful about.' And, you know, thinking about it, maybe I should have had a social worker present. [Anne, aged 20]

When I had my foster-parents the police never used to mess me around because they [foster-parents] were whites and they were standing by me. But when I ran away their [police] comments were just plain racist, they told lies and they took a lot of liberties. But you see, they were in a position to take those liberties because if you're alone and haven't got nobody, people can do with you as they feel. [Kim, aged 28]

Research evidence suggests that young teenage women who come to the attention of the police and criminal courts are escalated up the sentencing tariff more swiftly than boys. In the minds of the young women who had been punished for absconding by incarceration in Secure Units, the distinction between 'Care tariff' and 'criminal-sentencing tariff' had been eroded years before they ever set foot in a criminal court.

ESCALATORY FACTORS IN THE YOUNG WOMEN'S JOURNEY FROM CARE TO CUSTODY

In 1983 Lorraine Gelsthorpe, in her evidence to the Social Services Committee (House of Commons, 1984) claimed that 'girls particularly end up being committed to Care Orders because there is really no adequate provision for them within the tariff system.' She continued:

There are about six or seven attendance centres specifically for girls in this country as opposed to around 100 centres for boys . . . . Practitioners comment that there are many fewer provisions for girls and that the provisions tend to be dominated by, or orientated towards, providing facilities for boys, this frequently occurs in intermediate treatment schemes.

(Gelsthorpe, 1983: 566)

These observations are supported by other research, good summaries of which are to be found in Campbell (1981), Edwards (1984) and Heidensohn (1985). Of particular relevance to the Care/Custody axis are the following findings: of Webb (1984) that girls are made subject to supervision orders for less serious offences than those committed by boys; of Dominelli (1984) that some courts are biased against giving women community service orders; of Milham et al. (1978) that 'several children, particularly girls, can find themselves stranded in [secure] remand provision which has no long-term programme'; and of Fisher and Wilson (1982: 137) who found that the female residents of a probation hostel 'tended to have less serious criminal records than the males, but to be similarly characterized by behaviour worrying to social workers, probation officers, the courts and various agencies which had dealt with them since childhood.' Hilary Walker (1985) has argued that even much probation practice is biased against the particular interests of female clients. Housing research suggests that women leaving institutions suffer disproportionately from the shortage of rented housing for single people (Department of the Environment, 1982; Austerberry and Watson, 1983).

In analysing the twenty-two interview transcripts I was particularly interested in discovering if there were indications that the women themselves had been aware of escalatory factors in their own passages from Care to custody; and also if their experiences in Care had had any special features directly conducive to law-breaking and/or criminalization. The older women had been well aware that the 'Care' factor had been influential in their early dispatch to Approved School.

> I went to this Assessment Centre and then to Cumberlow Lodge and just got assessed for this Approved School. I was actually put there for being 'out of parental control'. I didn't have any parents anyway. So I thought I was really hard done by, in a place with criminals. I was just sent there because I didn't have any parents. I thought it was mighty unjust. [Muriel, aged 30]

Yasmin was aware that she had been escalated through the system because of the narrower range of provision for women:

> The first thing they found me guilty for I was sent here [Bullwood Hall] straight away.[4] They didn't put me in a hostel, give me community service or anything like that. But boys, they go to a hostel or a probation hostel. Women – they ain't got no choice, just get slammed behind the doors. [Yasmin, aged 16]

Some women said that law-breaking had been endemic in some (but not others) of their Children's Homes. Others claimed that residential social workers had often known about their illegal activities but had turned a blind eye.

> They blank things like that. We done an off-licence when I was in a kids' home and they could see us coming up the back stairs with crates and they did nothing about it. It's a lot of hassle, a lot of paperwork, so they brush it under the carpet. [Muriel, aged 30]

> *Pat*: What about the Children's Home, didn't they realize you were thieving?
> *Yasmin*: I'd just say I got them from me mate and they used to believe me. 'Cos I'd lose my temper with them and they just couldn't cope with that [Laughs].

Audrey stressed that the relationship between children in Care and social workers is a very legalistic one – for instance, that the social workers at her Children's Home must have guessed that all her new clothes had been stolen but that, as they could not have proved anything, they had never commented on her extensive and expensive wardrobe. Several of the women expressed resentment at their belief that, whereas residential social workers reacted sharply to (and thereby amplified) trouble *within* the institution, they were prepared to condone illegal activities committed outside it. This was not to say that the women thought that residential social workers should have 'shopped' them to the police; rather that they should have privately confronted them with their delinquency. Yet it seems that for children in Care there is often no space for an informal response to their law-breaking. The escalatory effect that this might have on their criminalization in comparison with that of law-breaking children still protected by parents is suggested by NAYPIC's Charlie Maynard's response to a 1985 item in London's *Evening Standard* where it was reported that Hounslow's Director of Social Services had directed social workers to report all children on drugs (including soft drugs) to the police if they refused to abandon the habit:

> Calling the police in is more likely to cause more problems. I don't think a natural parent would just call in the police. These young people are treated differently because they are in Care.
>
> (Maynard, 1985)

And, as the women bitterly noted, because children in groups tend to come under extra police surveillance, and because also many police officers assume that all children in Care are delinquents, their Children's Homes had in any case received disproportionate amounts of police attention. Any law-breaking, therefore, had had a greater likelihood of coming to police notice than if the young people had lived elsewhere.

Finally, there was a strong conviction amongst the interviewees that because they were in Care, when they *had* appeared in court on a criminal charge, the magistrates had been mainly influenced by social enquiry reports prepared by social services departments. Furthermore, that because they were in Care, social workers, believing that they had already exhausted all the social service provision, had recommended a custodial sentence primarily to give themselves a break from their most difficult charges. *Could* such a reason possibly explain the finding by Thorpe *et al.* (1980: 74) that (in relation to Interim Care Orders, Care Orders, Detention Centre Orders and referrals to Crown Court for Borstal sentencing) social workers make 'three times as many custodial recommendations as probation officers'?

> They said to me something about Borstal training. That was never explained to me, I didn't know what that was. Then my social worker was going on about sending me somewhere in Brentwood . . . But you know, they weren't talking to me, they were just getting on with it. I was sort of sitting in the background. It was just the social worker talking to the judge. [Shirley, aged 20]

> If anything went wrong in our neighbourhood the police would be on our [Children's Home] doorstep and we'd go up to court for cautions. The social worker would be present but, even then, my social workers gave me the

impression that, if they put me in prison or something, it was easier for them. If the responsibility was laid on *them*, they didn't want it because they'd sort of run out of places for me. [Muriel, aged 30]

'And,' said Anne, 'If you're a girl too, and you get into trouble, people think it's worse. They don't understand'.

THE DEPARTURE FROM CARE

Lack of preparation for non-institutional living, loneliness, homelessness and poverty have been listed as the all-embracing problems confronting young people legally leaving Care between the ages of 16 and 19 (NAYPIC, 1983; Stein and Carey, 1984; Stein and Maynard, 1985). The need for 'continuing care' has also been stressed (House of Commons, 1984). What has been less well publicized is the practice of placing some young people in their own bedsitters, even before they officially leave Care. Four interviewees had been thus placed in bedsitter accommodation and four in hostels catering mainly for older people. They had all seen the moves as a form of disciplinary action taken against them because they had been 'difficult'. This interpretation is supported by the National Association of Young People in Care (NAYPIC) who in their evidence to the House of Commons Select Committee's Inquiry into 'Children in Care' made the following comments:

> We also know of cases where young people are simply thrown out of [Children's] Homes to fend for themselves for periods of time. This is obviously an unacceptable form of control. If parents did this they would get into trouble with social services and the courts.
>
> (NAYPIC, 1983: 15)

The majority of young people leaving Care do not commit crime. But Stein and Carey (1984: 14) did find in their study of seventy-nine young people leaving the Care of a social services department in 1982 that at the second interview 16 per cent had committed offences and 'a further 4 per cent were already in custody'. The women I interviewed certainly believed that their eagerly awaited departure from Care had been a significant turning-point for the worse in their criminal careers.

Given the volume of criticism concerning the dependency engendered by institutional living, it might seem inappropriate to criticize social services departments for giving troublesome young women in their Care a foretaste of independence by placing them in private, single accommodation. After all, many of them will have stated again and again that their main aim in life is to get the Care Order off their backs. Yet the biographies of the women in this study suggest that they were so placed, not as part of a planned and caring programme, but rather as a last resort when they had exhausted every other type of social services provision. In fact, because of their sense of difference, isolation and varying degrees of institutionalization born of unhappy experiences in Care, they were the least well equipped to cope either financially or emotionally with life in the lonely isolation of a bedsitter.

The haphazard treatment of rebellious girls in Care is well reflected in Yasmin's experience. When I interviewed her in Bullwood Hall, she was aged 16 and already serving her second Youth Custody sentence. In Care since 2 years' old, she had been in continuous trouble throughout her young life. Her childhood passage through Care had been one of constant movement from placement to placement until she was eventually locked up for several months in a closed unit. As soon as she was 16 she was, according to her 1984 Social Work Report, 'placed on her own in the community because of her need to attack boundaries.' After serving her first Youth Custody sentence she was placed in her own self-contained flat. The Report continues: 'Her move from custody into complete freedom proved too great a shock to her system and she resorted to glue sniffing.' Unfortunately that was not all she (and others similarly treated) had resorted to, as the following accounts indicate.

> I have £57 a fortnight, right? Then I have £25–£30 rent. Then I've got to buy my food and things for myself and things for my place. And that gets you nowhere. So then I go out stealing, don't I? I have to nick my own food. Out of here I eat hardly anything at all. Can't afford to buy new clothes, just nick 'em all. (Laughs). I've never been caught for stealing yet, but I think that eventually I will be picked up. [Yasmin, aged 16]

> Soon as I was 16, they moved me out of the Children's Home I'd been in for six years into a bed-and-breakfast place in a red-light district in Queensway. At the time there was girls coming in, different guys, money every night. I was getting offers of big money and I was saying 'No', because I wasn't even sure what prostitution was. Anyway, it turned out that this was to be my way of living. I went to the clubs they went to, I had friends and, to me, this was making my life. I started doing this and ended up getting arrested for soliciting every night of the week. [Donna, aged 22]

> I got beat up by one of the members of staff [at the Children's Home where she had lived for nine years] so they quickly moved me out to Bethnal Green and put me in a hostel for girls that were 18 to 20. I couldn't apply for any jobs 'cos I was only 14, you know, so basically it started from there . . . They never bothered finding a school. Somewhere around 9 o'clock you'd go out and weren't allowed back till 12 for dinner and out again after that. And I used to go round with this other girl and that's when I really found out about criminal things, shoplifting, nicking cars. The police used to pick me up for being missing and that's where the offensive weapon comes in. You know I was staying out all night, just

trying to look after myself. I was skippering [living rough]. I went back to
another Children's Home after one Borstal and they just bunged you out
in the morning same as the hostel 'and don't come back till 12'. So we just
used to drink and started shoplifting because we weren't getting enough
money. In the end, like, it was like we were making our money in crime.
[Shirley, aged 20]

Two women had been in trouble upon leaving their Children's Home because
they had taken their files without authorization; it was Muriel's determination
to know about her past that had projected her straight from Care to custody.

I didn't know my mother or my father. I was totally confused as to where I
came from. I thought I'd just been created. Issue! Government issue! I
was 18 and I got kicked out of Care and I wanted to know who my father
was and all that. I broke in there and the next day I was arrested and so,
you know, I was just put straight inside then. [Muriel, aged 30]

Carol, after five years in Rampton, became involuntarily pregnant immediately
upon discharge. Zoë, who had done so well at school that she had gone away to
college at 18, found that she had nowhere at all to go at all during her first
(Christmas) vacation. She was eventually allowed to return to the Children's
Home as an employee. Her story is worth telling at some length as it should
dispel any notion that it is only girls who have already been in trouble who have
difficulties upon leaving Care.

I was actually 18 in May, but I stayed at the Children's Home until
October. Then my social worker took me to college and I was left. That
was it. I had no contact with anybody whatsoever, not with the social
worker, not with anybody at the Children's Home. I wrote to them. I
think I had one letter in the first year, that was all. Christmas came, the
first term. I had to telephone them and ask if I could go and stay at the
Children's Home because I had nowhere to go . . . . I telephoned them
back the next day and they said, 'We've arranged for you to come and
work here.' So I actually went and worked there for my first Christmas
holiday. I went back to college after Christmas and I was in a terrible state,
failed the exams and left. The Matron and the Superintendent at the
Children's Home were disgusted, they didn't want to know me. The
Bursar at the College got me into the YMCA. After about six weeks the
girl I shared with . . . we had a terrible argument one night and they
threw us both out so I was virtually walking the streets. I happened to be
standing in a shopping centre one day and somebody said 'I know
somebody who rents rooms.' It was an old man. What they didn't say was
that it was also being used for prostitution . . . . After I moved in, there
was a certain amount of pressure put on me. They kept saying, 'You need
the money'. So I started soliciting myself . . . . Then one of the girls

went to London and she came back for a weekend and said, 'What, you're earning here for prostitution is nothing. I'm earning a hundred quid a day in London.' So I went down with her and we did very well at first. Then she got caught, I got caught . . .' [Zoë, aged 28]

Several women had come out of local-authority institutions full of hope that they could make a new start. Barriers to so doing had been:

Material   Most had come out of Care equipped with few educational qualifications into situations of high youth unemployment and an acute shortage of housing for young single women.

Ideological   The peripatetic and poverty-stricken lives that many were forced to lead in the poor material circumstances into which they had been precipitated made them particularly vulnerable to a custodial sentence, if found guilty of a criminal offence. For, as women's place is still ideologically constructed as being most properly within the private sphere of family, domesticity and home, women out with home and family are seen as being in need of particular surveillance and penal regulation (Worrall, 1981; Carlen, 1983a; Eaton, 1986).

Psychological   Ill equipped (both materially and by their previous experiences) for living on their own, many of the women had soon begun to think that crime was the only route to a decent standard of living. They had *nothing* to lose, they had *everything* to gain . . . and if they were caught? Many of their friends were already 'inside' anyhow.

CLOSED CIRCLE: A HOME FROM HOME . . . THEN PRISON

I'd gone through the two years at Approved School and I was very positive – at that point the best prepared for creating a future. But people weren't prepared to forgive and forget. I went for a job in a shoe-shop and started chatting to an assistant, one of the girls I'd gone to school with. She said, 'You've just come out, haven't you?' I said, 'What's all this lot, 'coming out'? I haven't been in prison, you know.' There really wasn't a future for me. I'd been sent to a hostel that was very squalid and run by a woman who was taking kids in Care. I was only 16. So I went back to Bath, then back to Truro. Then I went out robbing with the full intention of getting nicked. I didn't see any way of making any progress at all. Everywhere the doors were slamming. [Josie, aged 30]

All the women stressed that anyone who had been in Care could cope with prison. Della was only 15, but already she felt that she had sussed out institutional life.

> I was scared when I first went into Care and I was scared when I first come into prison. But, when I got to know everyone and everything, I just didn't care any more. [Della, aged 15]

Others went further. Jill was so tired of being on the run that, at 17, she had welcomed Borstal as a refuge. Nadia had also been tired of 'running' by the time she had reached 17.

> I didn't mind getting Borstal. I was really made up because all the girls I knew had got Borstal. I had nothing and no one outside. I think Borstal and Approved School – really – that's when the whole thing about being in prison and feeling like a bad person started. I saw that I wasn't really going to have much of a life and the people that I identified with were all people doing crimes and a bit of villainy. [Nadia, aged 35]

Muriel also thought that her Borstal sentence had pushed her towards a criminal identity.

> *Pat*: So you didn't mind Bullwood?
> *Muriel*: I did at first. Minded a great deal at first, but after a while it come Jack-the-Lad sort of thing. You get a tremendous ego in them sort of places and actually, with being released, it's sort of frightening, pretty frightening. 'Cos it's just not like that outside. You ain't got these sort of people tripping over, sort of going arse over head to do things for you. [Muriel, aged 30]

But fear of institutionalization was also a constant theme.

> They kept me in Holloway while they were deciding what to do and it was just like being in Care. Coming in prison has made me realize that I've got to stop finding security in places like Care, because some people they get to like it in here so much they want *this* [Bullwood Hall] to be their home. [Audrey, aged 18]

> To me prison's like another Children's Home really. That's how I look at it but in another way I don't want to look at it like that 'cos I don't want to get institutionalized. I want to get back out. You know, a lot of people come back and come back because they get the attention that they need, that they haven't had from Children's Homes – young girls my age. You can tell when you see them talking to officers that they need the attention. I'm settling in here but I don't want to settle in too good 'cos I want to get back out. [Shirley, aged 20]

In fact, at Shirley's last appearance at the Crown Court, a letter had been received from Holloway Prison saying that it was felt she was 'a girl who was in danger of becoming institutionalized with her history of living in Children's Homes followed by the custodial sentence.' Notwithstanding this cautionary note the judge had returned her to Bullwood once more.

At 35 Nadia looked back at her own teenage experiences and knew that the younger women's characterizations and fears of institutionalization were neither exaggerated nor ill-founded.

I went to Holloway [at 17] and, when I went in there, I remember feeling quite relieved that I'd been nicked. I was just getting scared – it was all the heavies all the time and I was getting into a lot of very sordid relationships. But then I think I started to get institutionalized. I didn't want to leave Borstal, so I ended up hitting this officer so I'd get a second Borstal. I had no one to go out to. I would just have had to go back to Playland, really. I felt frightened of leaving Borstal. I had all me mates back there and we had a good laugh. And I felt embarrassed about feeling like that, as well. I felt really ashamed that I felt like that. It's been very useful I've been able to say it, you know, be honest about it, understand it for what it is. [Nadia, aged 35; cf. O'Dwyer and Carlen, 1985]

At 16 Yasmin does not look forward to anything. Already she engages in self-injury so that she can stay longer at Bullwood Hall, putting off the day when she once more has to face life in her lonely bedsitter. Listen:

Yasmin: Last time I was here I cut my throat and my wrists and everything. I think about the past, what kind of life I've had and I just take it out on myself 'cos I like hurting myself. I like it when I bleed, know what I mean? I like to see my blood because I feel good that I've taken it out on myself.
Pat: Do you have any visitors when you're in here?
Yasmin: You're joking, joking. Who'll ever come to visit me? I don't have visits except for my social worker. I haven't got no one on the outside. I've got no one. When I was out, I used to think of all them girls inside. We really had a laugh with the officers. Funnily enough, when I'm in a Children's Home I think that all I've got is my social workers to look after me. Then when I go to prison that's all I've got, them officers to look after me. But I miss 'em a lot and I really wanted to come back to be here with them. But I'll tell you what, I'll probably lose all my remission this time 'cos it's coming to when I should go. I've lost twenty-one days so far and I'll probably lose the rest because I don't want to go. You can't refuse to go out of here 'cos they force you out. But it's worth a try. I'm quite

happy in that room with my radio. I could spend my life behind that door.

Pat: Is that the life you like?

Yasmin: It's the life I know, that's all.

CONCLUSION

The analyses of this chapter suggest that the paths from residential Care to the women's penal institutions are trodden most frequently by gender-deviant working-class women. Having already suffered either family breakdown or familial oppression, they are then further alienated and isolated both by Care's physical and ideological confines and by the psychological brigandry of its pseudo-scientific procedures of assessment, categorization and 'placing'. Determined to be neither 'put away' nor 'filed away', spirited young women in Care repeatedly abscond, 'cause trouble' and come to the attention of the police.

The authorities' response is to speed up the rebels' progress through the tariff of increasingly restrictive 'placements'. Those who 'cannot be contained' anywhere are finally seen as being 'beyond Care'. Isolated in bedsitters they are, in effect, told to care for themselves. Even those who remain in Care are often convinced that, in fact, no one cares. Uncared for and depressed, it is at this stage that many begin to think that, since no one has ever cared for them, they really 'couldn't care less' about themselves either. Marginalized by both poverty and isolation from family, friends and other non-institutional associations, catapulted out of Care into extremes of poverty and existential chaos, many young women also begin to believe that they have nothing to lose (and maybe something to gain) by engaging in criminal activity.

Once they involve themselves in the crime that provides a better standard of living, an outlet for their energies and talents, and a network of non-judgemental friends, the custodial machinery is soon reactivated. Picked up for some minor crimes, the still-very-young women are once more presented to the courts for 'disposal'. In court, their rumbustious careers through Care, together with their post-Care poverty and apparent social isolation, are taken as being evidence of an essential gender deviance (cf. Farrington and Morris, 1983a; Carlen, 1983a.) Imprisonment is thereafter seen as an acceptable and inevitable sentence. The prematurely institutionalized women who once hoped that Care might provide an alternative Home from home subsequently recognize each other in penal institutions all over the country. Another generation of state-raised working-class women has passed from Care to Custody.

5

MAKING A LIFE

When I was studying sociology and I got up to the crime bit, I thought it was absolute shit. People steal for different reasons, but *not* because something causes it. They don't *have* to steal but they look around and they think of ways to get what other people take for granted and they decide that the only way to get it is to steal. [Kim, aged 28]

In my Reports they describe me in two ways. One way I'm aggressive, fight against the system, acting out behaviour, things like that. Then, on the other hand, I've had a life in Care, things like that. They write it down, you know: two ways how I am [Yasmin, aged 16]

I actually heard irate fathers open their doors when I was a kid and say, 'I'm not having my Susan playing with your sort.' What kind of thing is that to say to a 7-year-old kid? They say you can choose, but I didn't choose to be born [the eighth child] to a fucking drunken violent maniac, you know. That's *'my sort'*. [Josie, aged 30]

Kim, Yasmin and Josie are not philosophers. Kim is a practising criminal, Yasmin a Youth Custody Trainee, and Josie an ex-criminal. Yet, because they have been so often called to account for their actions in numerous courts of law, psychiatrists' clinics and probation offices, the three women have frequently ruminated upon two sets of related questions, questions that have exercised the minds of philosophers for centuries. To what extent is an individual free to shape her own actions, identity and consciousness independently of the economic, ideological and political circumstances in which she finds herself? What is the relationship between criminal justice and social justice in general? These two sets of questions, the first relating to issues traditionally debated under the legend of free will versus determinism, the second relating to questions of class, inequality, culpability and the power to punish, have also played a major part in the theoretical analysis of the thirty-nine women's oral histories and the concomitant construction and deconstruction of their socio-biographies.

The fundamental belief informing this text is that *individual human will is but one factor, and not a major one, in shaping someone's life history*. At the same time, and like Kim, I do not claim that any *one* social condition will usually propel somebody into either law-breaking and/or the criminal justice or penal systems. Instead, it is argued that under certain (diachronic and synchronic) combinations of historically specific economic, social, ideological and political conditions an individual is more likely than not to enter the criminal arena.

In this chapter we shall see how certain conditions, political discourses and gender ideologies conditioned the thirty-nine women's sense of self and identity. For, although living their lives in circumstances not initially of their own making, they all transmitted an awareness that they had, nonetheless, subsequently been responsible for the specific acts of law-breaking in which they had engaged.

As they talked about the material conditions constitutive of their identities, the women indicated that much of their early non-criminal but deviant behaviour had been engendered by a series of refusals, most dominant of which had been the refusals to make the class deal and/or the gender deal. Refusal to make the class deal and/or the gender deal had left them with few alternatives but to commit crime in order to get a living (see Cook, 1987; Edwards, 1987); additionally, refusal to make the gender deal had made them more vulnerable to criminalization, once they had been apprehended for law-breaking.

REFUSAL OF THE CLASS DEAL

As mentioned earlier, thirty-two of the thirty-nine women in this study had been poor all their lives. Yet, although most denied that *in itself* poverty had been a sole cause of their law-breaking, all indicated that the interpenetration of class oppression with the cruder forms of patriarchal oppression (see below) had been experienced by them as being more than they could bear without engaging in some form of resistance. Furthermore, their stories suggested that, whether or not they had resisted them, these extreme forms of oppression had in any case contributed to the women's marginalization. As far as class oppression was concerned, the talk centred mainly on the interrelated phenomena of poverty, powerlessness, boredom, isolation and an excess of official surveillance.

Vague consciousness of class differences had been transmitted to the women when they had come into contact with 'respectable' working-class families, with middle-class families and with middle-class schools. Lena and Josie both said that their families had been seen as 'rough'; Donna that she had always felt ashamed that her mother was a prostitute; and both Nicky and Dawn that they had felt stigmatized by their working-class accents when they had attended middle-class grammar schools. Indeed Nicky thought that her troubles had started then.

The headmistress called my mother up the school and said 'Nicky has an appallingly over-exaggerated Cockney accent.' My Mum's reply was, 'Well, I was born in Stoke Newington, my husband comes from West Ham and Nicky was brought up in Northolt.' But the attitude towards me was like a sort of class prejudice, without a doubt. [Nicky, aged 27]

Yet the women's sense of class difference only extended to a recognition that there were many people about who had much more money to spend than they or their families had. They had seldom realized (until they were much older) that access to money also gave access to entirely different life-styles. In fact Josie only became aware of it when, as a teenager, she began to break into other people's houses!

I broke into this house and there was this beautiful rug on the wall. That's when I first found it amazing, people putting rugs on their walls! (Laughs) [Josie, aged 30]

Experience of the cold, hunger and despair of grinding poverty had been more immediate and endemic, and most women who had been in Care, as well as many who had not, could vividly recall the bleakness of life on the dole. Mary, turned out of home by her mother at the age of 16, had eluded the Care of the local authority by alternately living rough on her own or shacking up with some man. Her memories were similar to, and no more extreme than, those of several others.

We had no heat and it was winter. We used to go out and get loads and loads of snow to try and make tea, and in the end we were sitting there with a candle and we used to try and get all this snow in a frying pan over the fire and we used to cook like that . . . . We moved around a lot, and we were sleeping rough. I remember we used to be on a lot of laybys and I was 'on' once and I had to throw away my clothes because I didn't have any sanitary wear with me. And the police kept coming along, 'What you doing here? You've gotta move on.' So we'd move on somewhere else. Then in the morning we used to walk down town and pinch a bottle of milk off a doorstep. [Mary, aged 27]

Living like this, some women had been far removed from the Christmas-card image of cosy family life. Others, especially those who had been in Children's Homes, had often not realized how poor they were until they had left Care. Then it had dawned on them with shock that they were in no position at all to change things. At 18 Muriel had recognized that, being out of Care, she no longer had a claim on anybody.

When I did this robbery I was living in a tiny, tiny, little cage – well, it was like someone's toilet and it really depressed me no end. There was no one to have a go at. I was out of Care and there was just no one. I had no *right* to go and moan at any one. [Muriel, aged 30]

Even when women did have a *right* to claim from the DHSS they expressed hatred at being forced into the role of suppliants before what often appeared to them to be an arbitrary authority. As Cindy remarked, the experience of many women was that 'social security is not a thing that you can *rely* on. So it's no bloody big help.' Powerlessness had been endemic in all their relationships with social services. Many saw social workers (rather than the police) as being the most coercive of the state's officials. Hazel's comment, 'There's always been social workers ever since I can remember; I mean, I was in Care so *I* had a social worker and then he [her son] was in Care so *he* got a social worker,' well summarized the all pervasive experience of state regulation that most of these women had experienced throughout their lives.

Not only did the women have no claim on *anybody*, they also had no claim on the consumer goods and pastimes represented as being necessary to the 'good life'. With no money to spend, the spending of time in itself became a killer. Crime was as important for the excitement it provided as it was for the money. Audrey explained: 'You see, the thing is, right? When you're living off the dole, it's not the money that makes you go out and steal. It's the boredom of not having anything to do.' Drink, drugs, crime, suicide attempts, or self-mutilation had engraved meaning on what had seemed to be meaningless lives. 'On the dole', said Jean, 'you don't live, you just exist from day to day', while Queenie's sentiments were echoed by many others when I enquired about their hopes for the future: 'How I feel at the moment', she said, 'it wouldn't bother me if I dropped dead tomorrow.'

But, despite the frequent talk of attempted suicides, accidental overdoses, futility and injustice, these women had not had histories of 'giving-up'. Their socio-biographies, as constructed in their talk, revealed a constant urge to struggle – to *make* ends meet, to *take* on inequity, to *make* their lives. They had done so by engaging in the series of resistances that had not only driven them even further beyond the margins but also strengthened their resolve to renegotiate the re-entry contract only on their own terms. Their capacity to break free of any possible ideological constraints against law-breaking stemmed from four main interrelated sources: their residence in wholly ideologically marginalized areas; their economic and political marginalization; and their conviction, born of their multidimensional experiences, that the only way for some people to get anything in this society is by helping themselves to it, regardless of the legality of the methods used; and finally the contemporary political discourses about social welfare and citizen rights that engendered in the women the conviction that, as the state had failed to fulfil its political commitment to *them*, their own law-breaking could, in part, be justified.

IDEOLOGICAL MARGINALIZATION

A high proportion of women in the study had had their entry into crime facilitated by upbringings in institutions or areas that had, early on, imbued them with a sense of ideological marginalization – of being beyond the confines of 'normal' or 'straight' society. As was argued in Chapter 4, all twenty-two of the women in Care had experienced a sense of 'difference' and 'isolation' as teenagers, though several of them had also known that their own families and neighbours had had a very low commitment to being law-abiding. Della, for instance, had been very happy with her travelling family until they had objected to her stealing, a situation seen as most unfair by Della whose nine brothers had all served terms of imprisonment for theft. Lisa, Bobby and Mary, though not introduced to larceny and fraud by relatives, had nonetheless found their mothers to be ready partners in crime – as the following narratives indicate. I had asked Lisa how she got involved with villainy.

> It started when I was about 6, that was just through hanging about the streets. There was a gang of us, all mucking about together. We used to do silly things like going to Woolworths and nick. We were just terrible: annoying people, breaking windows, going over to cemeteries. My Dad worked nights and my Mum was always out. I was truanting during the day and my Mum knew about that. She said, 'Well, if you ain't going, that's up to you.' Sometimes I feel she should have been more strict, but at the time it was great. It was good that I could go home and my Mum knew I was doing it. She used to like it because we'd bring her things home as well. She didn't say, 'Don't do it', just 'Be careful, don't get caught.' If I got caught, it didn't matter because my Mum knew so I wasn't scared of that. All the other kids used to say, 'I wish my Mum was like that.' When I first got caught, I was with my Mum. 'Cos, when she saw what I was doing, she said, 'Well take me out.' So we took her out – my cousins, my Mum and me – and then one day we got caught. [Lisa, aged 21]

Bobby's mother had been equally acquiescent.

> Sometimes I used to go home and say 'Mam, here's a fur coat' and she used to laugh. I nicked me Mam's mate a leather jacket for Christmas. They think it's funny some of the things I do. I mean, the things my brother's nicked for me Mam! He's got her a telly and a video! When I got sent here, me Mam went whacky. She hit a policeman. I thought, 'Mam, you stupid woman.' [Bobby, aged 15]

Other women, especially those still involved in crime, claimed to me that, in the areas they were presently living in, *everyone* was so poor that *everyone* was on some kind of fiddle to get by. 'They're all villains round here,' said Queenie. 'No one points at you,' said Jean 'because they know why you do it, they're all in the same boat.' Additionally, of course, even if the women had never lived in areas entirely composed of people who saw law-breaking as a necessary or justified mode of survival, the women's terms of imprisonment or other institutionalization had, by the time I met them, resulted in all but one (Monica) having numerous connections with people for whom law-breaking was a normal way of making a living.

ECONOMIC AND POLITICAL MARGINALIZATION

Economically and politically the women were marginalized by their present unemployment and their past records. Yet each was adamant that she would not take a 'crap job', 'put up with shit from a boss' or 'take a flat on some run-down estate'. Josie commented at length on the poor chances of survival ex-prisoners have in the present economic climate:

> What chance does a 16–17-year old stand to be suddenly dropped out into a world that's not gonna take them, (a) 'cos they've got a criminal record, (b) because you know they're gonna have some social problem? What chance do they stand of getting anything? I've run back to prison on several occasions because I just didn't see any way of making any progress at all. I was slung in some sleezy bedsit where me bed was like a hammock and everything stank. [Josie, aged 30]

Queenie made a similar point.

> There's three and a half million people unemployed now. So me, with a criminal record, where am I going to get a job? I wish to God I could get a job, so long as it's not factory work. I don't like factory work, because it puts me in mind of prison, it does. [Queenie, aged 43]

Without money, jobs and access to leisure activities, always dependent upon the DHSS, and sporadically under the supervision of social workers, the women were conscious of being ground down not only by poverty, but also by a powerlessness. Whichever way they turned, they seemed to come up against an official blockade of all legal routes out of the poverty trap. For instance, several of the younger women had enjoyed and successfully completed Youth Training Schemes – before being slung back into unemployment at the end of the year. No less than six had been involved with volunteer organizations engaged in various community projects – until cuts in local authority funding had closed them down. Many had gained some educational qualifications whilst in prison – and had found upon release that these were absolutely useless to them as far as employment prospects were concerned. And so on. Marginalized thus from childhood onwards, no wonder that, at almost every stage, the women had engaged in resistance to and refusals of a class deal that had, in fact, left them destitute. Small wonder too, that those resistances had repeatedly involved law-breaking and/or criminalization.

RESISTING POVERTY, CLASS REGULATION, RACISM AND POWERLESSNESS

The women in this study were not class-conscious in the classic political sense of believing that they had a relationship of mutual interest with all other working-class people. But they did have a strong sense of injustice, oppression and powerlessness. Their 'false consciousness' therefore did not inhere in any inability to see through the rhetorics of market 'equality' and welfare 'rights'. Rather it manifested itself in their continuing belief that their extreme marginalization could be changed by an individualistic response to their poverty and oppression – and often by a criminal response that in practice was most damaging to those in the same oppressed situation as themselves! Constant emphasis on the assertion of rights (to material goods), equality, individuation and independence can be traced out in the following accounts. They indicate how the women's strong sense of material deprivation, oppression and powerlessness again and again provoked them into dishonesty or violence.

Resisting poverty

Although twelve of the women had seen poverty as being a pre-emptive condition partly responsible for their initial entry into crime, only five (Prue, Kay, Nicky, Jessie and Monica) could say that poverty had *not* been a contributory factor in their later law-breaking. Prue had begun her long series of post-office frauds at a time when she had had a good job in the Civil Service; Kay, Nicky and Jessie had only engaged in serious crime after they had become addicted to heroin; and Monica's shoplifting had commenced after she had started to indulge in secret and heavy bouts of drinking. The other thirty-four women all claimed that at least some of their crimes had been occasioned by either a necessity born of poverty or a perceived need born of consumerism. Most, like Carol and Cindy, had begun stealing in childhood.

> I used to pinch food and take it home. My Mum and Dad never had no money to buy us anything. At Christmas we never had no toys or nothing and that's more or less why I went out pinching. I knew me Mum and Dad couldn't give me what I wanted. [Carol, aged 27]

> You're growing up and you want nice things and you want to go out. Your parents can't afford it, so you go out and take something from a shop. [Cindy, aged 22]

As we saw in Chapter 4, the departure from Care had precipitated many young women into a life of poverty and isolation for which they had been totally unprepared. Donna claimed that in such a situation she had had absolutely no alternative but to engage in prostitution.

I had no one in the world to turn to. The only thing I could do was go on the streets. I told the judge, 'I don't do this just for money or to buy myself gold and clothes. I do it to be able to eat and sleep somewhere for the night.' I was just making enough money for the hotel and to eat. If I was doing it for a week's hotel, I would need £100 or £150. But I wasn't getting all that in one night – just a bit at a time, paying the hotel daily. It was rough. [Donna, aged 22]

Being unemployed was mentioned most frequently as being a cause of poverty and its accompanying boredom and isolation – and not only by the women themselves. Cynthia's probation officer, writing a Social Enquiry Report for the Court, summed up the reasons for Cynthia's crimes in two bleak sentences: 'Miss G's living situation is dull and she has little prospect of increasing her income. Lack of money is her main reason for committing offences of dishonesty.' Kim told it 'like it is' for her – and many others.

I don't wanna go out there and thieve, right? But then I wouldn't have anything at all in my cupboard. So I say, 'Well, I'll have to suffer like everybody else – because everybody else *is* suffering.' But sometimes it kind of gets on your nerves, suffering (because I like nice things), and then I say, 'Oh! blast it. I know how to do it, I'll go out there and get it.' [Kim, aged 28]

Could they *justify* their crimes ? Yes. They did not want *more* than everyone else – just a fair share. The financial capacity to 'be comfortable' was the desire put forward most frequently, the modest requirement to be able to buy at least some of the goods that are pushed at women from all sides.

You haven't got any money. You go down town and see people buying this and that and you think, 'God, I wish I could buy that.' Then you go in the shop and you pinch it. I mean, when I moved here, I never had no carpets, I never had no three-piece, I never even had – erm you know, those thingies – erm, *wardrobes* upstairs. We used to sign on on Thursdays and get his money on a Saturday. Sometimes it never used to come till the Monday. So we was left starving. How can you tell my kids – one's 5 and one's nearly 6 – when they're crying and hungry, that they have to wait till Monday? If I didna pinch it, we'd have to go round scrounging. It were horrible [Jean, aged 26]

DHSS failure to make Supplementary Benefit payments regularly was also seen as precipitating all kinds of dishonesty.

I was living in Hackney and they had a strike for so many months and I couldn't even pay my bill. I never used to get a Giro or nothing. The first couple of months I lived there everything was all right. I just signed on and I got them to pay my rent instead of paying it myself, right? Then I found out that they didn't pay no rent for two weeks and I kept getting letters from the council saying I was in arrears. So I went and there were pickets outside. They were on strike and I couldn't do anything about *that*. I kept signing on but I didn't get my dole money. And I just thought, 'I ain't bothering to sign on any more.' Someone introduced me into cheques and I just went out and started doing cheques. [Sheila, aged 22]

Motherhood increased the women's problems. Initially, having children had made them determine to be law-abiding in future. To risk a prison sentence when they had only themselves to think about was a chance they were willing to take; once children were involved it was a chance they could not afford to take. So reasoned most of the mothers. At the same time, having children increased their poverty and underlined the inequity of a social system that condemns 1.7 million children to live in families on or below the poverty line (National Children's Home, 1986: 6). With normative pressure on them from neighbours, social workers, schools and a generally child-oriented consumerism, it is not surprising that many mothers were soon employing their criminal skills again – but this time either to feed their children or, as some insisted, to give them the best.

When I had the children it was my job to go down town everyday and pinch them something. Especially when they were starting back to school. It was never clothing for myself, always for the kids' school – you know, T-shirts, socks and trousers, all that kind of thing. [Queenie, aged 43]

I got this house when Sylvie was 7 months old. I was still paying off my electricity bill that we'd had the first winter 'cos Sylvie had had bronchitis and I'd had heating on twenty-four hours a day. I got myself into a complete and utter mess within six months of being in this house. I got rent arrears; I had gas bills. I'd managed to pay my electricity bill off and I had a coin meter installed for my gas. They set it so low that I was virtually getting nothing for my money. A lot of the time, once Sylvie had gone to bed, I was sitting with no fire. I was freezing cold. I started shoplifting. [Zoë, aged 28 – lone parent]

When I got Timothy I felt as though I *had* to shoplift. He had to have everything. I didn't want him to want for anything. Everything I had, I'd pinched for him. [Jean, aged 26 – lone parent]

I was trying to get my baby in a nursery so that I could go back to work, but the social worker I had wasn't much help, so the only thing I could do was steal. That was when I *really* began to steal. I used to shoplift all my food, clothes and things for the baby. [Kim, aged 28 – lone parent]

At the time of interview only twelve of the thirty-nine said that they had definitely turned their backs on crime. The remainder thought they would either 'choose' to return to crime or 'drift' into it. Tara listed what so many saw as being the strategic factors that always influenced them when they weighed up whether or not to commit a crime. They were the knowledge that they could commit and usually get away with a particular crime; the refusal to be entirely dependent on the DHSS (or a man – see below) and the refusal to remain in poverty.

> I knew I could thieve. I knew that, if I wanted it, I could go out there and get it, so I did. I've always wanted the money and I've wanted it *there*, you know. Not like signing on the dole and waiting weeks for it. I wanted it *there* when I wanted it. I *could* stop [stealing] if I wanted to but I refused and, now that I've got the baby, I wanna get all I want. Because I'm not gonna struggle with her and I don't want *her* to struggle. I want her to have the things that I never had to make me go out there and thieve it. You understand? [Tara, aged 21]

(A fourth factor – the refusal to put up with any form of physical, verbal or other ill-usage was mentioned by those women who feared that they would commit further crimes of violence.)

The fact remains that the majority of women in poverty do not land up in a court of law. Is it because they are law-abiding or is it because, when they do break the law, there are factors that operate against their criminalization?

The women I interviewed claimed that most poor women have to engage in some kind of 'fiddle' at some time in their lives in order to 'get by'. At the same time the researches of Box (1983) suggest that, although young adolescent girls probably do commit as much crime as their male peers, women in all other age groups commit less crime than men. Why then had *these* women become criminalized? Poverty alone would have most likely been insufficient cause for their law-breaking *and* criminalization. Their marginalization and concomitant absorption into the criminal Gulag had also been conditioned by:

1 their (often spectacular) refusals of the official state regulation that (in a majority of cases) had intruded into their lives from an early age and which for many had become the visible and tangible evidence of the oppression of the 'class deal'.
2 their sense of powerlessness in face of coercive assistantial regulation that violated prevailing discourses concerning citizens' rights to both welfare and privacy.
3 their refusal to shift responsibility on to a male by making the gender deal.

Resisting class regulation and racism

A recurring debate in Marxist and socialist analyses has asked why working-class people put up with exploitation. And the answers have usually been based on some variant of either that their exploitation is hidden from them by ideology or that any resistance is ultimately repressed by force. In the lives of the women in this study, however, unusual combinations of unusually adverse circumstances had forced on the women an acute awareness of the inequitable social relations that had oppressed them. This awareness had occurred because (1) in their cases it had not been occluded by the constraints of family or gender ideologies; (2) the women had been forced at an early age into confrontation with 'policing' by the state's regulatory apparatuses; (3) the women had placed the blame for their visible oppression on to those agents of social control with whom they had most frequently come into contact, i.e. social workers and had subsequently refused to be regulated by those same agents. Yet, by thus refusing to co-operate with social workers, they had also made themselves less eligible for social-work representation as clients worthy of further welfare regulation. Rejected as candidates for assistantial regulation, they had become more eligible for regulation by the criminal justice system.

The women's *resistance* to class regulation and racism can be traced out in their views on families, Care, work (or in most cases unemployment), welfare agencies, police, courts and prisons.

Family   The family is a major mechanism of social control, not only for its younger members but also for adults. The ideology of the rewards of familiness is one of the strongest forces of ideological control. It occludes and helps reproduce both class oppression and the exploitation of women. Its regulatory success with individuals, however, depends upon people perceiving their own families as being sources of at least *some* rewards, either material or psychological. The women in this study had experienced few material or psychological benefits within their families. Twenty-two had spent all or part of their lives in Care, twelve of them seeing their entry into Care as being an escape from difficult family situations. Fifteen had experienced physical abuse and four sexual abuse within their families of origin. Eight had been battered by husbands or cohabitees. Four of those who had never been in Care had left home in their teens, two because of their fathers' beatings and two because of their fathers' sexual abuse (in one case sexual advances, in the other incestuous sexual intercourse). Subsequently, neither Care nor school had been able to compensate for their oppression within the family and their eventual refusal to put up with that oppression.

Care   As we saw in Chapter 4, eleven of the twenty-two women who had been in Care claimed that their minor (and often non-criminal) early misbehaviour would never have escalated into 'criminal careers' at all, had they not been in the Care of the local authority. Thus, though many spoke with nostalgia about the good times they had had in individual Children's Homes and remembered some social workers with affection, their talk also suggested that they distinguished sharply between their approbation of specific residential institutions and social work personnel and their total rejection of the statutory relationship which, as children in Care, they had had with the state. At an age when the ideology of familiness had led them to believe that it is desirable for children to be brought up in families normatively bound by mutual ties of affection, they themselves had been reared in institutions constituted by law and within formalized relationships of statutory and subordinated clientage and regulatory supervision. 'I've always felt guilty and angry about my past,' said Yasmin, 'No one's cared for me or showed any respect for me, so why should I show any respect for anyone else? Since I've been in Children's Homes I've always fought against the system and I'm still fighting it.'

> Pat: (to Josie) Did the social workers keep in touch with you when you were at Approved School?
> Josie: Yeh. This woman came once every three months. But I associated her with one of the women who used to take me to Children's Homes. She was just one of those people that had always been taking me somewhere against my will. [Josie, aged 30]

And this anger at always and *only* being constituted as objects of the professional and bureaucratic labours of agents charged with the regulation of state-institutionalized children had persisted. Again and again the women who had been in Care told me that they would not be *indebted to*, that they would not be *tied* to, and that they would not be *dependent* upon, anyone. In Care this twofold quest for independence and relationships based on equality, mutuality and a non-indebted reciprocity had, as we have already seen, resulted in many young women bolting from their various Children's Homes or CHEs as soon as they had set foot inside them. What they had *not* foreseen at that stage was that there were a decreasing number of places in both ideology and society that they could bolt *to* without compromising the imaginary independence that was increasingly endowing them with a sense of identity – a sense of identity that was otherwise being denied them by their marginalization. By the time I interviewed them, all the older women had realized that running from Children's Homes had got them nowhere, that the sources of their oppression had been much deeper. 'I only went to one Children's Home' said Tara, and 'I broke out of that. I've been running one way or the other ever since.'

School Twenty-nine women had truanted from school. The older women merely remembered they had found it 'boring' or 'irrelevant'. The younger ones also claimed that there had been little point in being educated for the dole. Several who had been in Care had in effect left school before the statutory leaving age because they had been moved to a different Children's Home where the social workers had 'not bothered to find a school for the last six months or so.' Others, as we saw in Chapter 4, had been moved into hostels prior to reaching school-leaving age and no one at all had appeared to take responsibility for their day-to-day supervision. When they *had* attended school, they had, according to their own accounts, often created classroom havoc, in some cases with the express aim of being excluded. Four had been expelled from one or more educational establishments, four more had experienced temporary suspensions and three had simply refused to attend school and eventually had been provided with home tutors. The only two who volunteered the information that corporal punishment had been a feature of their school's disciplinary regime also told how they had had no hesitation in meeting violence with violence.

> They were going to give me six straps and I refused them, so they suspended me. When I went back to school, I kept doing physical violence to the other girls – girls get on my nerves – and one day when the teacher sent me out I kicked the door down and they expelled me. [Daphne, aged 15]

> She caned me across the hand. I'll never forget it. I stood there and said, 'Have you finished?' and she said, 'Yes'. Then I took the cane and caned her. I got kicked out of the school for that. [Jill, aged 21]

Although they had not been *very* critical of their teachers (generally pointing out that they had not been at school often enough to feel strongly about the *details* of their schooling), the two who had been to grammar schools claimed that they had been made to feel out of place because of their non-middle-class accents. Two of the black girls had sensed that the teachers had had lower expectations of them than they had of the white.

Others, both black and white, said that, even if they had attended school, the education on offer would not have equipped them with the knowledge or qualifications to get good jobs. Subsequent experience of unemployment and sporadic work in low-paid and low-status jobs had reinforced their previously held suspicions that working-class kids are schooled for working-class jobs (Willis, 1977; Messerschmidt, 1979; Harrison, 1983).

Work Thirty-seven of the women were questioned about their educational qualifications and twenty-three said that they had none. Eleven of the total thirty-nine had never had a paid job (three were still at school) and, of those who had been in employment, only nine had been continually in full-time work for a year or more. Four of the black girls who did have qualifications were angry that, owing to racism, they had had great difficulty in getting jobs; they had eventually taken jobs unrelated to, or not commensurate with, their qualifications; and, even when in work, they had neither been promoted nor received wage increases at the same rate as white employees.

Like I say, when I first left school – now this is God's truth! – I could type really fast and I went to this bureau. They sent me for an interview and they wanted a girl who could do so many words and I could do that. And when I got back, this really nice girl called me into the office and I goes, 'Have I got the job?' She goes, 'No. But don't let your spirits drop down.' I goes, 'Why haven't I got the job?' She says, 'Well, if I tell you, promise you won't tell anybody 'cos I'll get the sack.' I said, 'Tell me.' She goes, 'It's because you're black.' [Stephanie, aged 22]

The majority of those who had been in Care had not had any kind of permanent paid employment, either because they had gone straight from Care to custody (and had thereafter been refused jobs because of their criminal record) or because they had left Care ill equipped to compete in the shrinking labour market of an extended economic recession. Most, however, were adamant that in any case they would not work under factory discipline, an exploitative discipline mirroring the oppressive constraints that they had already suffered in the family, the welfare and the penal systems. Doing voluntary work was frequently mentioned as being one way of circumventing the exploitative constraints of wage labour. 'When you do voluntary work', said Audrey, 'the space is yours. Okay, you don't get paid but you sort of teach yourself and learn a lot.' Dawn tersely summarized what others said at greater length: 'Factory work is prison, anyway. No thank you.' (cf. Melossi and Pavarini, 1981).

Assistantial Regulation   Since the 1940s, when Beveridge's Welfare State ideal was premised on the right to relief of need, the practice of social work has focused on the policing of families in general (Donzelot, 1979) and the pedagogic regulation of women in particular (Wilson, 1977). The earlier language of 'rights' and 'needs' has been narrowed to that of a moral economy of 'claims' and 'entitlements'. In exchange for material assistance, women, especially mothers, have been subjected to tutelary supervision (Donzelot, 1979) and regulatory surveillance (e.g. see Cook, 1987 for discussion of how women claiming supplementary benefits as lone mothers have been constantly harassed by DHSS 'snoopers' employed to detect fraudulent claims).

The women in this study who had already either refused or been denied family, child-welfare, pedagogic and wage regulation were both prime candidates for, and vehement opponents of, assistantial regulation in later life. Dawn pinpointed the roots of that opposition when she said: 'I've always been anti-authority, especially anti-social workers; 'cos when I was younger they were always against me, not for me – always putting me in the Police Court.'

The women's talk was studded with expletives against social workers whom they had eventually made formal complaints against, turned out of the home or even assaulted and/or taken hostage. They themselves most frequently explained this violent resistance to assistantial regulation by reference to their own experiences of two major types of social-work intervention – the policing of parenting and maternity; and the extension and tightening of the assistantial screw.

The policing of parenting is one of the many unenviable tasks that social workers are legally obliged to perform. Policies aimed at reducing the number of children removed from their parents have also resulted in an increase in the number of parents under regular (and sometimes daily) supervision in their own homes. Although the need for such close monitoring is often predicated upon parental histories of child-abuse, child-neglect, drug-abuse and/or general instability of life-style, given the promotion of the privatized family ideology, it is inevitable that the parents themselves resent the intrusion. The policing of maternity is particularly resisted by those women who, brought up in Care themselves, have hopefully imagined that their own homes will one day provide a refuge beyond official domination and/or parental abuse and restrictions.

> A couple of days after I'd had Sylvie the medical social worker from the hospital came to see me and I told her to piss off. She was trying to get me to have Sylvie adopted, saying that I wouldn't be able to cope. I just told her to go away and she never came back again. [Zoë, aged 28]

> At nine o'clock every morning we used to get a knock on the door and it would either be the probation officer, the social worker or one of them type of people . . . one woman used to time it so that she turned up just as I was changing his bum. She used to say I wasn't doing it right. I just said 'Well, you're not his goddam mother are you? I'm his mother, not you,' and kicked her out of the house. All that the present social worker is interested in is getting my kids adopted. But I'm putting up a fight. There's no way I'm going to let them take my child from me. [Norma, aged 22]

> They just stormed into the house and took my child. I actually held a social worker and nearly had her out of the window. [Jeanette, aged 30]

The above complaints were about the policing of parenting. A more general complaint concerned the widening of the welfare net (Cohen, 1985), accompanied by its multidimensional tightening of control on all aspects of its clients' lives.

Every woman who had experienced both probation and social services supervision said that she preferred probation officers to social workers. The specificity of the probation task results in probation officers being consulted on problems that are often kept from social workers for fear that potentially damaging information will be used against the informant in a totally different context. It was suggested that whereas probation officers deal directly and straightforwardly with problems as they arise, social workers retain information to put forward as evidence of instability when entirely different issues (e.g. housing, child custody or even a sentence) are at stake.

> I find a probation officer a lot more straightforward than what a social worker is. Social workers will give you an answer but in a roundabout way, whereas probation officers will just tell you what they think and, if you don't like it, then that's your fault. But probation officers are straight with you. I think that's why a lot of people like probation officers more than social workers. [Hazel, aged 29]

Additionally, several women had found (to their cost) that, even when they had resigned themselves to statutory probation supervision, the expected benefits had not been forthcoming. Jill, for instance, had come out of Styal Youth Custody Centre (at the age of 17) with her recently born baby, having been told by her probation officer that self-contained accommodation had been found for her in her home town.

> *Pat*: Did anyone meet you out of prison?
>
> *Jill*: No. I had to find my own way home [200 miles] with my babe. A nurse and an officer took me to the station. I had my cases and everything, the babe and the babe's stuff. I got all the way to S. and then my probation officer met me at S. station. She just took me straight to the Homeless Families' Unit. I knew she was going the wrong way because the estate where I was supposed to be going was the other side of town. I just went mad. I did, I went mad. I went to my cousin's. I said, 'Look after the baby for me.' I give her clothes and nappies and milk and, to put it bluntly, I just pissed off. I did, 'cos I just couldn't take no more. I was on licence and everything, but I just didn't care because it was a big let-down. From then on I didn't care about anything or anybody because I got into trouble again. [Jill, aged 20]

A basic distrust of social workers was put forward by several women as an explanation for why they would rather steal than seek financial support from social services. That had been Zoë's position at the time of her last crime. She said, 'It was at a point where there was no food in the house. My probation officer had suggested to me several times that I get in touch with social services. But I'm afraid I can't stand interfering social workers.' Yet, despite suspicions that the state's financial assistance always has to be paid for by recipients' acceptance of increased supervision, the women were aware that resistance to assistantial regulation also exacts a price. Dislike of general surveillance had resulted in some going to prison rather than agreeing to probation or community service orders. In consequence of their histories of resistance to *all* official regulation, by the time I met them very few could have been represented in court as convincing candidates for non-custodial sentences.

Police   All women were asked whether they thought they had received better treatment from the police than maybe they would have done had they been men. All said no, though several added that they had not been treated badly. Friendly treatment was attributed either to a paternalism towards young people or to the 'special' relationship of mutual watchfulness that had developed between the police and certain 'gangs', troubled or troublesome areas, and individuals already 'known' to police and courts. Additionally, a few women claimed that, as they themselves had never given any trouble when questioned or arrested, the police had 'never tried to be funny' with them either. However, the majority expressed dislike or hatred of the police and this was usually put down to police harassment of, or discrimination against, the following groups: people living on run-down housing estates where the residents have all been stereotyped as criminal; children in institutions; young girls who are visibly gender deviant; and women engaged in prostitution or the purveyance of other sexual services. A few women admitted that they had always taken a confrontational stance towards all 'authority' figures and that they themselves had most probably provoked the police into violent retaliatory measures. But it was police harassment of black people that was mentioned most frequently as being both unprovoked and provocative. Shirley and Sheila gave graphic examples.

> They used to call me slag and nigger. Like one of my [white] friends, Fred, was standing at a bus stop with this girl who's black and I was walking up to meet them. The police pulled up in a van, jumped out and called Fred a 'nigger-lover'. Fred's not colour-prejudiced at all. But it seems like the Old Bill are. Then again, a lot of my friends are boys, so when they get nicked I get nicked and the police treat me the same way. They rough me up, handcuff me and kick me about. [Shirley, aged 20]

> When they find out my 'previous', then it's, 'Oh you black cunt', passing down the line. Then 'What colour's your mum' and I says, 'She's white.' 'Oh, black man's whore' and all that [Sheila, aged 22]

Finally, many mentioned a police sexism that had resulted in spurious references to arrested women's sexual orientation, sexual activities and sexual relationships. Supporting evidence for these accusations has recently been forthcoming from a number of sources (Carlen, 1983a; Chambers and Millar, 1983). In a significant number of incidents the women involved had not even been engaged in law-breaking, merely in activities that the police had defined as unwomanly.

With the exception of Kay, Monica and Prue, each of the women fell into one or more of the categories of people known to be susceptible to police harassment or special surveillance. Moreover, by virtue of their law-breaking and their sex, *all* were likely to be seen by police as being gender deviant. It is not, therefore, surprising that again and again some women referred to incidents in which they had either verbally abused or even assaulted the police. It is arguable that this resistance to 'the law' had reinforced police typifications of the gender contrariness of law-breaking women. Certainly it would have increased the chances of those particular women attracting police attention in the future.

Penal regulation   Given their histories of resistance to a variety of informal and formal regulatory controls, it was unlikely that the women would easily succumb to penal regulation. Of the thirty-seven who had served custodial sentences, sixteen admitted to being extremely disruptive while in penal institutions and two more had absconded from open prisons. Yet, although nineteen said that they usually served their sentences quietly and without trouble, not one of the interviewees saw imprisonment as a deterrent or reformative influence. All those with histories of institutionalization said that prison held no terror for them, while, as we saw in Chapter 4, some women who were extremely isolated or harassed by poverty outside prison actually welcomed their custodial sentences as providing temporary respite from loneliness and/or a debilitating struggle to make out against all the odds. A few women, like Muriel, Nadia and Josie, had, in their youth, seen imprisonment as enhancing a criminal image constitutive of a positive, strong, exciting and independent identity.

As I have previously argued elsewhere (Carlen, 1983a, 1985 and 1986) and demonstrated in 1985 (O'Dwyer and Carlen, 1985), much of the violence in women's prisons is a response to the rigid disciplinary regimes and fear-inducing techniques employed by officers to restrain unruly prisoners. Similar conclusions have also been reached by Gibbens (1971) and Mandaraka-Sheppard (1986).

One of the most disturbing features of the research reported here was the discovery that young girls like Yasmin, whose behaviour in Care had already resulted in their being sent to Secure Units and mental hospitals, could at 16 end up in a prison where the methods used to restrain them are as crude today as (according to the older women in the study) they were fifteen years ago. Listen to Yasmin's description of the series of measures that had been taken to stop her acts of self-mutilation and violence towards others:

> I was sent to a Place of Safety for a year and a half. I was in there to stop me hurting myself. I was cutting up, taking overdoses and things like that. When you blew up, you got the needle. The cells were padded . . . . Oh God! I went crazy when they took me in there, especially when I saw those cells and blinking needles. I hated it. It was a nuthouse. It took me so long to get out of there. Kept having Court Orders slapped on me. [Later] I went to another lock-up place and I jumped out of the bloody window. Cut all my arms and everything.

At Bullwood Hall Yasmin had spent long periods 'down the block'.

> The reason why I fight against them is because I get scared. I wouldn't
> mind if one or two officers came in here and took me down the block. But
> it's never one or two. The whole lot come in, right? And so then I get
> scared, I panic. So then I hit out to get 'em away from me. And, when I'm
> in front of the Governor, I'm not gonna say I was scared – not in front of
> three officers – 'cos then I would look a fool.

However, lest it be assumed that these techniques are employed solely for
girls like Yasmin whose records might be thought to justify such precautionary
measures, it should be pointed out that several officers were always in
attendance to escort any prisoner to the block. Nicky was serving her first prison
sentence and was only on Report for ignoring an officer's order to get to her cell
instead of going to the lavatory to change a Tampax. She was, nonetheless,
escorted to the block by the full complement of officers.

> Seven-thirty in the morning, along came the heavy mob to take me down
> the block. Two of the gym teachers and about four officers came. It's
> normal. They always send gym teachers in case someone puts up a fight.
> [Nicky, aged 27]

And the crude distinctions made by prison staff between behaviour requiring
punishment and behaviour requiring treatment is nicely revealed in a report on
Yasmin written at Holloway Prison in 1984. It stated that 'any further
self-injury will result in location in hospital – any damage to property should be
dealt with by the disciplinary staff.' The report had been occasioned by an
incident in which Yasmin, alone in a cell, had smashed a light bulb before
proceeding to cut her wrists with its fragments. She had been 15 years old at the
time.

Many women, particularly the older ones, saw it as an act of resistance to do
their sentences quietly, to refuse to allow themselves to be provoked into
behaviour which would draw on them humiliation and punishment. Yet this did
not mean that they had any more respect for the penal regime than had the
younger, often wilder girls. True, some women said that they wanted to give up
crime because they could not face another prison sentence. But not even these
gaol-tired women believed that fear of prison alone would in future keep them
out of the penal institutions. 'It's what you've got outside that keeps you out,'
said Josie and this sentiment was constantly expressed by others.

Powerlessness

> *Yasmin*: Some people find it exciting to get into trouble, it's different.
> *Pat*: Did *you* find it exciting?
> *Yasmin*: Yeh, I found it *very* exciting. I found it different. Instead of

walking round the streets being all nice and things like that, why not change, be horrible for once and do all mischievous things?

Pat: Do you still find it exciting? Or has that worn off?

Yasmin: I don't know. Sometimes I find things exciting what I want to do. You know, if I'm bored, I can go out and get into trouble.

Pat: When do you get bored.

Yasmin: In the evening I get bored, in the evening.

Pat: Is that because you haven't got the money to go places?

Yasmin: Yeh, plus we ain't allowed to go into most of the places anyway. It's the way we have our hair cut. 'Cos a lot of us go around, have our hair cut like this – Mohican – and we're not allowed into most of the places.

The words 'boring', 'bored' and 'boredom' figured often in the interviews. Not because the women were inarticulate. Rather, the words captured the emptiness of the wretched material situations that are doled out to increasing numbers of people marginalized by the class deal. Despite their many acts of resistance the women were always having it brought home to them that, without adequate material back-up, their best attempts at self-regeneration would fail. At those times a majority of them knew of only one way to relieve their pain – by resorting to violence towards themselves or others.

Pat: Had you decided when you came out this time that you weren't going back?

Josie: Oh for sure, this time. Oh God, yeh. But I did go through stages where I thought, 'Right, what I'll do is get drunk for a starter. I'm feeling pretty pissed off so I'll get drunk.' I'd smash things up. I mean, I fully expected the Hostel would throw me out. You know, I'd do something to *enforce* a change. I suppose that had just become my way of saying 'I'm not happy.'

Josie was describing what, over the months of the research, I had come to call the 'sod-it syndrome'. For as the older women talked, again and again they described situations in which, sometimes after months of going straight, of coping against all the odds, the four-hundredth blow had made them say 'Sod it,' had occasioned an outburst of violence, a return to an addiction, the start of a new and flamboyant thieving spree. How their particular form of problem-solving shaped their crimes has already been outlined in Chapter 2. Now, therefore, a discussion of the other fundamental refusal that had been partly responsible for the fashioning of their lives – their refusal of the gender deal.

REFUSAL OF THE GENDER DEAL

The idealized notion of familiness that can partly occlude the exploitative nature of the class deal can also occlude the exploitation of women inherent in the interplay of class deal with gender deal. For, despite the fact that 'housewives' have never been paid for the domestic work that frees men for wage-labour and is also preconditional to the renewal of their labour power, working-class women have often been forced to acquiesce in their own exploitation because of both the material powerlessness of their class and the ideological effectivity of patriarchal domination. The actual emotional rewards of motherhood have been emphasized and amplified by ideologies which have taught that such rewards should compensate women for the poverty induced by the class deal and the subordination inherent in the gender deal. Regulated by these all-embracing ideologies of motherhood and the female 'caring' roles, women have been *deterred* from committing serious crime because they, more than men, have been taught to consider themselves the guardians of domestic morality. They have also had *less opportunity* to commit serious crimes because first, as daughters, young women are likely to be under closer supervision than young men; later, as mothers, they are physically restricted by the care of young children and elderly relatives .Even when working-class women have been employed outside their homes their (low) earnings have seldom made them financially independent. Within the home their conformity to familial discipline has been induced by patriarchal ideology and enforced by male violence (cf. Dobash *et al.*, 1979). Sure, under certain conditions (e.g. male full employment and familiness based, variously, on bonds of affection, religion, mutual respect and *equally* shared interests) many women have believed that the emotional rewards accruing from home, marriage and family have been well worth the price paid in terms of their own domestic, marital and familial subordination. Conversely, however, when young girls have been brought up in situations where absolutely no rewards (and many severe disabilities) have been seen to emanate from familiness, when, too, the technologies of gender discipline have been unusually harsh or oppressive, women's adult consciousness has been constituted within an immediate experience of the fundamental oppression inherent in the gender deal; and they have resisted it. Thus it was with the majority of the thirty-nine women interviewed.

In talking of men, the women focused mainly on their own experiences as victims of male violence and male sexual abuse. Fathers had engaged primarily in physical violence, though three women volunteered information concerning their fathers' sexual abuse of them.

> He'd say that he wanted me to cuddle him. He'd say that, if I didn't open the door, he'd beat me up. It just got to the stage when he used to ask me to just rub him up. Well I didn't know what he meant or what it was, so I used to do that before I went to school. He used to say, 'Here you are,' and give me some money, and I used to get five Park Drive from the shop. [Mary, aged 27]

It got to the habit where I'd come through the front door, and he'd be waiting behind the door, and he'd bash me at the back of the head and say 'Take your knickers off and let me smell 'em' and all that kind of thing. One night (and this is when I did leave home) he came home paralytic drunk and tried to get into bed with me. I was screaming me head off. Me Mum came up and dragged him off. Mum said, 'Don't tell anybody 'cos they'll put him away'. . . . . What really hurt [was when] me Mum said, 'You'll have to go.' By rights *he* should have been put away. [Queenie, aged 43]

The sheer hatred that some of the women felt for their fathers was revealed in the strong language used to describe the batterings they had experienced at their hands.

He was a swine to us when we were younger . . . . I'd finished working at the factory but he didn't believe I'd got another job, so he beat me up. I'll always remember it. He was a bastard. Excuse the language, but he was. [Jean, aged 26]

He's belted me with the buckle-end of a belt, he's kicked me all over the house. Excuse me, he was a pure bastard. [Queenie, aged 43]

It's just that he's a fucking lunatic guy. He used to smack me up the wall. He used to stand on my head. He was a big geezer. I used to think my head was gonna snap like an egg; it was just gonna crack, 'cos I could feel that amount of pressure. I had really long hair then, down past my arse, and he'd swing me round by it. [Josie, aged 30]

And it had always been when the women reached puberty that the fathers had become both violent and possessive. (cf. Christina and Carlen, 1985).

When I was really little there was always big dolls at Christmas. When I got to 14 or 15, I could see the drastic change in him, as if he hated me. [Queenie, aged 43]

I got on really well with my father till I was – what they call it? Puberty? I was a footballer and I was a tomboy and we used to do everything together. Then I started going out with girls down the Youth Club and it sort of changed my family life. He used to kick me around and beat me up. [Nicky, aged 27]

Jean had been badly beaten by her male cohabitee and six other women had been battered by husbands, male cohabitees or boyfriends. (Eight of the thirty-nine women volunteered the information that they were lesbians and accordingly had not had husbands, male cohabitees or boyfriends. Nonetheless, four of them had been either physically, or sexually, abused by males.) Only Mary saw her husband's jealous violence as a sign of affection. All the others had been embittered both by the actual violence and by the taken-for-granted way in which bystanders had responded to it. Several gave vivid descriptions of how their mothers had been powerless to intervene against the male tyrant in the home. Carol ruminated on how 'useless' the police had been when they came. Jean told how police had threatened that her children would be taken into Care if she again called them to the house complaining of her cohabitee's violence.

Yet violent assault had not been the only way in which men had attempted to rule some of these women. Forbidding them to mix with anyone else at all had been another favoured mode of control (cf. Hunt, 1980). Sadie, for instance, was desperately lonely whilst her husband was in prison, but she did not join the various women's groups recommended by her probation officer because she knew her husband would be furious if he were ever to find out. 'He won't let me go out on my own or with other women,' she explained. Jean, too, having expanded on the same topic, concluded that 'They're all like that, men. They're like my Dad. Want to know what you're doing, what you're not doing.'

The women had resisted. Leaving home had been the obvious escape route for young girls whose fathers were abusing them. But the flight from home had often had disastrous results.

> I started to work on the buses and I was getting good money so [when her father had begun physically and sexually to assault her] I thought, 'Sod this,' and I left home. I got myself a little bedsitter and then I finished on the buses and started shoplifting. [Queenie, aged 43]

The eight women who said they were lesbian merely stated a sexual preference for women, though Jill claimed that it had definitely been her father's violence and her step-father's sexual abuse that had put her off men.

At the time of interview, Jean no longer took her father's verbal abuse quietly.

> He tries to tell me what to do but I call him all the bastard names under the sun. (Excuse me language). He's only been round about twice. I call him a bastard 'cos that's what he is. I hate him for what he's done to my mother. [Jean, aged 26]

Some women had gone further. Sheila had stabbed her mother's boyfriend after he had stabbed her mother. Nicky had assaulted a policeman in retaliation for his violence towards her. All of the women beaten up by male partners claimed that at least on some occasions they had fought back . . . . And *still* their dominant attitude to men in general was one of fear.

> 12.30 at night . . . and he [her father] petrified the life out of me. He was standing there paralytic drunk begging me to come home. I just pushed him away. Even when I think about it now it gives me the horrors. [Queenie, aged 43]

I am afraid of men. I am *literally* afraid of men. [Jill, aged 20]

I'm frightened of some men, not all men, but some men. [Yasmin, aged 16]

Pat: Would you still put up with anyone battering you?
Jean: No, I wouldn't. I'd kick their faces more like. Men are different than women. Puddled, men are. I don't like men. I'm frightened of 'em.

Only Queenie said that she wished she had been born male, though all the others said that they thought men had a much better life than women. For, even when they had been keeping home with a man, most of the women had had the main responsibility for managing the house, children, cooking and whatever little money there had been.

Women have a harder life, far harder. Men are with their mums till they leave home. Then they get married and the wife's got to do everything – housework, cooking and cleaning – plus women have to do it when they're at home with their parents, anyhow. [Carol, aged 27]

Mothers and/or housewives not only resented the immense amount of work expected of them, they were also bitter about being tied to the house twenty-four hours a day.

A man finds it a lot easier to get out. But with a woman you're sitting in the house, inside four walls and you get depressed. [Monica, aged 44]

Several made the point that even nowadays it is still more socially acceptable for men to go out alone in public than it is for women. As Queenie stressed, when family responsibilities become too much for men, they 'just bugger off to the boozer'. Zoë thought that under the Thatcher Government the position of women had worsened.

Women have been pushed back into the home because the unemployment situation is so bad that women have been made to feel that they're not entitled to work, that they should give up their jobs and stay in the home so that men can work. It's this thing about men being providers and women being the little woman at home to look after the children and cook the meals. It sickens me. I mean, case in point: my insurance agent came the other week to renew a policy for me. He said 'You've finished work, haven't you, you're a housewife.' I said, 'No, I'm not married to a house, I'm not a housewife. I'm a childminder.' I said, 'If you want to be really stupid, I'm a domestic engineer, but I'm not a housewife.' I'm unemployed but I'm not an employment statistic because I have a child. If a man was left alone with a child, he'd have to go and sign on, but I'm a woman, a second-class citizen. [Zoë, aged 28]

Mary believed that this traditional notion of a gender-appropriate division of labour is also incorporated into modern policies directed at the regulation and assessment of parenting.

> It's me that's gotta do everything. *Me* that's gotta prove myself, do this, do that. Yet she's *his* daughter too. He can just go out and get drunk, for all they care. [Mary, aged 27]

All the women thought there was a greater social stigma attached to being a female than to being a male criminal, and all attributed it to the ideological representation of women's 'proper place' as being in the home. It has already been suggested (in Chapter 4) that parents are more alarmed at the teenage deviance of daughters than of sons and that social workers are more concerned with the behaviour of mothers than of fathers. The women that I interviewed thought that these general concerns with the greater need to regulate and control women were carried over to the courtroom, the prison and, amplified, back again into the bleak world of the woman ex-prisoner. Talking of the criminal courts, Cindy held firm to her oft repeated assertion that women who choose to live independently of men are disadvantaged when they come to court (cf. Carlen, 1983a; Eaton, 1986, 1987):

> Courts feel that it's more normal for men to commit crime. But they don't realize how hard it is out there for women. It's harder for a woman, especially if she's got kids. I'm a person, I don't depend on nobody, but they look on it as wrong. [They think] women shouldn't be into them kind of things, that's why they come down harsh on you. [Cindy, aged 22]

Sally agreed:

> You're seen as evil and wicked and bad. 'Cos women are supposed to be in the house, aren't they? Looking after your husband and the kids, not out committing crimes and taking drugs. I think they're a lot harder on women than on men. [Sally, aged 35]

Jeanette argued that this harsher attitude towards women has resulted in the more rigid disciplinary regimes operative in the women's prisons (see Carlen, 1983a; Mandaraka-Sheppard, 1986).

> We're made to feel that it's not something a woman should do, be in prison. The system is trying to say women shouldn't get into trouble, should not be in prison, and therefore we are meant to suffer a little bit more. [Jeanette, aged 30]

Finally, Zoë ruminated on the double standard that sees men's crime as normal, women's as out of place.

> It's this thing about a double standard again for a man and a woman. If a man commits a criminal offence, okay, he's a bad lad and he goes away and does his time. But he comes out afterwards and it's 'Are you all right

mate?' 'Come and have a drink.' 'It wasn't too bad, was it' Whereas, the day I came back, everybody avoided me. Nobody wanted to talk about it all. *Because I was a woman and especially because I'd got a child* [Zoë, aged 28]

Ideology, identity and everyday life

Production and social reproduction are central to the social order and to the individual's identity within it. Ideological discourse is directed, from childhood onwards, to the performance of the productive and reproductive roles which gendered class subjects are expected to perform. Familial ideology is especially significant in constructing a self which is congruent with dominant conceptions of the activities and capacities involved in present or future roles . . . . But what happens to those who do not appear to occupy these central roles? What is the effect of subordinate marginality on personality?

(Leonard, 1984: 181)

The thirty-nine women had been reared in material and ideological conditions they had early perceived as giving the lie to the class and gender deals constitutive of their actual exploitation and powerlessness. Individualistic resistance had not reduced that powerlessness. Instead it had engendered a series of regulatory and penal responses that had pushed *all* of them further to the margins and *many* into an outsider status from which they either could not, or did not wish to, escape.

The three 15-year olds interviewed at Bullwood Hall seemed to have no idea that their early criminal careers might affect their future lives adversely. Each talked of 'having fun for a few years' and then either 'getting a job' or 'settling down like everyone else.' By contrast, all thirty-six of the older women thought their criminal or penal careers had differentiated them from other women in several ways, the two major ones being their strong desire for independence from men, and their outlawing from both the labour market and, in some cases, assistantial regulation.

Although several of the older women admitted to a commitment to community politics and the women's movement, all insisted that their political beliefs had developed after they had already become involved in crime. Again and again they stressed that from an early age they had experienced a sharp desire to be independent of other people's control and particularly the kind of ideological controls that required them to put up with an unjust distribution of goods and income and/or a restricting 'feminine' lifestyle. Tara's comment is typical of the women who insisted that they had never intended to be materially dependent upon a male.

No, I'm not a feminist, no. I'm just headstrong, very headstrong. I know what's what and, if I want something, I don't need a man to get it for me. [Tara, aged 21]

Yet, although they had not wanted to be dependent upon men, several said that, in adolescence, at least, they had found the company of young men more liberating than that of young women. Mary, looking back to adolescence, spoke for many who in their early teens had refused to be contained within the trammels of adolescent femininity.

> I just found women boring. Blokes outside used to call me one of the lads. I used to go round drinking with them and I had more of a laugh than with women. [Mary, aged 27]

Sally and Nadia also insisted that from an early age they had been 'different'. When I asked Sally if she had ever envisaged having a home and children of her own, she replied, 'I wouldn't even entertain the thought of that kind of life.' Nadia said:

> It was like I was a feminist even then, before I even knew what feminism meant. You know, about being treated the same and why couldn't I do woodwork instead of sewing which I hated. I always used to get chucked out of sewing. [Nadia, aged 35]

Crucially, the early sense of independence had been nurtured in circumstances where toughness was a condition of survival. This was insisted upon most strongly when the women talked about their sexual orientation and self-concept as women. Jeanette, for instance, insisted that her resistance had not been in opposition to, but a condition of, strong womanhood:

> I do believe that women are not given the same opportunities as men but I'm a fighter, a survivor. I'm not fighting it, being bitter, being hard or being a toughee. I'm fighting it because I'm a woman and believe I should be treated with respect so that I can show respect back. [Jeanette, aged 30]

The eight lesbian women stated their sexual orientation as a fact and without further elaboration. What they and some of the others were anxious to explain was that fighting and aspects of self-presentation like wearing men's clothes and being tattoed had had *nothing* to do with their sexual orientation, *everything* to do with the need to survive street and institutional life.

Tattooing had usually been done to indicate membership of a deviant subculture and to enhance a veneer of 'hardness', although several of the twelve women who drew my attention to their tattoos also expressed regret that the difficulties of tattoo removal meant that they had for ever to bear the visible marks of their adolescent quest for identity and difference. Lena simply said, 'I think I just had 'em done to make me look hard. To let people think I'm a hard girl.' Adopting men's clothes, however, had usually been a behaviour born of pragmatism: women on the run from institutions had experienced so much sexual harassment that the most obvious solution had been to present themselves as men. When that had not worked, physical violence had; and, as Josie explained, pride in survival could become an identity in itself.

> We were barred from every pub because, you know, it was very much a
> man's world there. We were getting all sorts of trouble so we used to
> fight. I could never say now that I resisted the wrongs of women, like. It
> wasn't because of my political beliefs. It was just the way things were and I
> made the best of any situation. As far as we were concerned, when we
> walked down the street we were like seven-foot high criminals. We felt
> 'We're different than anybody else.' It was all we knew. It was the only
> world we were accepted in. [Josie, aged 30]

By the time of interview the attractions of the criminal underworld had palled
for many of the women. At the same time, direct entry to the conventional
world of work and consumerism had not been open to most. Indirect entry via
male-related domesticity and/or motherhood was rejected by the majority.

Except for the three youngest girls, all the women were very realistic about
their future chances in the labour market. Lack of educational qualifications,
having a criminal record and high unemployment had already rendered the
majority of them workless and penniless. They knew that their work prospects
were unlikely to get better. The only immediate and legitimate way 'back in'
was via men or motherhood and, though they were aware that both housing and
supplementary benefit policies favour women making the gender deal (Cook,
1987), it is not surprising that *these* women, most of whom had fought (often
literally) for their independence, were scornful of those options.

> You get some women, they have a kid, right? And then they get together
> with a man, just for the sake of getting a council house. Then, when they
> get there, the man goes out and does what he wants to do and she stays
> indoors all the time. What kind of life is that? What kind of *woman* is
> that? [Audrey, aged 18]

Jill and Cynthia *did* admit that they had thought a child would give them a sense
of security but they had soon realized their mistake; by the time of interview Jill
had already had her child adopted, Cynthia was hoping that hers would be
placed for adoption in the near future. All the women who were married said
they would never marry again. Even women like Jean and Zoë who were
devoted to their children had reservations about motherhood.

> Sometimes I wish I hadn't had the kids when I was so young, when I was
> 19. I could have made something out of my life instead of just looking
> after kids. [Jean, aged 26]

> You're only living for someone else. I've got a life in the respect that I've
> got to make sure that she [her child] has a life. But eventually she's gonna
> grow, she's gonna go away and I'm still going to be sitting here. Twelve
> years' time I'll only be 40, so I feel that in the end I've still got to get
> myself sorted out, because I haven't got a life. [Zoë, aged 28]

So whither had the women come in their lonely quests for identity and independence?

Some who had been in Care were still struggling to prise more information out of social services departments reluctant, or unable, to give them further details about the whereabouts or, in some cases, country of origin, of their parents. They described the pain of believing that, because their parents were 'unknown', they themselves were without identity. At 20 both Donna and Shirley were still angry that so little was known about one parent, that there was so little contact with the other. Additionally Shirley described the identity crises that may arise from being of mixed parentage in a racist society.

> I think the worst thing that has happened to me is not knowing my identity, not knowing who my father is. [Donna, aged 20]

> You try and find your own identity. My mother's white but trying to know who your Dad is . . . . I don't know how to explain it – but it's hard for half-caste people. Where I live there's not many black people about. All my friends are white anyway, and they used to say 'Don't let them call you nigger.' Yet in a black community they say 'Oh, you're a white.' They don't accept you. So in a way it's hard, really. [Shirley, aged 20]

Finally, Nadia poignantly recalled her own childhood sadness and the pain of youthful marginalization when she jokingly explained the origin of her name.

> I got adopted when I was 9. Originally my name was Deborah Naylor and my name's now Nadia Cox. Yes, they asked me [but] in fact, if they had said, 'Do you want to be called Dracula?' I would have said 'Yes,' if it had meant them having me. [Nadia, aged 35]

ASYMETRICAL CONTRACTUALITY, MARGINALIZATION, RESISTANCE AND EXCLUSION

> Victoire Rivière, the mother, is an exemplary case. No doubt because as a woman and even more so as a wife married to thwart by rule a rule which itself was irregular, she felt that any contract remained a trick, an institutionalised assault – as if in a frozen, arrested, perpetual combat. She set herself up as the everlasting canceller of contracts, perpetually put them in doubt, and shifted their signs by setting them moving again – which is tantamount to repudiation and challenge.
>
> (Peter and Fauret, 1975)

Analysis of the thirty-nine women's attempts to make their lives livable in extremely adverse circumstances points to the promise of asymmetrical contractuality as being a major co-ordinating and coercive principle in the complex of discourses wherein working-class women's respectability is conventionally constituted.

Historically, the promise of asymmetrical contractuality has been a central constituent of hegemonic control in societies characterized by various forms of grossly exploitative social relations. People visibly exploited by a society's supposedly contractual relations have again and again acquiesced in the myth that their real rewards are stored up in some other place – ultimately, of course, in Heaven but meantime, on this earth, in their 'characters' if they are working-class men, in their 'femininity', 'motherhood' and 'personal relationships' if they are working-class women. However, because they had been born into *extremely* adverse material conditions, Yasmin and most of the other women had not had the bitter pill of class exploitation sugared by even the *promise* of the rewards mythically attributed to the gender deal. Furthermore, whereas their early refusals of the class deal had resulted in their lacking the education and 'good character' that are the necessary prerequisites of employment, their concomitant or subsequent refusals to believe in the rewards of the gender deal had left them also lacking the moral collateral (of proper femininity, familiness and motherhood) demanded of women without men who seek to claim in full their statutory welfare rights. Outraged by such marginalization and excluded by the very conditions of that marginalization from any collective political response to it, many of the women had proceeded to carve out a personalized ideological space wherein they had, over the years, become so individualistic and socially aloof that, by the time of interview, they themselves had begun to wonder if, rather than being merely marginalized, they were not, instead, totally outcast. Their individual answers to that question had ultimately been dependent upon their own cumulative experiences of both law-breaking and the official response to it.

6

WOMEN IN POVERTY AND IN CRIME: OPTIONS AND POSSIBILITIES

> When people say they're stopping crime, it's not because of the gaol sentence they've done, it's because of their children or boyfriends or the ones they really love. But bird hasn't got anything to do with it, bird doesn't stop them. [Stephanie, aged 22]

> I don't believe I could have done another sentence, but that wouldn't have kept me out if I'd come out to the same sort of situation that I had on every previous occasion. Then I still wouldn't have stayed out, whether I could take the prison sentence or not. In order to keep them out, you actually have to give them something outside. Otherwise, a life of surviving in there seems preferable to life out here where there's just nothing. [Josie, aged 30]

When they talked with me in 1985 and 1986, twelve of the thirty-nine women claimed that they had turned their backs on crime for good. Conversely, twelve others asserted that they were by then committed to a life of crime or, at least, the pursuance of their own particular crime-line in the future. A further fifteen said that, although they desperately wanted to lead a 'normal life', they were afraid that, if they were to be 'realistic', they would have to assess their chances of being crime free in the future as being slim. They twenty-seven women in the two latter groups were those who, in effect, believed that their chances of ever enjoying prosperous law-abiding lives were practically nil.

Is it possible, therefore, to respond to deviant girls and criminal women without narrowing their options to such an extent that, both for material and psychological reasons, they feel that, as they are always/already outsiders, there is a certain inevitability about the continuance of their criminal and penal careers? To help answer that question this chapter first summarizes (Table 6.1) just *how* the combined law-breaking and criminalization of working-class women can effect a further narrowing of already meagre life chances. Then it discusses alternative ways of confronting women's crime and proposes some

TABLE 6.1   Narrowing options: interactive sequences in the outlawing of deviant girls and law-breaking women

Outlawing	Interactive Sequences
From family	Guilt or anger about physical or sexual abuse; entry into residential Care; or running away from home.
From education and employment	Truancy from school; absconding from residential Care; or failure of social workers to find a school for the student.
By drugs	Attractiveness of drug-taking in the short-term can lead to formation of habit, estrangement from family and non-drug users, and eventually criminal activity for the purpose of funding the drug habit. Young people in Care who are discovered using drugs may be escalated into the criminal-justice system more quickly than young people still living with their families. Poor women who offend are unable to pay for the private treatment which sometimes keeps better-off drug-users out of prison.
By residential Care	Loss of contact with family and non-institutional associations; identity problems stemming from constant assessment and categorization; escalation into criminal-justice system. Isolated and vulnerable upon leaving residential Care.
By sexist responses to unconventional behaviour – often pursued in quest for excitement	Early criminalization likely if young girl engages in behaviour defined as masculine. More likely to be reconvicted if convicted at an early age (NACRO, 1986b) and more likely to become institutionalized. Once on circuit of absconders some young women attempt to 'pass' as male for self-protection; others tattoo themselves in order to signify either 'hardness' or 'deviant' status.
By welfare surveillance	Social work intervention in relation to adolescent female status offences, assistantial regulation of women's poverty, and the state policing of motherhood can together alienate women from local-authority social services and other welfare agencies, thereby increasing the likelihood of their receiving a custodial sentence if they should appear in court.
Imprisonment	Learning more crime skills; further debilitation of physically and mentally vulnerable women; loss of material goods, accommodation, children, friends, etc., can lead to institutionalization (i.e. inability to live outside institution).
Record	The criminal career produces the criminal record that is such a barrier to employment that some women become convinced that their only way 'back in' is through men or motherhood, a conviction that can lead to even more disastrous results than the previous criminal convictions did!

reforms of those parts of the welfare, judicial and penal systems that presently respond so ineptly to it. Finally, and most importantly, there is a consideration of the more fundamental political and economic changes prerequisite to a rethinking of criminal justice for women within a programme of social justice in general (cf. Carlen, 1983b).

NARROWING OPTIONS

In 1981 Marsha Rosenbaum wrote:

> In analysing the career of the woman addict, I found her career is inverted. Heroin expands her life options in the initial stages and that is the essence of its social attraction. Yet with progressively further immersion in the heroin world, the social, psychological and physiological exigencies of heroin use create an option 'funnel' for the woman addict . . . . Ultimately, the woman addict is locked into the heroin life and locked out of the conventional world.
>
> (Rosenbaum, 1981: 11)

Amend the above quotation by substituting 'crime' for 'heroin' and 'woman criminal' for 'woman addict', and it well describes the careers of that tiny minority of young female law-breakers who go on to become recidivist criminals.

In Chapter 4 I charted the narrowing options of young women in Care (Table 4.3, pp. 76–78). Now Table 6.1 lists the interactive sequences that cumulatively facilitated the beliefs of twenty-seven of the thirty-nine women that they had become such outsiders that either they could not get 'back in' or that they did not want to.

The twenty-seven women, who felt that they were now irretrievably beyond the pale, also believed that, regardless of what they themselves did, their criminal record had marked them as non-employable for life; and/or that, regardless of their present good intentions, they would again get into some kind of criminal trouble once they either returned to their old haunts or became overwhelmingly depressed by the dullness of a law-abiding and poverty-stricken existence 'on the dole'. Said Cynthia,

> My future's finished. I'm a criminal now and with my record – I mean I've been charged thirteen times – I can't get a job unless I say, 'Right, I have been in trouble' and own up. Some interviews I say, 'No, I ain't been in trouble.' I need to marry an Arab geezer with all the money [laughs] but that will never happen. [Cynthia, aged 19]

Zoë detailed her experience at greater length:

> The things that I was interested in when I was younger are closed to me now because of my criminal record. I could never go back into teaching – that option isn't open to me any more because I've got a conviction for possession of cannabis – The best job I've ever had was working for —— [a

nationally known entertainments company]. I worked in the offices doing bookings. I lied on the application form because it said, 'Do you have any criminal convictions apart from driving offences?' and I put 'No'. And then we had a spate of thefts there and, unbeknown to us, we were all investigated by security – they're all ex-policemen. Well, their friends in the police force came back and said, 'You've got a right one here – prostitution, theft, deception, fraud, drugs, the lot!' So I was sacked. Several years ago, when I was trying to get myself sorted out, I tried to apply for nursing and the Director of Nursing said there was no way they could take me on. You have to have a clear record for five years and I don't know whether I can wait that long, just sitting on my butt doing nothing. I had thought about trying to get back into something to do with food but more on the business side of it. But I'd have to have a City and Guilds qualification and I can't get a grant for that because it's not classed as something you get a grant for. I can't do it and stay on the dole because it's a full-time course! I just feel that I've completely wasted my life, just ruined it. [Zoë, aged 28]

Zoë has seven O levels and three A levels. What chance for the majority of the thirty-nine who have no educational qualifications at all? Their only hope is to lie when asked about their record. Most decline to because they already know someone who *has* lied and consequently lives in fear of being found out. Muriel and Monica, for instance, were living in such fear. Muriel explained how she got the job which she loves but dreads losing.

Now I've got a job, I want to keep it. It's the longest job I've been in but they don't know I've got a criminal record. I didn't declare it. [Muriel, aged 30]

Others were less concerned about the obduracy of the criminal record, more demoralized by their previous recidivism and doubts about their ability to keep to the straight and narrow when confronted once more with poverty, isolation and boredom.

A lot of people say, 'No, I'm not going to do it again,' but when you go out there and things are hard, you just *have* to do it again. [Stephanie, aged 22]

There's women in prison today who've got young children. They say they are going to change and start a clean slate. But, when they go back into society, they find they've got bills, certain things that need doing and they haven't got the money. Then, once they've been put into prison for stealing, they're going to do it again – and make it doubly worse and they'll always end up coming back into prison. [Audrey, aged 18]

The effect of imprisonment on future decisions to commit crime was mentioned frequently by those who thought they would either choose to break the law or drift into law-breaking again.

> I was quite worried when I had to go in but, when it was over, I felt all right. I thought, 'Well, if I come back again, at least I know what it's like. [Sadie, aged 20]

> I've done my bird, I ain't boasting but I'll do another bird again. And next time for something constructive. Not one where I get nicked and everything is returned to them. Next bird will be a bird where I'll have something to come out to. [Cynthia, aged 19]

And Jean thought that things were only made worse when already poor women were fined for stealing.

> Sometimes they'll ask a pound, sometimes two pounds. With me, like, the last one was two pounds a week, wasn't it? I know it's not much but, when you come to paying it, you've got other things you've got to pay for. You want things. I mean, if you didn't buy 'em, you'd pinch 'em, wouldn't you? Well, I would, anyway. I shall probably end up in gaol. [Jean, aged 26]

In 1985 nearly 30 per cent of all women received into prison to serve sentence were serving sentences for fine default! Seear and Player comment:

> Although the length of time such women spend in custody has been reduced over recent years, the number passing through the system has increased, so that in 1984 more women than in any previous year were received into prison for fine default and were kept there under sentence.
>
> (Seear and Player, 1986)

The women who had been addicted to heroin when they were received into prison were particularly dubious about their futures.

> A lot of people end up back on the gear. It depends on the area you're living in. [Anne, aged 20]

> They always say that, if you go in prison and come off heroin, then you'll always go back on it because you've come off it without your own will. All I think to myself is that I can't wait to get out there and have a bit. Because prison's made me even worse, I think. [Jessie, aged 20]

Sally was adamant that she would only be law-abiding if the law were to be changed in such a way that she could get as much heroin as she needed.

Most of the twelve who said they intended to continue law-breaking stated this intention baldly and with no further elaboration than the observation that 'doing cheques', shoplifting – or whatever – was their way of earning a living.

Tara, though, like Cynthia (above), explained more fully her view that she could still expand her narrowing options if she committed more sophisticated crimes.

[My parents] are in America and in the last four years the bonds have just dropped. I've become so independent that I don't even want to know them. I wanna get on with my life and get what I want. When my kids go into the nursery, I'll go out and get money without getting caught. I know myself now. Before I had Sasha I began to know myself and what I want: which is my own flat, my own car and my own identity as a woman – you know – struggling or doing whatever she wants to do. And I'm getting there. [Tara, aged 21]

And who knows? Cynthia and Tara *may* eventually join the ranks of those unidentified law-breakers (mainly of the white-collar and corporate variety) whose anonymous existence perennially disproves the old adage that 'crime doesn't pay'. But for the rest of those thirty-nine women the future is bleak; and, I would argue, most bleak for Daphne, Della and Bobby, the three 15-year olds already doing time in Bullwood who gave no indication that they had any awareness whatsoever that their options were narrowing fast.

And what of the women who had already given up crime? To a woman they claimed that although prison is no picnic – and in several cases had become more difficult to take as they had got older – fear of imprisonment in itself would not have kept them out of trouble. *In every case they had stayed out of prison because of what they had going for them on the outside – not because of fear of another custodial sentence.* Thus Josie and Muriel could both look back with gratitude to the probation hostel that had given them the space and material help to enable them to believe that, after all the years in institutions, an alternative way of life *might* be possible.

I've got something out here now and that's what I'm staying out here for. [Josie, aged 30]

I was lucky enough to be liked there [at the probation hostel]. But yeh, I do think it did help me, sort of, get me out of the prison bit. They helped me get a flat and they gave me a lot of support. I got the job as a road sweeper the week after. [Muriel, aged 30]

What changes, then, could be made to ensure that fewer women get into the welfare/penal institutional complex in the first place; *and* that those who do are not solely dependent upon 'luck' or opportunity and incentive to cut free of at least some of the *most* debilitating, disabling and outlawing effects of being women in poverty and in crime?

BROADENING OPTIONS

A major aim of this book has been to provide a detailed ethnography of the perennial outlawing of a small minority of women who, once they have come to the attention of the authorities (either because of their parents' inability to care for them, or through their own deviance or law-breaking), are caught up and mangled by the regulatory machinery of the welfare and penal systems until both they themselves, and those who repeatedly judge them, have few grounds for optimism about their chances of not falling foul of the law in future.

Table 6.1 charts the major career points at which such outlawing can occur or be further endorsed. (Though obviously not every stage is applicable to every career discussed here.) It will now be argued that the response to deviant or law-breaking women could be very different at each of these stages, so different that the options of women already in trouble might be *broadened* – rather than narrowed still further.

OUTLAWING FROM FAMILY: SUMMARY AND POLICY IMPLICATIONS

> We've never had any love in our family. [Dawn, aged 23]

> The male siblings have appeared in court on several occasions and the influence over the years of observing the delinquent behaviour of the family has presented Della with a picture of criminality as being the norm.
> (1984 Social Inquiry Report on Della, aged 15)

> The issue is whether government will continue to encourage the social forces that so often split, stress and isolate families, or whether it will work to create a protective and supportive framework of public policies that can cushion families against those undercutting forces and – more actively – help develop the conditions under which patterns of tolerance, reciprocity and understanding can flourish . . .
> (Currie, 1985: 246)[1]

In recent years a number of criminological studies have indicated that, once women break the law, they are judged not only in terms of the seriousness of their crimes but also – and often predominantly – in terms of their conformity to idealized notions of proper femininity and women's proper place in the idealized nuclear family (cf., in particular, Carlen, 1983a and Eaton, 1986). Most recently, commentators writing from a wider range of perspectives have pointed to the hypocrisy of a government that makes repeated calls for the promotion of 'family values' (whatever they might be!) at the same time as not only making swingeing economic cuts that fall most heavily on already poor families, but also taking the increasingly punitive actions against unemployed young people that further add to family tensions and divisions (see Chapter 1). In referring to the 'outlawing' of increasing numbers of young and not so young women from 'the family', I am not, however, referring so much to the fact that some women are rejected by their already overburdened families once they have been in trouble. Rather, I am referring primarily to my arguments (already outlined in Chapter 4) that, as a result of prevailing ideologies concerning the normality of the conventional nuclear family: (1) sentencers see troublesome young girls in Care as being potential recidivists because they are without family and therefore gender decontrolled; and (2) single women are not seen as heading 'proper' families at all (Cook, 1987: 28). A more material effect of this 'outlawing' from family is the isolation and ensuing vulnerability experienced by young women once they leave the care of the local authorities for good. What should be done?

1 *There should be adequate state financial support for all household units –* single, single-parent, communal, conventional nuclear, extended or what-ever – regardless of whether or not they conform to the traditional and idealized concept of 'the family' (cf. Currie, 1985; Birley and Bright, 1985).

2 *Residential Care (or life 'on the run' from it) should cease to be seen as being the only alternative to 'family life' for young girls wishing to gain some independence from their families.*

   A network of hostels (maybe attached to schools) should be made available for the use of young persons aged 13+ wishing to be away from their families for either shorter or longer periods.

3 *Sheltered housing, grants for setting up home, and a network of specifically post-Care hostels should be established for the benefit of young persons leaving residential Care.*[2] And, as young women presently find it more difficult to get accommodation than do young men, in the short term at least, priority should be given to the provision of low-rent housing for young women either leaving Care or setting up home on their own – and without 'families'!

OUTLAWING FROM EDUCATION AND EMPLOYMENT: SUMMARY AND POLICY IMPLICATIONS

Just as it would be wrong to blame social workers *per se* for the women's alienation from welfare agencies, so too it would be wrong to attribute blame to schools and teachers for the women's lack of education. For, although some truancy may be blamed upon schools' failure to engage the interests of their pupils, the women in this study had, in the main, stayed away from school either because they had more pressing problems to deal with at home or because they were already involved with law-breaking activities which they wished to pursue during school hours. Once in residential Care several young women refused to attend the new school found for them near their Children's Home. Others ceased going to school simply because no new school had been found or (if they already had a record of bad behaviour) because no school in the area would take them. A few, moreover, were of the opinion that their local schools would have only provided a second-rate education in any case (though they offered little evidence to support this opinion). More made the point that, even if they *had* attended school, present unemployment rates made it unlikely that they would have ever been able to get a job commensurate with the extra burden of schooling undertaken. The view put forward most frequently was that education had not been seen as being a major priority for these particular young women in Care – that they had already been seen as no-hopers.

They wasn't really bothered with whether I went to school or not. Deep down, I don't think they were bothered at all. [Jill, aged 21]

They were allright, except they couldn't do anything with me. I suppose they think that Approved School's the first step down, innit? And you can't get out again. [Sally, aged 35]

At present, the English education system is structured as a set of narrowing options for all but the privileged few. Once a person misses a rung on the educational ladder, it is very difficult to get a leg up again. So had it been with these women, way before they had come to believe that their criminal records had knocked them off the ladder for good. In 1985 and 1986 all but Monica, Muriel and the three 15-year-olds felt that their education and job prospects were bleak. Two reasons were given: one, that they had missed their chance educationwise and that it was by then too late to get any qualifications; two, that even though they had gained some qualifications in prison, these would be insufficient to gain them employment outside.

Two fundamental changes in education and employment policies should be made. First, and because, at the present time, the living conditions of some young people are *so* poverty stricken that as teenagers they are in no fit state to compete with their better-off counterparts already shooting along the examination paths to higher education, it should be an axiom of social policy that no one should ever lose for good their chances of education. It should then follow that college and examination systems would be geared to people studying at every stage of their lives. (See also Box, 1987: 202 on the importance of education in broadening people's options.) Second, all job-training schemes should be linked to the creation of worthwhile jobs. For, although the majority of the women in this study said that they 'hated' or would not do factory work or 'shit jobs', many of them described voluntary work that they had done and liked – for example, working with children, working with old people, working with community groups, etc. As Elliott Currie has argued in the American context, 'the need for good jobs rather than just *any* job is one central theme in any employment policy that fits what we know about work and crime' (Currie, 1985: 267; cf. Box, 1987). Another would be to ensure equality of employment practice and protection for both women and men.

Those who at certain times *choose* to be out of the traditional paid labour force in order to fulfil other worthwhile tasks e.g. child-rearing, care of the elderly, and disabled, etc., must also be supported, both financially and by other types of social recognition in the form of a wide range of communal back-up facilities, e.g. canteens, leisure centres and nurseries. However, and again as Elliott Currie has argued, 'the logic of the private economy runs counter [to this type of] anticrime policy. Left to its own devices the private economy tends to disrupt local communities, to eliminate vast numbers of jobs, and, even though it may create new ones in great numbers, leaves a drastic mismatch between workless people and available opportunities for work' (Currie, 1985: 268). The social costs of a market economy that engenders a public commitment to greed, cut-throat competition, and irresponsible gambling on the stock market, together with contempt for those who 'fail to make it' in such a system, are to be seen not only in the statistics for 'street' and property crime, they are also revealed in the increasing number of white-collar criminals prosecuted for 'insider dealing' and fraud (see Levi, 1987).

OUTLAWING BY DRUGS: SUMMARY AND POLICY IMPLICATIONS

It is not a major aim of this book to locate and unravel all of the very complex issues related to substance abuse. However, as at the time I met them, six women were still addicted to heroin, two (at least) still had an alcohol problem and others said that they had suffered from some kind of addiction in the past, I shall now briefly summarize the women's views both on the part drugs had played in narrowing their options and also on the shortcomings of the few and far-between facilities designed to help them.

All who had taken drugs remembered the positive aspects of their drug-usage.[3] The 'blanking off' of extremes of misery seemed to be the most highly valued effect of heroin, whilst alcohol was lauded more for its facilitation of conviviality and an increase in social confidence. Glue alone was remembered with abhorrence – and, unlike ex-users of other drugs, none of the ex-glue-sniffers appeared to contemplate the possibility of a return to that particular habit. Other drugs were either valued for their various pleasure-inducing properties or for their capacity-increasing effects (for example, the wakefulness engendered by 'speed'). Some women had also valued the camaraderie of what they referred to as 'the whole drug scene'. Yet, for most, the glamour of the 'scene' and the positively experienced effects of the drug had been relatively short lived. The pleasures of heroin-usage in particular had soon been outweighed by the need to 'work' non-stop (usually, in the case of these women, in law-breaking activities) in order to fund an increasingly expensive habit. Others became aware that the effects of, for instance, their glue-sniffing or drinking were making other people shun them.

Women on heroin were the most critical of the social response to their addiction. Their particular grievances concerned:

1 the fact that they had been given no drugs therapy while in prison;
2 their belief that, as heroin addicts, they would have avoided a prison sentence if they had been rich enough to register at a private fee-paying residential rehabilitation centre;
3 the fact that so few places are available on state or charity-funded residential rehabilitation programmes;
4 the fact that the rehabilitation centres that do have free places available are often run according to a punitive ideology that some women experience as degrading them still further;
5 the fact that, whilst the pains of imprisonment had aggravated their condition, their penal confinement had also equipped them with a variety of new criminal skills and contacts wherewith they would be able to finance and feed their addictive habits in future.
6 the lack of rehabilitative facilities to help ensure that, once addicts had come off heroin, they kept off.

Although it is likely that a substantial number of heroin users do *not* fall into the arms of the law, Picardie and Wade reported in 1985 that, in the view of at least one treatment centre, 'prison continues to be the major source for the "treatment" of the majority of drug users in this country' (Picardie and Wade, 1985: 8). The women whom I interviewed were derisive of the notion that imprisonment would force them to abstain from drugs. Shirley (although not an addict) had been offered heroin for the first time when she was in Holloway. Others frequently made the point that 'if you go in prison and come off heroin, then you'll always go back on it because you've come off it without your own will' (Jessie, aged 20). Picardie and Wade, moreover, claim that;

the most convincing evidence that prison is bad for addicts is in the heroin overdose figures: 10 per cent of people who die from heroin overdoses do so after coming out of prison. They do not realize that their tolerance to the drug has been reduced by their forced withdrawal and go straight back to the level of dose they were taking before.

(Picardie and Wade, 1985: 83)

And it is not surprising that they *do* want to go back to that level of dose, given that the poor usually come out of treatment centres, hospitals or prisons to absolutely no back-up facilities whatsoever.

> They don't give you any help at all. See, magistrates say, 'Oh, we're gonna help you,' but their idea of help is prison or a nut house which I can't see is gonna help anybody . . . . Psychiatric wards in General Hospitals . . . just withdraw you slowly but then that would be it. I never got offered any help to get a place to live or a job or anything . . . . All that time I didn't live anywhere. I just lived in derelicts. [Sally, aged 35]

More fundamentally, a constant complaint was that women in particular did not (or would not) like the type of treatment offered by some of those more established and well-known treatment centres which aim to make drug-users confront the state to which the drug has brought them. Women who already had low self-esteem felt that they needed to be 'buoyed up' rather than 'brought down' by treatment.

> They really put you down; they haven't got any respect for you. You go lower and lower. I'd rather be in prison . . . . But I do know people who have gone to hospital outpatients and come off that way. [Jessie, aged 20]

And, according to Picardie and Wade, there are statistics to

> show that during the seventies more opiate addicts in the UK were likely to be abstinent after five years than in Europe and the United States, possibly because of our out-patient drug-clinic system. *Yet in 1980 Patrick Jenkin showed no commitment to strengthening our resources: 'I do not have to tell you that all this (treatment and research) is of course in competition with other more immediate and perhaps more obviously popular needs.'*
>
> (Picardie and Wade, 1985: 70. My emphasis.)

If the experiences of the women in this study are representative of other law-breaking addicts, then it seems that, as far as women offenders who are also heroin (or other drug) addicts are concerned, changes of policy need to be made in at least four major areas. They are:

1 *Sentencing*   Drug addicts should be sent to prison only because of the seriousness of their crimes – not because the judge or magistrate erroneously believes that imprisonment in itself will 'cure' addiction.
2 *Prisons*   All imprisoned drug (including alcohol) abusers should be offered treatment/counselling whilst in prison, though it should be made clear to them that such treatment/counselling must be followed by their involvement in a continued programme of 'throughcare' once they leave prison. (If imprisonment were to be reserved for the most serious women criminals – as suggested by Seear and Player in 1986 – then such programmes for imprisoned women drug abusers would not be so expensive.)
3 *Throughcare for addict ex-prisoners*   Programmes of treatment for women addict ex-prisoners should be established together with a network of other

support services. Community drug teams, similar to those described by Dr John Strang, consultant in charge of the drugs clinic at Prestwich Hospital, Manchester, are an example of the type of service that would particularly benefit addict ex-prisoners whose legitimate options have been narrowed by drug abuse. According to Dr Strang, community drug teams

> are not the entire service, they act as local agents provocateurs – they are the key which open the doors to general hospital beds . . . . They have the links with local GPs, adult education, housing departments, they can persuade local polytechnics to take on ex-drug addicts. They must be a full-time committed team to bring about a change in the whole fabric of services.
>
> (Dr John Strang, quoted in Picardie and Wade, 1985: 86)[4]

4 *Treatment*   A variety of treatment models should be employed to meet the varying needs of different women. For, as the Advisory Council for the Misuse of Drugs reported in 1982:

> [As] there is no typical addict, it follows that there is no single treatment or rehabilitation strategy confined to one discipline or service which will be effective for all individuals. Each individual drug misuser's problems must be assessed and the most appropriate match made to the services available.
>
> (Quoted in Picardie and Wade, 1985: 84)

But existing provision favours males simply because many of the few services presently available are not suitable for *women*. This is because: (a) several women addicts have been so badly abused by males that they are not prepared to join mixed 'concept' houses or other treatment programmes that cater for both men and women; (b) some women addicts are not prepared to leave their children in order to enter residential rehabilitation programmes; and (c) women with already low self-esteem are not prepared to enter into aggressive forms of treatment which they see as degrading them still further.

As for recidivist drinkers, it might be worthwhile investigating the possibility of forming specialist teams of workers trained to provide a 'guardianship' service for them. The tasks which such teams might undertake could include:

(a) being on call to visit and ensure the physical safety of any of their clients taken to a police cell when unconscious or incapable;
(b) being available to sort out problems with hostel, DHSS, hospital and other officials;
(c) in general being available to ensure some continuity of care and rehabilitation at times when the recidivist alcoholic offender is not herself capable of so coping.

The aim of such a scheme would not be to 'cure' alcoholics but to divert them from the judicial and penal processes. The major reasons for diverting alcoholic offenders from the judicial and penal processes are:

(a) that, each time a rootless alcoholic offender goes to prison, she loses any gains (e.g. hostel place, furniture, belongings, relationships) which she might have made since the previous period of imprisonment.
(b) that, while the prison is seen to be the only and inevitable place for rootless alcoholic offenders, existing agencies will continue to pass the buck and new strategies for coping with this group of offenders will neither be demanded by the public nor explored by the authorities.

OUTLAWING BY RESIDENTIAL CARE: SUMMARY AND POLICY IMPLICATIONS

In Chapter 4 it was suggested that residential Care can itself have deleterious effects on women's subsequent careers, the major reasons being:

1 that 'girls particularly end up being committed to Care orders because there is really no adequate provision for them within the tariff system' (Gelsthorpe, 1983).
2 Care's overemphasis on 'assessment' which results in some young people believing that they are in Care as a consequence of some (unknown) individual pathology, rather than as an effect of a social situation beyond their control.
3 Care's movement of some children and young persons from placement to placement which prevents the young people from establishing long-standing friendship ties. This can precipitate them into a quest for excitement and friendship in circumstances of risk and danger which their sheltered life in Care has not equipped them to cope with.
4 Care's punitive response to misbehaviour within Children's Homes as contrasted with the 'turning of a blind eye' to criminal behaviour outside the Homes. This can result in young people being escalated through the whole gamut of secure places in the Care system without anyone pointing out to them that it is their criminal behaviour which, if continued, will eventually land them in very serious trouble indeed. The punitive response to bad behaviour within Children's Homes can also result in the absconding that almost inevitably leads to law-breaking.
5 The failure of some Authorities to ensure that young people in their Care have adequate information about all aspects of sexual activity. This lack of sex education can obviously have disastrous effects for young women – and their ensuing offspring.
6 The failure of the Care system to prepare young people for non-institutional

living. This can result in post-Care money problems and depression of such magnitude that some young people see law-breaking and maybe a subsequent return to institutional life (but this time in a penal institution) as attractive alternatives to isolation and penury in an inner-city bedsit. What should be done?

While it is recognized that some of the problems of some children in the care of the local authorities stem from experiences that they had *before* they were ever admitted to residential Care, it does seem that at least some aspects of Care exacerbate those problems. Certainly the analyses of Chapter 4 suggest:

1 that young people in Care need to be provided with much greater stability of residence than many whom I interviewed had experienced;
2 that increased provision should be made to prepare young persons in Care for adult life, including sexual activity and non-institutional living;
3 that there should be less emphasis on assessment and categorization of young people in Children's Homes;
4 young people should be seen as being in need of care way beyond the time when their Care Order finishes. A range of services, e.g. befriending schemes, residential weekends and post-Care-contact social workers, should be on offer to young people leaving Care for at least ten years after the Care Order has been lifted.

Moreover, it is also suggested that the task of those working in Children's Homes would be made much easier if increased state support for types of household units other than the 'family' resulted in such a multiplicity of styles of domesticity and intimacy that Children's Homes could be seen as being but one type amongst several styles of living – and not, as often happens now, be resented as the state's ultimate filing cabinet for unwanted, unfortunate or delinquent children.

OUTLAWING BY SEXIST RESPONSES TO UNCONVENTIONAL BEHAVIOUR: SUMMARY AND POLICY IMPLICATIONS

The 1980s have seen the publication of a plethora of articles and research monographs on women's experiences of the courts (either as lawyers, defendants or witnesses) which report that women in the criminal-justice system are discriminated against by a judicial logic shaped by outdated typifications of both femininity and women's proper place in an idealized nuclear family (see, for example, Pattullo, 1983; Carlen, 1983a; Edwards, 1984; Eaton, 1986; Chambers and Millar, 1987 and Adler, 1987). It is therefore suggested that:

1 *There is a case for sensitizing court personnel to the stereotyping that precludes consideration of contemporary women's actual gender problems* (even when the magistrate is a woman – see Worrall, 1987a) and to the courtroom practices that particularly inhibit women.

2 *There is a case for the radical rethinking of the concept of culpability in terms of what a reasonable woman (often with prior experience of her relative powerlessness in face of male violence) might be justified in doing in certain circumstances.* For example, it is often implied in rape cases that the female victim was blameworthy because she did not put up enough of a fight (cf. Chambers and Millar, 1987 and Adler, 1987): or women who stab their husbands, because they know from experience that they cannot defend themselves with their bare fists, are often seen as being more culpable because they have used a weapon (cf. Carlen, 1983a).

OUTLAWING FROM WELFARE BY EXCESSIVE WELFARE SURVEILLANCE: SUMMARY AND POLICY IMPLICATIONS

In Chapter 5 I described how it had come about that, by the time I met them, many of the women were so antagonistic towards social workers that it was unlikely that any traditional-type social-work intervention could be effectively made into their lives in future. Even more unlikely was it that social workers themselves would be particularly sympathetic to clients who had already used many different strategies to evade supervision (see Worrall, 1987b) and who, in some cases, had even used physical violence to obstruct them in the course of their duties. Yet most of the women recognized that in addition to more realistic levels of financial support, they did need some kind of emotional/psychological or even just neighbourly practical support to help them sort out their (often extremely tangled) affairs. Others readily admitted that their troubles had become so acute that they should seek expert assistance. Still they were reluctant to turn to social workers. Those who had been in Care blamed social workers for setting them on the road to dependency.

> Even when I had social workers they wanted to rule my life for me. They weren't saying 'What do you want to do, Donna?' They were saying, 'You are going to do this.' [Donna, aged 22]

> People weren't particularly concerned with what I wanted, just what they wanted for me. I think I would have done a lot better if people would have allowed me to take my own course of action. I was in a Children's Home and they made your decisions for you and you had to do it. [Zoë, aged 28]

Those who had either sought welfare assistance or had it imposed on them in later life thought that there had been a gradual increase of social-work control over *all* areas of their lives. What, then, could be done to help ensure that those most in need of welfare support do not become those who are also most alienated from the agencies empowered to provide it? As I have already suggested steps that could be taken to reduce the stigma, alienation and isolation of young women both in, and recently out of, Care I shall here limit discussion to consideration of the difficulties confronting social workers charged with the task of supervising mothers' child-rearing practices and probation officers charged with supervising adult women offenders. In both cases I shall be recommending a diminution of individual casework and an increase in community provision and group-oriented methods of supervision.

It should be obvious to most people that social workers are faced with an impossible task when they are expected to prevent parental child-battering through home supervision. All the women in this study who had been battered themselves knew that they had only been safe once they had been taken in to residential Care or had left home of their own accord. And Norma, one of the most badly beaten children, had grown up knowing, too, exactly how to evade social workers concerned that she was, in her turn, battering her own children. Yet we have also seen in this study how the (sometimes longed-for) entry into Care can also bring other problems, psychological and emotional scars more lasting than those incurred from physical assault. It is for this reason that there is presently (November, 1987) great public disquiet about suggestions that some local authorities in Britain, rightly concerned about suspected sexual abuse of children, are taking precipitate action in removing suspected victims from their parents. Obviously parents will be alienated from, and unco-operative with, social service departments that are not seen to be giving parents a fair hearing in such cases. A more immediate day-to-day concern for individual social workers is with how best to supervise those *known* child-batterers and child-sex-abusers whom, through supervision, they are supposed to prevent offending again.

The abuse of children in Britain is fostered by a fundamentally flawed social organization which isolates adults and children into small privatized groups wherein children have to bear alone, and for much of the time unprotected, the full brunt of the domestic violence caused by adult tensions, frustrations and misery. Today, in the late 1980s, many of those adult tensions and miseries stem from unemployment, poor accommodation and a hopelessness born of the knowledge 'that those strutting down the corridors of power [have] replaced compassion for the disadvantaged with a passion for market forces' (Box, 1987: 8). At the same time, and as I argued in Chapter 5, the popular notion of familiness has been constituted within ideological and political discourses that promote a private/public distinction celebrating the myth that the governance of family and domesticity should (and does) remain beyond the purview and regulation of the state. Social work supervision of parenting – and mothering in particular – is therefore resented by women (and fathers) who, given prevailing ideologies about family privacy, also believe that they have a *right* to be bitter. In such a situation it seems that social workers can only be expected to supervise abusing parents effectively and with minimal friction if they are supported in their task by a whole range of back-up facilities, pre-eminent among them being full-day nursery provision where offending parents could be required to attend with their pre-school children. Such provision could have the following advantages: it would enable the parents to share the burden of child-rearing both with professionals and other parents; it would enable the social worker to share the burden of supervision with other professionals; and it could reduce the likelihood that the parents would see themselves as being locked in a personalized conflict with one individual social worker.[5]

OUTLAWING BY IMPRISONMENT: SUMMARY AND POLICY IMPLICATIONS

The majority of imprisoned women are in gaol for relatively minor crimes. The effects of imprisonment on already poor women's lives are such that one would expect no one in their right minds to send such minor offenders to prison 'for their own good'. Yet, on those rare occasions when sentencers do justify prison terms, this is often exactly how they explain their sentences – particularly on young girls and drug takers. However, girls and women who are already beset by a variety of problems are further outlawed from society once they serve a term of youth custody or imprisonment. This outlawing occurs in three major ways.

Prison is a school for crime

> I know more now than before I came into prison. I know about burglary, how to cut off burglar alarms, how to pick pockets. A girl here who's made a lot of money out of shoplifting showed me how to make a little thing out of a hairclip to take the buzzers off. And that judge says it's done me good! [Kay, aged 21]

> When I was in Holloway they put me on a hospital wing and that is the first time I came in touch with heroin. Some of the girls gave me heroin in Holloway. You go into prison for punishment; you come out junkies and lesbians. [Shirley, aged 20]

> I knew about cheques but not about drugs. Everybody [in prison] goes for medicines and they used to take phenegol, valium, modegon – that's where I know all these names from. Then I began to get some valium for myself [Kim, aged 28]

I think it's wrong for 15-year-olds to be put in here [Bullwood Hall] with older people. It's a bad atmosphere and you're just looking over your shoulder all the time. (Della, aged 15. Cf. Genders and Player, 1987 on the Prison Department's extraordinary policy of mixing youth custody trainees with older women prisoners.)

All you learn in prison is kiting [forging cheques], smuggling [drugs] and crotching [hiding stolen goods in one's crotch]. Basically, I thought about prison, 'What a waste of human life.' [Yvonne, aged 37]

Prison debilitates

Josie O'Dwyer (O'Dwyer and Carlen, 1985) has already given what is probably one of the most vivid accounts of the pains, tensions, debilitations, violence and degradations inherent in the disciplinary regimes of the women's prisons. Her account of women prisoners' self-mutilations, mounting tensions, sense of nothingness and sometimes, paralysing or rampaging fear and anger were echoed by many of the thirty-nine women. Lena explained to me why she had slashed her face:

The other week we wasn't getting hardly any association. If you're locked in a lot, you get mad and you don't know what to do with yourself. You just laze about, go to sleep. I done my face because I was down, things on me mind. I can tell when it's coming on. I get a funny feeling in my stomach and I want to cry. [Lena, aged 21]

Daphne, like Yasmin (see Chapter 4, p. 105) was, at 15 years old, already acclimatizing herself to solitary confinement (cf. Christina and Carlen, 1985).

I've got used to it, so it's allright. I don't mind being locked in. All the better! I go to sleep and I think about when I get out. I dream. I always dream about the Children's Homes. [Daphne, aged 15]

Kim claimed that Styal prison was such a hard prison that life outside had become increasingly irrelevant as she had just concentrated on her own survival. (cf. McShane, 1980; O'Dwyer and Carlen, 1985 and Mandaraka-Sheppard, 1986).

When you're in Styal, leaving Styal is irrelevant. It's getting through that sentence. That is the only place where I never used to think 'What's gonna happen when I come out?' You only think about what is gonna happen while you're there. [Kim, aged 28]

And, as we have already seen in Chapter 5, Yasmin, for one, was already learning to climb the prison hierarchy by fighting the officers. Nicky described what so many other ex-prisoners report daily concerning the punitive and debilitating atmosphere in the women's gaols.

It's the revenge aspect. You've had your liberty taken away but that seems to be insufficient for them. They have to get at you in other ways as well. And it obviously doesn't help because a lot of the girls here come back again and again. It's a total mixture in women's prisons. You've got lifers mixed up with remand prisoners and people in for petty crimes and drugs, all mixed up. When they do go out they can't cope because they're institutionalized – but also they've learned a lot from being inside. They're going out with hatred in their hearts because of the way they've been treated in prison. [Nicky, aged 27]

Imprisonment aggravates poverty and its related problems

Most of the women in our study were either single parents and thus the sole breadwinner for their children, or totally dispossessed of any home and family.
  (Genders and Player, 1987: 171; referring to research conducted in five female penal establishments over a two-year period.)

The interviews with women and an investigation of their backgrounds revealed at least one common element existing in women prisoners before they were involved in criminal activities: this seemed to be their financial difficulties and their inability to find other ways of livelihood.
  (Mandaraka-Sheppard, 1986, referring to interviews with 326 prisoners in six women's prisons in 1980–1.)

When already poor women go to prison they usually lose their accommodation, what few possessions they have and often, and most devastatingly, the custody of their children. In NACRO's study of twenty-nine people's post-release experiences it was found that:

People generally suffered a decline in housing standard post-release; for the women it was more severe. The majority – 81% – were in secure housing before imprisonment, a figure which declined to 45% post-release . . . .The women were more likely to mention money and bills related to housing as problems they faced on release. Fifteen out of 22 mentions (i.e. two thirds) of such problems came from women, even though they were only one third of the sample.
                                                          (NACRO, 1986a)

Josie O'Dwyer and Judi Wilson were speaking both from their own experience and from that of women known to them when they wrote:

Prison is not only damaging during the course of a sentence. Coming out has its own problems, and the snowballing effects of imprisonment are felt long after release. Women are often let out of prison very early in the morning not knowing where to go or even in which direction. They may have the equivalent of one week's rent with which to find accommodation. They will have nothing for fares, food, fags or finding friends . . . . Many women will have entered prison as a result of being homeless . . . . A majority will have had histories of institutionalization . . . . A high proportion [will] have children in Care placed there because of their mother's imprisonment. Regaining custody can be a new battle, one that . . . occurs in circumstances where all the odds – especially the financial ones – are against them.

(O'Dwyer, Wilson and Carlen, 1987: 87)

Anne, Sally and Hazel also spoke from experience.

Prison leaves you really sort of bewildered. All of a sudden you're thrown out into the big wide world and, if you did have anything, you've lost it. The second time I came out I felt very strange and lonely. [Anne, aged 20]

Say you go into Holloway and you've got three suitcases with all your possessions in – they won't keep 'em, not at all. You can only have three sets of clothes. So you lose everything. [Sally, aged 35]

One woman I knew lost her house because social services wouldn't pay the mortgage while she was in prison. When she came out, she'd got nothing. [My young son] didn't understand why he couldn't see me while I was in prison and then it took me five years to get him home. But, as I said, social workers seem to have this attitude that, because women are in prison, they're not really bothered about their kids. [Hazel, aged 29]

SENTENCING

Seear and Player (1986) list a number of sentencing changes that could effect reduction of the women's prison population, one of the most valuable suggestions being that 'by law no woman should be sent to prison for [certain] identifiable, non-violent offences' (Seear and Player, 1986: 6). Additionally they suggest that women should not be imprisoned for non-payment of fines, that only exceptionally should they be remanded in prison before trial, and that alternatives to imprisonment should be found for the mentally ill. All these proposals have been made before, and the history of the modern criminal justice system suggests that exhortation alone will not change sentencing practices rooted in a groundless faith in imprisonment as *the* magic cure for crime. Therefore, and as Seear and Player themselves recognize, statutory change is required to effect a more rational and coherent system of sentencing (cf. Ashworth 1983, Shaw, 1987).

PRISON REGIMES

> I know that to the guy lying in prison it's not so much the actual physical
> conditions that count but the treatment [s]he receives from the prison staff.
>
> (Boyle, 1977: 263)

As I have travelled round talking to prison staff I have become more and more
convinced that prison regimes (whether for men or women) will not be
improved until prison officers are formally given a greater role in their development. As far as women's prisons are concerned, I have repeatedly heard very
positive ideas for change put forward by women officers who have then told me
that, under the present hierarchical and centralized staff structure, they will
have little chance of having their ideas taken seriously by the powers that be. Be
that as it may, it seems that, as a priority, programmes should be developed
which aim to reduce the debilitating tension and anxiety suffered by women
prisoners. These programmes could include at least the following: more life-
and career-skill courses (as opposed to domestic and mothering courses); more
opportunities for association both informally, in groups, and with people
coming from outside the prison; and more effort by the Prison Department to
contact volunteer professionals willing to give legal, housing, educational and
other advice to prisoners – together with the necessary rule changes to allow
them into the prisons. These measures should also be seen as possibly con-
tributing to a reduction in tension and anxiety by non-pharmaceutical means.

Mothers in prison are a group whom the prison authorities should be
particularly concerned to send out stronger both mentally and physically than
when they went into prison. In this connection the Prison Department should
examine the many US projects that involve having children fostered near their
mothers' prisons (Baunach, 1985). Additionally, all prisoners should be allowed
to meet their families regularly in pleasant surroundings as well as being able to
telephone them from payphone call boxes on the reverse-charge system.

In a society with a rational anti-crime sentencing policy it would not be
necessary to make a special case for imprisoned mothers. Imprisonment,
whether for men or women, would be seen as being such an extreme form of
punishment that *all* deemed to merit it would, in the interests of the society that
sentenced them, be given every kind of support while serving their sentence[6]
and, additionally, be seen as needing continued financial and psychological
support once released.[7]

OUTLAWING BY CRIMINAL RECORD: SUMMARY
AND POLICY IMPLICATIONS

Crime causes such misery that it is not surprising that the known law-breaker is
regarded warily, that the ex-prisoner is shunned. Yet, before one is tempted

into believing that this fear of the convict is a universal element of human nature, it should be noted that it is usually the poor and the powerless who suffer most from the stigma of having a criminal record. In fact, even as I write newspapers and television are covering a story which once again illustrates Edwin Sutherland's point that white-collar criminals seldom suffer all-round social stigmatization for their misdeeds:

> The man sacked by the Government as deputy chairman of the London Docklands Development Corporation was yesterday appointed by its board to virtually the same job but with a new title.
>
> Mr John Mills, a former Labour councillor, was dismissed by the Environment Secretary, Mr Nicholas Ridley, on Monday night, shortly before Granada TV's World in Action reported he had been convicted and fined for selling "gold" jewellery made of brass.
>
> Yesterday an informal board meeting of the corporation appointed Mr Mills, aged 49, as a special adviser to its chairman, Mr Christopher Benson.
>
> A spokesman for the LDDC confirmed that the new post would involve virtually the same work he did as deputy director.
>
> But Mr Mills would not be sacked again by the Government, he said.
> (*The Guardian*, 2 December 1987. Cf. Levi, 1987, 327–9)

And even if, as Levi argues in his most recent book *Regulating Fraud*, (1987) there is on occasion *some* stigmatization of the fraudster, the examples he gives – being left out of the Queen's Honours List and being thwarted in an attempt to take control of Harrods – point to a different order of stigmatization than that which had been experienced by the poverty stricken women whom I interviewed and who believed that their criminal past had rendered them outcast forever. Yet the case of white-collar crime does not reveal only that 'The rich get richer and the poor get prison' (Reiman, 1984); it also suggests that all ex-criminals could have a better deal. And it is essential that they should. If they don't, those ex-prisoners who wish to lead law-abiding lives will become increasingly embittered as their best attempts to earn a living are repeatedly frustrated by the stigma of a criminal record. Several things could be done.

First, all prisons should have a rehabilitation officer employed specifically to get jobs, accommodation, education courses, child-care arrangements and any other special counselling or treatment facilities required, set up for women *before* they leave prison (see Wright, 1985 on the need for a prisoners' advice and law service). Such officers could build up lists of sympathetic employers, accompany women to interviews and keep in touch for as long as the ex-prisoner required them to. A start in this direction has already been made by the National Association for the Care and Resettlement of Offenders (NACRO)'s Women Prisoners' Resource Centre (WPRC). But such essential work should *not* (as in the case of WPRC) have to depend on charity funding. The rehabilitation of ex-prisoners should be seen as a state responsibility.

Second, all women serving long sentences (over one year) should be found paid employment outside the prison for at least the last six months prior to their release. I have seen such a scheme working in the Norma Parker Women's Prison in Australia and the Superintendent there told me that not only had employers been relatively easy to find, but the women themselves had both contributed to their prison board while working *and* saved quite substantial sums which would provide them with *some* financial protection when released.

Third, a programme of information about crime and punishment should be initiated. This might create the more enlightened ideological climate which would most probably be a necessary prerequisite to changing the public's view of women criminals as doubly deviant – that is, as being both bad persons *and* bad women. If the public were to be more accurately appraised of the characteristics of its prison population, then it might be in a better position to make judgements about the desirability and necessity of continuing to maintain such a costly network of penal institutions (cf. Dodge, 1979: 239).

POVERTY, CRIME AND CRIMINAL JUSTICE

> The criminal justice system is likely to work best when it is used least. It should not be used routinely, but exceptionally. With this major tenet as a focus for criminal justice and crime control policy, we can start to attack crime at its real sources, and allow the criminal justice system to operate effectively.
>
> (Pontell, 1984: 112)

After statistically analysing 'ecological linkages' between inequality, crime and punishment, Henry Pontell came to the conclusion that 'the *deterrent value of criminal sanctions depends upon conditions prevailing outside of the criminal justice system itself* (1984: 36, emphases added). Having qualitatively analysed the turning-points in the criminal careers of thirty-nine women I have come to the same conclusion. Even so, it is still important to campaign for a rational and humane penal system – and not only in pursuit of the three ideals of liberty, equality and fraternity that Stephen Shaw (1987) invokes in his excellent *Conviction Politics: A Plan for Penal Policy*. A rational and humane penal policy is also important because its opposite narrows the options of convicted law-breakers to a point where they are more likely to commit crime in the future. I have already proposed a number of welfare and policy changes that might result in the future options of deviant or criminal women being broadened rather than narrowed. In 1987 Stephen Shaw outlined a most succinct and comprehensive agenda for the implementation of a rational penal policy. I shall now conclude this book by examining the more fundamental, structural and ideological changes that need to be made if, in the future, fewer (rather than more) women are to be caught up in criminal careers. Three major changes – one purely structural and two structural–ideological – are proposed. Each, if realized, should result in a reduction in women's dependency upon male-related domesticity, while the second and third would involve decreases both in individualistic social organization *and* in the representation of women as being primarily consumers – rather than producers.

First, and as a prerequisite for all women to have better lives, and especially for women in poverty and with criminal convictions to have a chance of surviving without resorting to crime again, changes need to be made in policies relating to housing, social security, tax, wage and pension structures and, in particular, to the wages and working conditions of the part-time, mainly female, work force. Such policy changes should be directed at realizing a situation where women would no longer be expected to be dependent upon males and a concomitant male-related domesticity.

Financial independence, though important to all women, is of especial importance to women, like the ones in this study, whose previous experiences (e.g. of male violence and family lives torn apart by poverty-stricken living conditions), histories of institutionalization or present sexual orientation make them reluctant to link their fortunes with a male in the future. Yet, despite previous bad experiences of 'family life', some women already in trouble with the law and with a host of other problems stemming from poverty and a generalized feeling of marginalization, are, nonetheless, led by existing social policies to believe that their only way 'back in' again is via men or motherhood. Once they act on such beliefs, the outcome is usually disastrous – as the women I talked with knew only too well.

The second change that could immensely benefit women (and men) would be a move towards a more community-oriented type of provision for families engaged in child-rearing – and other types of care (see also Messerschmidt, 1986: 186–90). This is not to argue that an already oppressive 'family discipline' should be replaced by an even more coercive 'community control'. Rather that 'community' should be given equal value with 'family' and that the former should be used to 'ventilate' and enrich the life of the latter. The undesirable distinction between public and private morality might begin to disappear if networks of communal facilities were to enable people to establish their own best methods of child-rearing (and other domestic and community tasks) with *specialist assistance* as required – but with minimal *supervision* by social workers. The latter could instead by employed by community associations, with the families themselves being the primary definers of their own needs.

There would still have to be state controls to protect children from possible adult violence but the move in social policy in general could be towards the 'facilitating controls' of increased community provision, production and support. Fundamental reorientation from the private to the more public realms of social organization is not only a desirable socialist goal, it is also *necessary*. For while the present 'Englishman's home is his castle' ideology predominates, 'disciplinary welfare' surveillance will never adequately protect children whose violent parents are being continually outraged at the regular 'intrusion' of social workers into their homes. However, a less privatized system of child-rearing would only work if it were to be designed, funded and accepted as a desirable mode of organization for *all* communities and families. If implemented in piecemeal fashion, it would probably turn out to be just another device for 'containing' (i.e. oppressing) the poor and the marginalized.[8]

Thirdly, criminologists and politicians concerned with the relationships between criminal justice and social justice need to develop more sophisticated models of culpability, responsibility and accountability. Undoubtedly some readers will be tempted to accuse the present author of proffering a deterministic explanation of the crimes of women in poverty, of attempting to absolve them from responsibility for their actions. Yet a morality is socially constructed, as is a sociological argument; and the former cannot be read off from the latter. The analyses presented here claim only to indicate that, under certain, relatively rare *combinations* of otherwise general economic and ideological conditions, some women are more likely than not to choose to break the law and/or be imprisoned. Such analyses do *not* assume or imply that the women involved have no choice. To indicate the conditions that socially overdetermine the law-breaking and/or criminalization of some women is a task for social theory; argument about the degree of their culpability or the most judicious method for calculating it are tasks for political jurisprudence. Moreover, under present conditions of class exploitation, sexism and racism, questions of individual culpability will in any case ultimately be decided in the courts after a calculation of the political feasibility (or not) of appearing to imply that specific clusters of social disadvantage license crime (cf. Carlen, 1983b; Carlen and Worrall, 1987: 2 and Box, 1987: 31). Yet we still need to understand the actions and ideologies of the offender and her sentencers. As Stephen Box has put it:

> A demand for justice must go beyond retribution for the offence and reparation for the victim. It has to include a demand for *understanding* the offender. It needs this not in the hope that the offender will then be excused, condoned or justified. Nor does understanding the offender necessarily shift the blame to the victim. The demand for understanding is necessary because *although people choose to act, sometimes criminally, they do not do so under conditions of their own choosing*. Their choice makes them responsible, but the conditions make the choice comprehensible. These conditions, social and economic, contribute to crime because they constrain, limit or narrow the choices available. Many of us, in similar circumstances might choose the same course of action.
>
> (Box, 1987: 29, emphasis in original)

Quite so. And the question then becomes, what might encourage them (and, possibly, us) to act otherwise? For it is not enough to point out that working-class crime is intra-class and for Labour MPs to jump on the law-and-order bandwagon and make opportunistic calls for stiffer sentences. Of course, Jock Young is right to point out that 'the offender should be ashamed, he/she should feel morally responsible within the limits of circumstances, and rehabilitation is truly *impossible* without this moral dimension' (Young, 1986: 29). But whence does morality emanate? It should be the product of a society seen to be committed to reducing inequality and of communities seen to be committed to the welfare of *all* their members. Without reciprocal commitments between those who offend, their victims and their judges, it is unlikely that those who break the law will feel shame. Shame is usually the product of the transgressor's conviction that by her actions she has diminished the stock of social good. Many of the women in this study had had very little experience either of other people's goodness or of the world's goods. It was only when some of them began to experience them that they started to believe that a life without crime might be both desirable and possible.

Finally, a word about women's imprisonment, poverty and social responsibility. In so far as prisons debilitate, women's prisons feed off their own product. But it is an indictment of British Society at the end of the twentieth century, and not of the penal system itself when women tell me that they will go out to a world that has even less to offer them than the prison. Certainly fewer women should be sent to gaol and, of course, prison regimes *could* be changed to make them less debilitating. But sentencing and prison reforms are not enough. Years ago, when I worked in an ex-prisoners' campaigning group, we had a poster depicting a prison and bearing the slogan 'The buck stops here'. In fact the buck does not stop at prison.[9] It stops with a government whose present policies on social security, health, housing, education and employment are likely to ensure that in the future many more young women will be sentenced to lives of poverty, and that many more will be outlawed by careers in crime.

APPENDIX

THIRTY-NINE WOMEN: DEMOGRAPHIC CHARACTERISTICS

As this was a qualitative rather than a quantitative investigation not many demographic details were systematically collected. Yet many of the interviewees, when considering significant factors or turning-points in their lives, did mention similar processes or events that had obviously had significance for a significant number of them. In this section it is indicated which information was obtained in answer to a direct question and which was obtained as a result of the woman mentioning it spontaneously.

Age

Obtained by direct questioning – see Table A.1

Marital status, number of children and whereabouts of children of the Bullwood Group

Obtained by direct questioning. Only one of the twenty women interviewed at Bullwood was married, though several of the single women cohabited with men whom they referred to as their husbands. Between them, six of the twenty women had eight children.

Norma was married and when out of prison lived with her husband, the father of her two infants, both of whom had been taken into Care on Place of Safety Orders prior to the offence for which Norma was serving her sentence. At the time of interview the elder child had been adopted and the younger was living with foster-parents.

TABLES A.1 and A.2   Tables relating to demographic characteristics

A.1			
Ages of women interviewed in 1985			
Age in years	No. of women	%	
14–16	4	10.25	
17–20	7	18.00	
21–24	11	28.20	
25–29	6	15.30	
30–39	7	18.00	
40–49	4	10.25	
50–59	0	0.00	
60 and over	0	0.00	
Total	39	100.00	

A.2		
Ages of female prison population under sentence on 30 June 1984*		
Age in years	No. of women	%
14–16	23	2.00
17–20	198	16.80
21–24	238	20.20
25–29	235	20.00
30–39	298	25.30
40–49	124	10.50
50–59	46	3.90
60 and over	15	1.30
Total	1177	100.00

* Adapted from Table 1(b), *Prison Statistics*, England and Wales (1984) (Cmnd. 9621) p. 8.

Note

As I was dependent upon volunteers, there was no attempt to make the ages of my group of interviewees proportionally representative of the age structure of either the female prison population under sentence at any one time or of the ages of women convicted in the criminal courts in any one year. Tables A.1 and A.2 are included purely for the interest of any statistically minded reader who might wish to compare the age structure of the 1984 group of interviewees with that of the female prison population on 30 June 1984.

Cindy   was single but cohabited with the father of her two children who were staying with her parents whilst she was in prison.

Dawn   was single but cohabited with the father of her one child, a 4-year-old daughter. As the father had been arrested and imprisoned at the same time as Dawn, the child had been taken into Care when her parents were sentenced and at the time of interview was living with foster-parents.

Mary   was single but had been living with her child (a 5-year-old daughter) and the child's father until the time of her arrest, when the child was taken into Care and placed with foster-parents.

Cynthia   was single and normally lived alone with her baby son who was being looked after by one of her friends whilst his mother was in prison. Cynthia hoped to place him for adoption as soon as she had served her sentence.

Jeanette   was single and normally lived alone with her one child, a 12-year-old daughter who was living with a family friend whilst Jeanette was in prison.

Marital status, number of children and whereabouts of children of the Contact group

Obtained by direct questioning. Five of the twenty women in the Contact Group were married at the time of interview, though several others were living with men whom they referred to as their husbands. Eleven of the Contact Group (the five married women, together with seven of the single women) had fifteen children between them.

Carol   was married with no children but had had a baby when she was an unmarried teenager. The baby had been adopted and at the time of interview Carol lived with her husband.

Monica   was married with one teenage son by her first husband. At the time of interview the son lived with the maternal grandparents and Monica lived with her second husband.

Queenie   was married with two teenage children who at the time of interview lived at home with her and her husband (their father). When their mother had been in prison, the children had been placed with several sets of foster-parents.

Lisa   was married, though she did not live with her husband. At the time of interview her 3-year-old daughter lived with Lisa's mother-in-law who had also looked after the child during the mother's imprisonment.

Sadie   was married and usually lived with her husband, the father of her two infants. At the time of interview the children lived with their mother but the father was in prison. During Sadie's own short period of imprisonment the two children had been cared for by her mother.

Jill   was single and had recently given birth to a baby in prison. The baby had been adopted. Jill had no other children.

Tara   was single (and pregnant) and at the time of interview lived in a hostel with her one child, a baby aged six months.

Jean   was single and lived by herself with her two junior-school-age children. She had never served a term of imprisonment.

Zoë   was single and lived by herself with her one child, a 4-year-old daughter.

Kim   was single and at the time of interview lived alone with her one child, a 10-year-old daughter who had been in Care during her mother's imprisonment.

Hazel   was single and at the time of interview lived in a hostel with her one child, an 8-year-old son who had been in Care for several years as a result of his mother's ill-health and imprisonment.

Sally   was single and as a teenager had had a baby who had been adopted.

Experience of residential institutions

In answer to direct questioning and as part of narrative. Questions relating to the age of school-leaving and the number of qualifications gained proved to be quite irrelevant to the actual childhood and teenage experience of a majority of the women, and most frequently resulted in long and convoluted accounts of constant movement between a variety of residential institutions, absconding, truancy, 'living rough' and being 'on the run'. Discussion of the women's major non-school experiences during their official school-age years might help the reader to understand why, so often in answer to my question, 'When did you leave school?', I received a wry smile and the slow reply: 'Well, you see, it wasn't exactly like that . . . what you have to understand is . . .'

Twenty-two of the thirty-nine convicted women (ten of the Bullwood Group and twelve of the Contact Group) had been in residential Care (or at the time of interview were still in residential Care) prior to attaining school-leaving age (16 years). Six had been in Care from infancy (2 years old or under) to the age of 18. Fourteen of the others had spent at least three years or more in Care (most

TABLE A.3   Reasons (sometimes more than one) given by thirty-two (out of thirty-nine) women to explain their interrupted schooling

Reason for interrupted schooling	No. of women giving this reason
Truancy	25
Absconding from residential institution	14
Constant movement between residential institutions, foster-parents/parents	22
Temporary suspension from school	4
Expulsion from school (resulting in change of school or cessation of education)	4
Home Tutor (after refusing to go to school)	3

TABLE A.4   Educational qualifications and work experience of the thirty-nine women

Name (age)	Formal qualifications	Jobs held	Other (non-criminal) skills mentioned
Daphne (15)	None	Still at school	—
Della (15)	None	Still at school	—
Bobby (15)	GCE A level in Art	Still at school	—
Yasmin (16)	None	Unemployed – never had job	—
Tricia (17)	None	Unemployed – never had job	—
Audrey (18)	None	2 low-paid factory jobs	—
Cynthia (19)	3 GCE O levels	Office junior for 7 months	—
Shirley (20)	None	Painting/decorating-temp.	—
Jessie (20)	None	2 temp. clerical jobs	—
Sadie (20)	None	Unemployed – never had job	—
Anne (20)	2 GCE O levels	Unemployed – never had job	—
Jill (21)	None	Unemployed – never had job (job of childminder obtained but not begun at time of interview)	—
Lisa (21)	None	Unemployed – never had job	—
Kay (21)	GCE Art O level, CSE English, A level fabric and textile design	Window-dresser (13 months)	—
Lena (21)	None	Unemployed – never had job	—
Tara (21)	3 CSEs	Unemployed – never had job	—
Cindy (22)	None	2 part-time manual jobs	—
Stephanie (22)	Typing qualifications	Nanny 1 year/2 temp. jobs	—
Sheila (22)	CSE Maths, 2 Pitman typing certificates	Clerk/typist, window-dresser	—
Norma (22)	4 O levels, 1 Pitman typing certificate	Catering for 2 years	—
Donna (22)	None	Unemployed – never had job	—
Dawn (23)	None	Unemployed – never had job	—
Jean (26)	None	Factory (1 year) shop assistant	—

TABLE A.4—continued

Name (age)	Formal qualifications	Jobs held	Other (non-criminal) skills mentioned
Mary (27)	None	Factory (3 years) various seasonal jobs	—
Carol (27)	None	Cleaning jobs	—
Nicky (27)	None but gained scholarship to public school, aged 11 (later expelled)	Gardener, wages clerk, play leader, always worked	Writes for pleasure
Zoë (28)	7 GCE O levels, 3 A levels	Factory	Cookery/needlework
Kim (28)	3 GCE O levels, 1 A level	Dancer/show girl	—
Hazel (29)	None	Machinist	Writes poetry
Muriel (30)	None	Always worked – variety skilled manual jobs	—
Jeanette (30)	Certificates for Art	Always worked as receptionist	—
Josie (30)	GCE O level Art	Unemployed/had job for Prison Campaign Group for 6 months	Writes
Nadia (35)	None	Community work	Community work
Sally (35)	None	Unemployed – never had job	Typing, acting
Yvonne (37)	Information not sought	Croupier, singer – freelance	Song-writing
Queenie (43)	None	Factory work, bus conductress	—
Monica (44)	Typing certificates	Secretary	Various secretarial skills
Prue (46)	7 O levels, 3 A levels	Civil service	—
Dee (46)	Information not sought	Factory work	—

frequently, all of their teens). Two of the three 15-year-olds had been in Care for two years. All of the women who had been in Care said either that they had truanted from day schools or that they had repeatedly absconded from some type of residential schooling. Additionally, seven of the women who had never been in residential Care said that they had truanted from school. Altogether fourteen of the women said that they had absconded on one or more occasions from residential Care. Of the seven women who said that their schooling had been uninterrupted, not one had been in Care during her schooldays (one had been in Care for a short period during infancy).

Lest it be thought that the poor school records of the young women in Care can be explained solely by reference to the reasons for their being taken into Care in the first place, perusal of Table 4.4 will show this not to have been the case; only six of the women had been taken into Care as a result of status offences that involved truancy or poor school attendance.

TABLE A.5   Women volunteering information that they had been physically abused

Name	Age at Interview	Assailant
Yasmin	16	Female prison officers
Audrey	18	Father
Cynthia	19	Grandmother and boy-friend
Shirley	20	Mother, male staff member of Children's Home and police
Sadie	20	Husband
Anne	20	Aunt
Jill	21	Father
Kay	21	Boy-friend
Lena	21	Mother
Tara	21	Boy-friend
Sheila	22	Mother
Norma	22	Mother, husband
Jean	26	Father, boy-friend
Mary	27	Mother, boy-friends
Nicky	27	Father
Carol	27	Father, husband
Kim	28	Grandmother
Josie	30	Father, male and female prison officers
Queenie	43	Father

Total: 19

Educational attainment and work experience

In view of the peripatetic lives led by at least twenty-two of the women during all or part of their schooldays, it is not surprising that many of them left school (often prior to the official school-leaving age) without any qualifications. All the Bullwood Group were asked whether or not they had liked school, but that was yet another question (amongst several!) that for many of them was irrelevant. 'Did you like school?' more often than not produced replies such as: 'Well, I was never really there, see?' or 'I never thought about it, I had too much on my mind at the time.' The twenty-two ex-truants in both Contact and Bullwood Groups were not enthusiastic about (what should have been) their schooldays. Hostility was directed less against the teachers and more against the system of 'schooling' itself. Repeatedly women made remarks such as 'I just couldn't bear sitting down all day, being told what to do,' or 'I never really knew what I was doing in secondary school, just going from room to room all day.' Boredom in lessons and regimentation in school were described most often as being reasons for truanting, though many women tried to be fair to their secondary schools by stressing that 'Primary school was all right. I never really gave secondary school a chance.' In fact, by the time they had reached

TABLE A.6   Women volunteering information that they had been sexually abused

Name	Present age	Age when abuse suffered	Assailant	Nature of abuse
Jill	21	Under 10	Foster-father	Sexual assault
Norma	22	13	Elder brother	Rape
Mary	27	12–16	(1) Father	Incestuous sexual intercourse
Zoë	28	Various	Clients	Sexual assault
		20	(2) Stranger	Attempted rape
Nadia	35	17	Stranger	Rape
Sally	35	Various	Clients	Sexual assault
Queenie	43	16	Father	Sexual assault and harassment

Total: 7

secondary-school age (11–12), many young women were either already feeling overconstrained by the combined disciplines of family and school or already overinstitutionalized by the combined restraints of residential institution and schooling. Furthermore, neither family/residential institution nor schooling had put much on offer for a majority of them. As all those under the age of 25 had also perceived their post-school work prospects to be nil, it was obvious that the labour market had held out no promises either.

Fifteen women (probably an underestimate) volunteered the information that they had suffered physical and (in four cases) sexual abuse in their families of origin (see Tables A.5 and A.6). Most of the women who had been in Care had thought that in reality no one 'cared' for them. Only a handful of the women (not one under the age of 27) had expected that the reward for a good school record would be a good job, though several remarked (or said words to the effect) that they 'would never work in a factory' or 'for a rubbish wage'. Sizing up their situations and prospects like this, many young teenage women had seen truanting and absconding as escape routes to worlds wherein they could be free of the ideological and physical trammels of family, social services, residential institutions and schools. Most frequently the women themselves summed it up with the deceptively simple and, as things turned out, movingly innocent statement, 'I just wanted to lead my own life.'

Victims of Physical and/or Sexual Abuse

A total of twenty-two (out of thirty-nine) convicted women had been the victims of physical and/or sexual abuse, mainly from family members both male and female (see Tables A.5 and A.6). (Excluded from these figures are incidents which the women themselves described as 'fights' or 'fighting', wherein they themselves had been the antagonists.)

TABLE A.7   Ages of women claiming to have a glue, heroin or alcohol addiction

Name	Age at interview	Age and duration of addiction	Drug involved
Della	15	14–15	Glue
Yasmin	16	15–16	Glue
Shirley	20	13–17	Glue
Jessie	20	14–present sentence	Heroin
Anne	20	16–19	Heroin
Jill	21	12–13	Glue
		16–19	Alcohol
Lisa	21	17–time of interview	Heroin
Kay	21	17–present sentence	Heroin
Lena	21	15–18	Glue
Dawn	23	18–present sentence	Heroin
Mary	27	16–present sentence	Alcohol
Nicky	27	18–25	Heroin
Hazel	29	Early twenties	Alcohol
Nadia	35	20–28	Heroin
Sally	35	16–time of interview	Heroin
Queenie	43	34–time of interview	Alcohol
Monica	44	36–42	Alcohol

Total: 17

TABLE A.8   Distribution between interview groups of women who had been conscious of being victims of racist attitudes

	Bullwood Group	Contact Group	Total
Women with 2 parents of Caribbean origin	3	2	5
Women with 1 parent of Caribbean origin	2	2	4
Women with Chinese father and English mother	0	1	1
Total	5	5	10

Drug usage

All thirty-nine women had at some time used illicitly obtained drugs and many had also engaged in heavy alcohol consumption. Of the thirty-nine convicted women the only ones who thought that drug-abuse had influenced their criminal careers were the seventeen who also claimed to have had an addiction or 'habit' (see Table A.7).

Victims of racism

Ten of the thirty-nine women said that at one or more points in their lives they had been conscious of being victims of racism. Of these ten women, five had two parents of Caribbean origin, four others each had a father of Caribbean origin and a European mother; three of these four mothers were English, one was German, and one had a Chinese father and an English mother.

Local authority care

Twenty-two of the women had at some time been in the residential Care of a local authority and twelve had insisted that being in Care had been partly responsible for their law-breaking and/or criminalization. The full ethnographic analysis is to be found in Chapter 4 and a summary presentation of the ethnographic analyses is given in Table 4.3.

NOTES

Chapter One

1 One of the greatest advances made by the symbolic-interactionist criminology of the 1960s was its insistence that law-breaking and criminalization are two separate processes, each requiring an entirely different explanation (Kitsuse and Cicourel, 1963). Although it was recognized that law-breaking would usually be one contributory factor in subsequent criminalization, the most innovatory contention was that criminalization and its effects might be major factors in subsequent law-breaking and/or further criminalization (Matza, 1968).

  Strictly speaking, any infraction of the criminal law is a crime, anyone convicted of a crime is literally a 'criminal'. Speaking strictly, then, 'criminalization' could be applied to the sequence of events occurring between any one act of law-breaking and the conviction of either is perpetrator, or the person thought to be its perpetrator. In this book the term will have a wider usage. It will refer both to the sequence of events between acts of law-breaking and convictions *and* to the snowballing effects of those events on the persons thereby convicted. In other words, it is given a meaning rooted in the symbolic-interactionist assumption that criminalization is a sequential process, with both objective and subjective conditions of existence, that determine the social meanings of a person's criminal career. Thus, whereas not all convicted law-breakers suffer the stigmatizing effects of conviction (for example, white-collar criminals, traffic offenders and tax dodgers are seldom disgraced, even though they may have several convictions), some young people perceive themselves as having been criminalized (i.e. punished for a crime), even though they have never been found guilty of any criminal offence. In this text unconvicted law-breakers and law-breakers convicted without incurring stigmatization are referred to as being *undercriminalized*. Law-breakers whose criminalization has been out of all proportion to the seriousness of their individual offences are referred to as *overcriminalized*.

2 *Oral Histories* According to James Bennett (1981: 283) 'the earliest presentations resembling oral histories were probably the speeches the Greek rhetorician Lysias (active in this work about 403–380 BC) wrote for his clients to deliver in court.' Since that time oral histories have provided the stuff of much forensic oratory. Today,

indeed, the oral history has become both the main mode of communication *and* tool of analysis between all kinds of professionals and their clients. Not only between those professionals who have clients upon whose behalf they have to speak in court (e.g. lawyers and probation officers) but also between doctors and patients (the medical history) and state officials and recipients of welfare benefits (the interviews that produce 'the file') – all those professionals, in short, whose job it is both to assemble *and* assess 'cases'.

In England the best-known forerunners of the twentieth-century harvesters of oral histories were Henry Mayhew, Henry Rowntree and Charles Booth. In the United States the first major uses of oral histories in relation to crime were collected by the group of sociologists who worked at and around Chicago University from the 1920s onwards. Throughout this century English working-class histories have been obtained orally by a number of writers and the oral history has also become a major medium in mass media representations of contemporary life. What are its attractions?

Bennett (1981: 17) argues that Mayhew's use of oral histories was already multifunctional:

Mayhew used oral history to:
1 express his own personality and interests
2 communicate between social classes
3 educate by entertaining
4 demonstrate authenticity of evidence
5 make a vivid impression on the reader
6 arouse emotion and thus rouse readers to action.

Apart from laying no claim 'to demonstrate authenticity of evidence' (point 4 in Bennett's list), I myself both approve of, and would hope to realize in this text, all those functions of oral histories. Yet I suspect that most proponents of the oral-history method would not approve my usage of the term 'oral history' at all. First, because the interviews were to some extent focused on topics chosen by me prior to interview. Second, because the interviews have not been reproduced fully and unedited in this text. In other words, what I did was to conduct focused interviews which were then used as *texts* (*not testimonies*) for translation into *socio-biographies*.

From oral histories to socio-biographies   The term 'oral history' rather than 'life history' is being used in this text because it is doubtful whether any of the women interviewed would think me justified in claiming that I had obtained their *life* histories during two hours of interviewing (two one-hour interviews each with those at Bullwood; one two-hour interview with each of the women in the Contact Group). Instead, I aimed only to obtain oral histories of their criminal careers. Each woman was told (though in a variety of words and ways) that I wanted her to describe her progress through law-breaking, police stations, courts and custodial institutions and to start her narrative from the point where she thought it had all begun. I also said (again in a variety of words and ways) that I wanted particularly to discover what they themselves saw as the major influences on and turning-points in their criminal careers, and that therefore I would interrupt with questions like 'Why do you think things got better?', 'What went wrong,', etc., though I would keep the questions vague enough not to put words into their mouths. Either at the beginning, during, or at the end of each interview, I checked out a list of questions relating to factual details that I wanted to collect e.g. demographic details, age of first criminal contact with the police, age of first conscious law-breaking, etc.

Not surprisingly, all of the women asked me what I intended to do with the taped interviews after they had been transcribed. Whilst desiring to spare them a lecture on theoretical analysis, I did attempt to tell them how I would use their stories. In reassuring them that all quotations from the transcripts would be made pseudonymously, I was also able to explain that no individual oral history would be reproduced in full. I stressed that, as I was a sociologist, I would be looking mainly to social factors in investigating why their lives had gone the way they had. That, in analysing the transcripts, I would first be trying to ascertain what each individual's career had in common with the thirty-eight others and that I would then attempt to describe and explain the variety of effects that these shared social factors had had on their criminal careers. A majority of the women seemed very interested in how I was going to make sense of their stories, though many of them thought the task impossible. They had attempted it so many times themselves that Muriel (unknowingly) spoke for many of them when she said:

> I did things for all different reasons. It's difficult to remember even how many foster-parents I had. I could sit here and say about this one, that one and the other one, and then about an hour later I'd think, 'Oh yeah, there was that one too'. I mean, at various times when I look back, I come up with a different thing each time. It all contradicts itself . . . it depends what sort of mood I'm in.

I assured Muriel and the others who expressed these doubts that I concurred with their belief that there was no 'truth of the matter', but that, if my method worked, a book would be produced which should both reproduce their own descriptions of the rich individuality and variety of their experiences *and* a sociological commentary on them. In fact, what I told the women was how I hoped to translate their individual (autobiographical) oral histories into a coherent socio-biographical analysis of women's criminal careers.

3 An exposition of control theory is to be found in Hirschi (1969). A brief summary is provided in the following quotation from Kornhauser (1978: 24) who writes: 'Social controls are actual or potential rewards and punishments that accrue from conformity to or deviation from norms. Controls may be internal, invoked by the self, or external, enforced by others . . . indirect controls are represented in the self by stakes in conformity, which consist of (a) the rational awareness of interests and (b) sentiments or attachments, both products of rewarding social relations.'

Chapter two

1 See Bardsley (1987) for some more examples of the variety of women's crimes.

Chapter four

1 With the exception of Carol who had not served a custodial sentence.
2 Norma, Donna, Jill and Carol had become pregnant whilst still in Care.
3 Playland was an amusement arcade that used to be situated in Coventry Street, just off Piccadilly Circus, London.
4 In fact, Yasmin was sent to Bullwood after her third conviction. She had previously been fined and had a deferred sentence, but her general point, that the range of provision for young women is narrower than that for young men, is correct.

Chapter six

1 I should like to thank Roger Matthews who brought Elliott Currie's book to my attention and Sheldon Messinger who kindly provided me with a copy of it.

2 Some such schemes already exist – for example, Rufford Road Independence Unit in Liverpool (see National Children's Home, 1987). The work of Handsworth Young Person's Accommodation Committee (HYPAC) in Birmingham is also informed by recognition of the specific needs of the *young* homeless (NACRO, 1985b). See also Daniels, Davy and Grant (1984) and NACRO, 1982).

3 Helen MacGill Hughes's book, *The Fantastic Lodge*, still provides (for me, at any rate) one of the most persuasive narratives concerning the reasons for taking heroin.

4 For a lively discussion of alternative approaches to the treatment of addictions see Picardie and Wade (1985), chapters 5 and 6.

5 For two constructive discussions about possible changes in supervision of women on probation see Walker (1985) and Worrall (1987b).

6 Two prerequisites for the reform of prison regimes would be a different type of training for prison officers and the setting of Statutory Minimum Standards for penal institutions (see Casale, 1984).

7 For details of some existing schemes see Pointing (1986) and also my forthcoming book, *Alternatives to Women's Imprisonment*.

8 In fact, most of the proposals made in this chapter could also turn out to be oppressive if implemented as isolated control devices rather than as part of a fundamental change towards a more rational and humane society.

9 Two useful booklets for prisoners and ex-prisoners are Lancaster (1985) and Hardwick (1986).

REFERENCES

Ackland, J. W. (1982). *Girls in Care*. Aldershot, Gower.

Adler, Z. (1987). *Rape on Trial*. London, Routledge and Kegan Paul.

Allen, H. (1986). 'Rendering them harmless: the professional portrayal of women charged with serious violent crimes', in Carlen and Worrall (1987: 81–94).

—— (1987). *Justice Unbalanced*. Milton Keynes, Open University Press.

Ardener, S. (1978). *Defining Females*. London, Croom Helm.

Aries, P. (1973). *Centuries of Childhood*. Harmondsworth, Allen Lane.

Ashworth, A. (1983). 'Reducing the prison population: the need for sentencing reform' in NACRO, *A Prison System for the '80s and Beyond*. London, National Association for the Care and Rehabilitation of Offenders.

Auld, J., Dorn, N. and South, N. (1986). 'Irregular work, irregular pleasures: heroin in the 1980s in Matthews and Young (1986: 166–87).

Austerberry, H. and Watson, S. (1983). *Women on the Margins*. London, City University, Housing Research Group.

Bailey, P. (1982). *An English Madam: The Life and Work of Cynthia Payne*. London, Jonathan Cape.

Bardsley, B. (1987). *Flowers in Hell: An Investigation into Women and Crime*. London, Pandora.

Barrett, M. and McIntosh, M. (1982). *The Anti-Social Family*. London, Verso.

Baunach, P. (1985). *Mothers in Prison*. Oxford, Transaction Books.

Beattie, J. M. (1980). 'The criminality of women in eighteenth-century England' in Weisberg (1980: 197–238).

Benn, M. and Worpole, K. (1986). *Death in the City*. London. Canary Press.

Bennett, J. (1981). *Oral History and Delinquency*. Chicago, University of Chicago Press.

Birley, D. and Bright, J. (1985). *Crime in The Community: Towards a Labour Party Policy on Crime Prevention and Public Safety*. London, Labour Campaign for Criminal Justice.

Bishop, C. (1931). *Women and Crime*. London, Chatto and Windus.

Blumenthal, G. (1985). *Development of Secure Units in Child Care*. Aldershot, Gower.

Booth, A. (1985). *Life on the Margins*. London, Communist Party.

Box, S. (1983). *Power, Crime and Mystification*. London, Tavistock.

—— (1987). *Recession, Crime and Punishment*. London, Macmillan.

Box, S. and Hale, C. (1984). 'Liberation/emancipation, economic marginalization or less chivalry', *Criminology*, 22: 473–97.

Boyle, J. (1977). *A Sense of Freedom*. Edinburgh, Canongate.

Braithwaite, J. (1983). *Corporate Crime in the Pharmaceutical Industry*. London, Routledge and Kegan Paul.

Briggs, A. (1967). 'The language of "class" in early nineteenth-century England' in A. Briggs and J. Saville *Essays in Labour History*. London, Macmillan.

Bull, D. and Wilding, P. (eds.) (1983). *Thatcherism and the Poor*. London, Child Poverty Action Group.

Burton, F. (1980). 'Questions of violence in party political criminology' in Carlen, P. and Collison, M. (1980: 123–51).

Campbell, A. (1981). *Girl Delinquents*. Oxford, Blackwell.

Campbell, B. (1984). *Wigan Pier Revisited: Poverty and Politics in the 80's*. London, Virago.

  (1987). *The Iron Ladies: Why Do Women Vote Tory?* London, Virago.

Carlen, P. (1976). *Magistrates' Justice*. Oxford, Martin Robertson.

  (1983a). *Women's Imprisonment*. London, Routledge and Kegan Paul.

  (1983b). 'On rights and powers: some notes on penal politics' in Garland, D. and Young, P. (1983: 203–16).

  (1985). 'Law, psychiatry and women's imprisonment: a sociological view', *British Journal of Psychiatry*, vol. 46, June, 618–21.

  (1986). 'Psychiatry in prisons: promises, premises, practices and politics' in P. Miller and N. Rose (1986). *The Power of Psychiatry*, Cambridge, Polity Press.

Carlen, P., Christina, D., Hicks, J., O'Dwyer, J., and Tchaikovsky, C. (1985). *Criminal Women*. Cambridge, Polity Press.

Carlen, P. and Collison, M. (eds.) (1980). *Radical Issues in Criminology*. Oxford, Martin Robertson.

Carlen, P. and Worrall, A. (eds.) (1987). *Gender, Crime and Justice*. Milton Keynes, Open University Press.

Carson, W. G. (1970). 'White Collar Crime and the Enforcement of Factory Legislation'. *British Journal of Criminology*. Vol. 10, 283–93.

  (1981). *The Other Price of Britain's Oil*. Oxford, Martin Robertson.

Casale, S. (1984). *Minimum Standards for Prison Establishments*. London, National Association for Care and Rehabilitation of Offenders.

Casburn, M. (1979). *Girls will be Girls*. London, Women's Research and Resources Centre.

Central Statistical Office (1987). *Key Data 87*. London, HMSO.

Chambers, G. and Millar, A. (1987). 'Proving sexual assault: prosecuting the offender or persecuting the victim' in Carlen and Worrall, (1987: 58–80).

Christina, D. and Carlen, P. (1985). 'Christina: in her own time', in Carlen *et al.* (1985).

Cohen, S. (1985). *Visions of Social Control*. Cambridge, Polity Press.

Cook, D. (1987). 'Women on welfare: in crime or injustice?' in Carlen and Worrall (1987: 28–42).

Coote, A. and Campbell, B. (1982). *Sweet Freedom: The Struggle for Women's Liberation*. London, Picador/Pan.

Cowell, D. *et al.* (eds.) (1982) *Policing The Riots*. London, Junction Books.

Cowie, J., Cowie, V. and Slater, E. (1968). *Delinquency in Girls*. London, Heinemann.

Crystal-Kirk, D. (1985). 'Bricks in the wall: an analysis of the current criminalisation of the poor', *Criminal Justice*, vol. 3, no. 3, August (1985) London, Howard League.

Currie, E. (1985). *Confronting Crime: An American Challenge*. New York, Pantheon.

Daniels, J. Davy, T. and Grant, I. (1984). *Towards Independent Housing*. London,

National Association for Care and Rehabilitation of Offenders.

Denton, G. (1984). *For Whose Eyes Only?* Bradford, National Association of Young People in Care.

Department of Environment (1982). *Single Homeless.* London, HMSO.

Department of Health and Social Security (1984). *Personal Social Services: Local Authority Statistics.* London, HMSO.

Ditton, J. (1977). *Part-time Crime.* London, Macmillan.

Dobash, R. *et al.* (1979). *Violence Against Wives.* London, Open Books.

Dodge, C. (1979). *A World Without Prisons.* Massachusetts, Heath/Lexington Books.

Dominelli, L. (1984). 'Differential justice: domestic labour, community service and female offenders', *Probation Journal* 3 (3), 100–03.

Donzelot, J. (1979). *The Policing of Families.* London, Hutchison.

Eaton, M. (1986). *Justice for Women: Family, Court and Social Control.* Milton Keynes, Open University Press.

Edwards, S. (1984). *Women on Trial.* Manchester, Manchester University Press.

   (1987). 'Prostitutes: victims of law, social policy and organised crime' in Carlen and Worrall (1987: 43–56).

Farrington, D. and Morris, A. (1983a). 'Sex, sentencing and conviction', *Journal of Criminology,* 23 (3), July, 229–48.

   (1983b). 'Do magistrates discriminate against men?', *Justice of the Peace,* 17 September, 601–03.

Field, F. (1981). *Inequality in Britain: Freedom, Welfare and The State.* London, Fontana.

Fisher, R. and Wilson, C. (1982). *Authority or Freedom?* Gower, Aldershot.

Foucault, M. (1977). *Discipline and Punish.* London, Allen Lane.

Freeman, M. (1983). *The Rights and Wrongs of Children.* London, Frances Pinter.

Garland, D. and Young, P. (eds.) (1983). *The Power to Punish.* London, Heinemann.

Gelsthorpe, L. (1983). Evidence given to House of Commons Social Services Committee Enquiry, *Children in Care.* London, HMSO.

   (1986). *Gender Issues in Juvenile Justice: An Annotated Bibliography.* Lancaster, Information Systems.

Genders, E. and Player, E. (1987). 'Women in prison: the treatment, the control and the experience', in Carlen and Worrall (1987: 161–75).

Gibbens, T. C. N. (1971). 'Female offenders', *British Journal of Hospital Medicine,* September.

Griffin, C. (1985). *Typical Girls.* London, Routledge and Kegan Paul.

Hagan, J., Simpson, J. and Gillis, J. R. (1979). 'The sexual stratification of social control: a gender-based perspective on crime and delinquency', *British Journal of Sociology,* vol. 30, I.

Hanawalt, B. (1979). *Crime and Conflict in English Communities, 1300–1348.* Massachusetts, Harvard University Press.

   (1980) 'Women before the law: females as felons and prey in fourteenth-century England' in Weisberg, (1980: 165–95).

Hardwick, D. J. (1986). *Serving The Second Sentence.* Birmingham, Pepar.

Harrison, P. (1983). *Inside The Inner City: Life Under The Cutting Edge.* Harmonds-worth, Penguin.

Hartmann, M. (1977). *Victorian Murderesses.* London, Robson Books.

Heidensohn, F. (1985). *Women and Crime.* London, Macmillan.

Henry, S. (1978). *The Informal Economy.* London, Martin Robertson.

Hicks, J. and Carlen, P. (1985). 'Jenny: in a criminal business' in Carlen *et al.* (1985).

Hirschi, T. (1969). *Causes of Delinquency.* Berkeley, University of California Press.

Holdaway, S. (1983). *Inside the British Police.* Oxford, Blackwell.

Home Office (1970). *Care and Treatment in a Planned Environment*. London, Advisory Council on Child Care.

Home Office (1977). *Fifteen and Sixteen-Year-Olds in Borstal*. London, Young Offenders' Psychology Unit.

Home Office (1985). *Prison Statistics England and Wales 1984*, Cmnd. 9622. London, HMSO.

Home Office (1986a). *Report of the Work of the Prison Department 1985/86*, C M 11. London, HMSO.

Home Office (1986b). *The Ethnic Origins of Prisoners*. London, HMSO.

House of Commons (1984). *Second Report from The Social Services Committee: Children in Care*, vols. I, II and III. London, HMSO.

Hudson, A. (1983). 'The welfare state and adolescent femininity' in *Youth and Policy*, vol. 2, No. 1, Summer.

   (1985). 'Troublesome girls: towards alternative definitions and policies', paper presented to European University Institute Conference, Florence.

Hudson, B. (1984). 'Femininity and adolescence' in McRobbie, A. and Nava, M. (1984).

Hughes, H. M. (1963). *The Fantastic Lodge*. London, Arthur Baker.

Hunt, P. (1980). *Gender and Class Consciousness*. London, Macmillan.

Ignatieff, M. (1978). *A Just Measure of Pain*. London, Macmillan.

Jenkins, E. (1949). *Six Criminal Women*. London, Sampson Low.

Jordan, B. (1983). 'The politics of "Care": social workers and schools' in B. Jordan and N. Parton (eds.) (1983) *The Political Dimensions of Social Work*. Cambridge, Polity Press.

Kitsuse, J. and Cicourel, A. (1963). 'A note on the use of official statistics', *Social Problems*, 11, Autumn: 131–9.

Kornhauser, R. (1978). *Social Sources of Delinquency*. Chicago, University of Chicago Press.

Lancaster, E. (1985). *Prisoners and the Welfare State*. Birmingham, Pepar.

Leigh, L. H. (1982). *The Control of Commercial Fraud*. London, Heinemann.

Leonard, P. (1984). *Personality and Ideology*. London, Macmillan.

Levi, M. (1987). *Regulating Fraud*. London, Tavistock.

Lock, C. (1987). '50p beggars who ponce for a kind of living', *Guardian*, 5 May 1987.

Lombroso, C. and Ferrero, W. (1895). *The Female Offender*. London, Fisher Unwin.

Mandaraka-Sheppard, A. (1986). *The Dynamics of Aggression in Women's Prisons in England*. London, Gower.

Mars, G. (1982). *Cheats at Work*. London, Unwin.

Mathiesen, T. (1980). *Law, Society and Political Action*. London, Academic Press.

Matthews, R. and Young, J. (eds.) (1986). *Confronting Crime*. London, Sage.

Matza, D. (1968). *Becoming Deviant*. New Jersey, Prentice Hall.

Maynard, C. (1985). Comment reported in *Evening Standard*, 13 September 1985.

McLeod, E. (1982). *Women Working: Prostitution Now*. London, Croom Helm.

McRobbie, A. and Garber, J. (1976). 'Girls and subcultures' in S. Hall and T. Jefferson, *Resistance through Rituals*. London, Hutchinson.

McRobbie, A. and Nava, M. (1984). *Gender and Generation*. London, Macmillan.

McShane, Y. (1980). *Daughter of Evil*. London, W. H. Allen.

Melossi, M. and Pavarini, M. (1981). *The Prison and the Factory*. London, Macmillan.

Messerschmidt, J. (1979). *School Stratification and Delinquent Behaviour*. University of Stockholm.

   (1986). *Capitalism, Patriarchy and Crime, Towards a Socialist Feminist Criminology*. Totowa, New Jersey, Rowman and Littlefield.

Milham, S., Bullock, R. and Hosie, K. (1978). *Locking Up Children*. London, Saxon House.

Morris, A., Giller, H., Szwed, E. and Geach, H. (1980). *Justice for Children*. London, Macmillan.

Murray, T. (1978). *Margaret Thatcher*. London, W. H. Allen.

NACRO (1977). *Children and Young Persons in Trouble*. London, National Association for Care and Resettlement of Offenders, 169 Clapham Road, SW9 (hereafter NACRO).

NACRO (1982) *Supported Housing Projects for Single People*. London, NACRO.

NACRO (1985a). *Mothers and Babies in Prison*. London, NACRO.

NACRO (1985b). HYPAC, *The Work of Handsworth Young Persons' Accommodation Committee*. London, NACRO.

NACRO (1986a). *They don't give you a clue*. London, NACRO.

NACRO (1986b). *Criminal Careers of People Born in 1953, 1958 and 1963*. London, NACRO.

NACRO (1987a). *Women in Prison*. London, NACRO.

NACRO (1987b). *Women, Cautions and Sentencing*. London, NACRO.

National Children's Home (1986). *Children Today*. London, National Children's Home.

National Children's Home (1987). *Children*, Winter 1987/1988: 9.

NAYPIC (1983). *Sharing Care*. Bradford, National Association of Young People in Care.

O'Dwyer, J. and Carlen, P. (1985). 'Surviving Holloway and other women's prisons' in Carlen *et al.* (1985a).

O'Dwyer, J., Wilson, J. and Carlen, P. (1987). 'Women's imprisonment in England, Wales and Scotland: recurring issues' in Carlen and Worrall (1987: 176–90).

Okely, J. (1978). 'Privileged, schooled and finished' in Ardener (1978).

Page, R. and Clark, G. (1977). *Who Cares?*. London, National Children's Bureau.

Pascall, G. (1986). *Social Policy: A Feminist Analysis*. London, Tavistock.

Pattullo, P. (1983). *Judging Women*. London, National Council for Civil Liberties.

Pearson, G. *et al.* (1986). *Young People and Heroin use in the North of England: A Report to the Health Education Council*. London, Middlesex Polytechnic.

Peter, J. P. and Fauret, J. (1975). 'The animal, the madman, and death' in M. Foucault, *I Pierre Rivière, having slaughtered my mother, my sister and my brother . . .* Harmondsworth, Penguin (1975: 175–99).

Picardie, J. and Wade, D. (1985). *Heroin: Chasing the Dragon*. Harmondsworth, Penguin.

Pointing, J. (1986). *Alternatives to Custody*. Oxford, Blackwell.

Pontell, H. (1984). *A Capacity to Punish*. Bloomington, Indiana University Press.

Radzinowitz, L. (1966). *Ideology and Crime*. London, Heinemann.

Reiman, J. (1984). *The Rich Get Richer and The Poor Get Prison*. New York, Wiley.

Richards, E. (1974). 'Patterns of Highland discontent' in J. Stevenson and R. Quinault (eds.) *Popular Protest and Public Order: Six Studies in British History, 1790–1920*. London, Allen and Unwin.

Richardson, H. J. (1969). *Adolescent Girls in Approved Schools*. London, Routledge and Kegan Paul.

Rosenbaum, M. (1981). *Women on Heroin*. New Jersey, Rutgers University Press.

Rusche, G. and Kirchheimer, O. (1939). *Punishment and Social Structure*. New York, Columbia University Press.

Sachs, A. and Wilson, J. (1978). *Sexism and The Law*. Oxford, Martin Robertson.

Salgado, G. (1977). *The Elizabethan Underworld*. London, Dent.

Scarman, L. G. (1982). *The Scarman Report*. Harmondsworth, Penguin.

Scull, A. (1979). *Museums of Madness*. London, Allen Lane.

Seear, N. and Player, E. (1986). *Women in the Penal System*. London, Howard League for Penal Reform.

Segal, L. (ed.) (1983). *What Is To Be Done About The Family?* Harmondsworth, Penguin.

Shaw, S. (1987). *Conviction Politics: A Plan for Penal Policy*. London, Fabian Society no. 522.

Smart, C. (1981). 'Law and the control of women's sexuality' in B. Hutter and G. Williams, *Controlling Women*, London, Croom Helm.

Smith, D. and Gray, L. (1983). *Police and People in London*. London, Policy Studies Unit.

Smithies, E. (1982). *Crime in Wartime*. London, Allen and Unwin.

Stanworth, M. (1985). 'Just three quiet girls' in C. Ungerson, *Women and Social Policy*. London, Macmillan.

Stein, M. (1983). 'Protest in care' in B. Jordan and N. Parton (1983) *The Political Dimensions of Social Work*. Oxford, Blackwell.

Stein, M. and Carey, K. (1984). 'A study of young people leaving care' in NAYPIC *Leaving Care – Where?* Bradford, National Association of Young People in Care.

Stein, M. and Ellis, S. (1983). *Gizza Say: Reviews and Young People In Care*. Bradford, NAYPIC.

Stein, M. and Maynard, C. (1985). *I've Never Been So Lonely*. Bradford, NAYPIC.

Stevens, P. and Willis, C. F. (1979). *Race, Crime and Arrests*. London, Home Office.

Sutherland, E. (1949). *White Collar Crime*. New York, Holt, Rinehart and Winston.

Taylor, L., Lacey, R. and Bracken, D. (1979). *In Whose Best Interests?* London, Cobden Trust and National Association for Mental Health.

Tchaikovsky, C. (1985). 'Looking for trouble' in P. Carlen *et al.* (1985).

Tebbit, N. (1985). 'My cure for our sick society', *New Society*, 15 November.

Thorpe, D., Smith, D., Green, C. and Paley, J. H. (1980) *Out of Care: The Community Support of Juvenile Offenders*. London, Allen and Unwin.

Townsend, P. *et al.* (1987). *Poverty and Labour in London*. London, Low Pay Unit.

Wakerley, A. (1984). 'Files' in *NAYPIC News*, issue 9, Bradford, National Association of Young People in Care.

Walker, A. and Walker, C. (eds.) (1987). *The Growing Divide: A Social Audit, 1979–1987*. London, Child Poverty Action Group.

Walker, H. (1985). 'Women's issues in probation practice' in H. Walker and B. Beaumont, (eds.) *Working with Offenders*. London, Macmillan.

Wapshott, N. and Brock, G. (1983). *Thatcher*. London, Macdonald.

Webb, D. (1984). 'More on gender and justice: girl offenders on supervision', *Sociology*, vol. 18, no. 3, 367–81.

Weisberg, D. K. (ed.) (1980). *Women and the Law*, vol. I. Massachusetts, Schenkman.

Wilden, A. (1972). *System and Sign*. London, Tavistock.

Williams, K. (1981). *From Pauperism to Poverty*. London, Routledge and Kegan Paul.

Willis, P. (1977). *Learning to Labour: How Working-Class Kids Get Working-Class Jobs*. London, Saxon House.

Wilson, E. (1977). *Women and the Welfare State*. London, Tavistock.

Worrall, A. (1981). 'Out of place: the female offender in court', *Probation Journal*, 28: 90–93.

Worrall, A. (1987a). 'Sisters in law? Women defendants and women magistrates' in Carlen and Worrall (1987: 108–24).

(1987b). *Nonedescript Women*. Unpublished PhD thesis, University of Keele.

Wright, M. (1985). *Kept in the Dark: The Need For a Prisoners' Advice and Law Service*. London, Prisoners' Advice and Law Service.

Young, J. (1975). 'Working-class criminology' in I. Taylor, P. Walton and J. Young *Critical Criminology*. London, Routledge and Kegan Paul.

   (1986). 'The failure of criminology: the need for radical realism,' in Matthews and Young (1986).

Young, J. D. (1979). *The Rousing of the Scottish Working Class*, London, Croom Helm.

NAME INDEX

SUBJECT INDEX